DEATH AND THE ROCK STAR

Death and the Rock Star

Edited by

CATHERINE STRONG
RMIT University, Australia

BARBARA LEBRUN
University of Manchester, UK

ASHGATE

© Catherine Strong and Barbara Lebrun and the contributors 2015

All rights reserved. No part of this publication may be reproduced, stored in a retrieval system or transmitted in any form or by any means, electronic, mechanical, photocopying, recording or otherwise without the prior permission of the publisher.

Catherine Strong and Barbara Lebrun have asserted their rights under the Copyright, Designs and Patents Act, 1988, to be identified as the editors of this work.

Published by
Ashgate Publishing Limited
Wey Court East
Union Road
Farnham
Surrey, GU9 7PT
England

Ashgate Publishing Company
110 Cherry Street
Suite 3-1
Burlington, VT 05401-3818
USA

www.ashgate.com

British Library Cataloguing in Publication Data
A catalogue record for this book is available from the British Library.

The Library of Congress has cataloged the printed edition as follows:
Death and the rock star / edited by Catherine Strong and Barbara Lebrun.
    pages cm. – (Ashgate popular and folk music series)
  Includes index.
    ISBN 978-1-4724-3091-5 (hardcover : alk. paper) – ISBN 978-1-4724-3092-2 (ebook) – ISBN 978-1-4724-3093-9 (epub)
  1. Musicians – Death – Social aspects. 2. Popular music – Social aspects. 3. Bereavement – Social aspects. I. Strong, Catherine. II. Lebrun, Barbara.

ML3916.D43 2015
781.64 – dc23

    2015010980

ISBN 9781472430915 (hbk)
ISBN 9781472430922 (ebk – PDF)
ISBN 9781472430939 (ebk – ePUB)

Bach musicological font developed by © Yo Tomita

Printed in the United Kingdom by Henry Ling Limited, at the Dorset Press, Dorchester, DT1 1HD

Contents

List of Figures	*vii*
List of Contributors	*ix*
General Editors' Preface	*xiii*
Acknowledgements	*xv*

1   The Great Gig in the Sky: Exploring Popular Music and Death   1
Barbara Lebrun and Catherine Strong

PART I   DEATH AND TABOO

2   The Afterlife of the People's Singer: Bodily Matters in a
Dutch Sing-along Culture   17
Irene Stengs

3   'I Don't Preach Premature Suicide': The Biopolitics of GG Allin   33
Ben Dumbauld

4   Difference that Exceeded Understanding:
Remembering Michael Jackson (Redux)   45
Susan Fast

PART II   MEDIATING THE DEAD

5   Mediation, Generational Memory and the Dead Music Icon   61
Andy Bennett

6   'From Death to Birth': Suicide and Stardom in the
Musical Biopic   73
Penny Spirou

7   Social Sorrow: Tweeting the Mourning of Whitney Houston   87
Taylor Cole Miller

PART III   THE LABOURING DEAD

8   Laneways of the Dead: Memorialising Musicians in Melbourne   103
Catherine Strong

9	Three Faces of Musical Motherhood in Death: Amy Winehouse, Whitney Houston and Donna Summer *Paula Hearsum*	119
10	En'shrine'd: Ushering Fela Kuti into the Western 'Rock' Canon *Abigail Gardner*	135
11	Post-mortem Elvis: From Cultural Icon to Transproperty *June M. Madeley and Daniel Downes*	149

PART IV RESURRECTIONS

12	Performing Beyond the Grave: The Posthumous Duet *Shelley D. Brunt*	165
13	There's a Spectre Haunting Hip-hop: Tupac Shakur, Holograms in Concert and the Future of Live Performance *Regina Arnold*	177
14	Post-mortem Sampling in Hip-hop Recordings and the Rap Lament *Justin A. Williams*	189

Index   *201*

List of Figures

2.1   A kiss for 'André' (23 September 2009 commemoration at the
André Hazes statue, Albert Cuyp Street Market, Amsterdam)   25
2.2   André Hazes fans at the commemorative ceremony of
23 September 2006 (Albert Cuyp Street Market, Amsterdam)   27

8.1   Artwork of Bon Scott in AC/DC Lane, Melbourne   107
8.2   Paul Hester Walk   113

List of Contributors

Regina Arnold received her PhD from Stanford's Program of Modern Thought and Literature. She is a former rock critic for *Rolling Stone, Spin, Entertainment Weekly* and other publications. In addition to her scholarly work in comparative media and ethnic studies, she is the author of three monographs on popular music: *Route 666: On the Road To Nirvana* (1993), *Kiss This: Punk in the Present Tense* (1997) and *Exile in Guyville* (2014).

Andy Bennett is Professor of Cultural Sociology and Director of the Griffith Centre for Cultural Research at Griffith University in Queensland, Australia. He has authored and edited numerous books including *Music, Style and Aging* (2013), *Cultures of Popular Music* (2001), *Popular Music and Youth Culture* (2000) and *Remembering Woodstock* (2004). Bennett led a three-year, five-country project funded by the Australian Research Council entitled 'Popular Music and Cultural Memory: Localized Popular Music Histories and their Significance for National Music Industries' between 2010 and 2012. He is a Faculty Fellow of the Center for Cultural Sociology, Yale University.

Shelley D. Brunt is a Senior Lecturer in Music and Media at RMIT University, Australia. She is a core member of the University's Digital Ethnography Research Centre (DERC). Her teaching and research interests are in the field of ethnomusicology, with a focus on popular music and media in Australasia. She has produced a number of publications on Japanese music, and Asian performing arts in New Zealand. Recent studies include a co-authored examination of an interactive digital Indonesian musical instrument (*Musicology Australia*, 2013), and an analysis of nation-building in a televised Japanese song context (2014). She is also the editor of a special issue on Asian popular music for the Australasian journal *Perfect Beat* (2011).

Daniel Downes is Associate Professor of Information and Communication Studies at the University of New Brunswick at Saint John, and Fellow of the Royal Society of Arts. An academic, musician and broadcaster, Downes has published articles on copyright, the structure of the new media economy, and the role of media in the construction of community and personal identity. His research interests include the relationships between Irish, Canadian and American musical practice and technology, and the role of intellectual property in the regulation of cultural industries and popular culture. He is the author of *Interactive Realism: The Poetics of Cyberspace* (2005) and co-editor of *Post-Colonial Distances: The Study of Popular Music in Canada and Australia* with Bev Diamond and Denis Crowdy (2008).

Ben Dumbauld is a PhD candidate at the Graduate Center of the City University of New York. His research interests include local and subcultural music economies, performance studies, music of Romania, gender studies and music production technologies. Currently he is working on his dissertation, which focuses on interrelations between performance and political/economic ideologies within the Romanian community in New York City. He was the recipient of the Joann Kealiinohomoku Award for Excellence in 2010, and has published in *Ethnomusicology Review*. He teaches at Hunter College and holds a position at Bronx Community College.

Susan Fast is Professor in the Department of English and Cultural Studies, at McMaster University, Ontario. Her research interests include representations of gender and sexuality, race and ethnicity, constructions of self and other, performance and performativity, and geopolitical violence/conflict in contemporary popular music. She is author of the book *In the Houses of the Holy: Led Zeppelin and the Power of Rock Music* (2001), and co-editor of *Music, Politics and Violence* (2012). Her current project, funded by the Social Sciences and Humanities Research Council of Canada, investigates issues related to gender, race and normative genre boundaries in rock music; part of this study concentrates on the burgeoning scene of all-female tribute bands in hard rock and heavy metal.

Abigail Gardner is a Principal Lecturer in Popular Music and Media at the University of Gloucestershire, where she works on music and ageing, music video and music documentary. She has spent many years researching and writing about PJ Harvey and is now looking at her recent output in relation to manifestations of Englishness. She is editor (with Ros Jennings) of *Rock On: Women, Ageing and Popular Music* (2012) and author of *PJ Harvey and Music Video Performance* (2015). She has written on Dolly Parton in J. Dolan and E. Tincknell (eds), *Aging Femininities: Troubling Representations* (2012) and is co-author of *Media Studies: The Essential Resource* (2014). She is a member of IASPM and the Centre for Women, Ageing and Media (WAM), an international research hub based in Gloucestershire. Current projects include research on intergenerational expectations and experiences of popular music for WAM, and an investigation into Black Metal fans and 'Vice' music documentaries.

Paula Hearsum previously worked as a music journalist and now lectures in popular music and journalism at the University of Brighton. She has previously written for publications such as *NME, The Times, Red, Everywoman* (Music Editor), *1015* (*The Times* supplement) and *Sounds*. Her published work also includes the biography *Manic Street Preachers: Design for Living* (1997) and articles in *The Journal of Mortality* and *The Journal of Celebrity Studies*. She is currently engaged in research and writing projects around media representation of both popular music and popular musicians in the areas of death, technology and socio-cultural contexts.

LIST OF CONTRIBUTORS

Barbara Lebrun is a Senior Lecturer in French Studies at the University of Manchester. Her research is in the area of contemporary French popular music and covers a wide range of interests, including record production, audience reception, the representation of gender and ethnicity, and the roles of performance and prestige. She is the author of *Protest Music in France* (2009), which won the 2011 IASPM prize for Best Anglophone Monograph, and the editor of *Chanson et Performance* (2012). She is currently working on the career and posthumous fame of France's best-selling female singer Dalida.

June M. Madeley is Assistant Professor of Information and Communication Studies at the University of New Brunswick in Saint John, Canada. She is interested in the content, production and reception of various communications media and applies a focus on class, gender, ethnicity and racialisation to her work. Her current research centres on gender and the audiences of comic books and manga, and she has published work on this topic in *The Journal of Popular Culture*. She is currently working on analyses of science fiction and fantasy fandom.

Taylor Cole Miller is a doctoral student in Media and Cultural Studies at the University of Wisconsin-Madison. His primary areas of research interest include mediated identity struggle in the matrix of oppression, rural and heartland audience studies, queer spectatorship practices, feminist media studies and television studies. He received his MA in Media Studies from the University of Texas at Austin, a BA in Peninsular Spanish Literature from the University of Kansas, and a BS in Journalism also from the University of Kansas. He is also a regular contributor for *The Huffington Post*.

Penny Spirou is Graduate Education Officer at the University of Notre Dame, Australia, a tutor in Media Studies at the University of New South Wales, and Senior Research Officer at Macquarie University. Penny has published in the areas of musical biopics, celebrity and stardom, digital media and film genre in journals including *Refractory*, *Metro Magazine*, *Comedy Studies* and *Studies in Australasian Cinema*. She is a member of IASPM-ANZ and is Book Reviews Editor for *IASPM@ Journal*. Penny is currently completing a manuscript based on her PhD research on contemporary American musical biopics, due to be published in 2015.

Irene Stengs, a cultural anthropologist, is a senior researcher at the Meertens Instituut in Amsterdam, where she works on ritual and popular culture in the Netherlands. New public rituals, commemorative culture, heritage formation and the relation between celebrity culture and everyday life in the Netherlands form her principal interests. In 2009, she published *Worshipping the Great Modernizer: King Chulalongkorn, Patron Saint of the Thai Middle Class* (2009). She also worked on the Dutchness of multicultural rituals in the Netherlands and edited *Nieuw in Nederland. Feesten en rituelen in verandering* (2012). Presently, she is working on a book on the phenomenon of André Rieu, the world's 'King of the Waltz'.

Catherine Strong lectures in the Music Industry program at RMIT in Melbourne, Australia. She completed her PhD in Sociology at the Australian National University in 2008, and since this time has also worked at Monash University in Melbourne and Charles Sturt University in Wagga Wagga. She has published a monograph, *Grunge: Popular Music and Memory* (2011), as well as articles in *The Journal of Popular Culture* and *Perfect Beat*, and a number of book chapters. Her research deals with various aspects of memory, nostalgia and gender in rock music, popular culture and the media. She is currently Chair of the Australia–New Zealand branch of IASPM.

Justin A. Williams is a Lecturer in Music at the University of Bristol. He received a BA in History and a BA in Music from Stanford University, MMus in Music from King's College London and a PhD from the University of Nottingham under the supervision of Adam Krims. He has taught at Leeds College of Music, Lancaster University and Anglia Ruskin University, and has been published in *Popular Music*, *Popular Music History* and *The Journal of Musicology*. He is author of *Rhymin and Stealin: Musical Borrowing in Hip-hop* (2013) and is editor of the *Cambridge Companion to Hip-hop* (2015).

General Editors' Preface

Popular musicology embraces the field of musicological study that engages with popular forms of music, especially music associated with commerce, entertainment and leisure activities. The Ashgate Popular and Folk Music Series aims to present the best research in this field. Authors are concerned with criticism and analysis of the music itself, as well as locating musical practices, values and meanings in cultural context. The focus of the series is on popular music of the twentieth and twenty-first centuries, with a remit to encompass the entirety of the world's popular music.

Critical and analytical tools employed in the study of popular music are being continually developed and refined in the twenty-first century. Perspectives on the transcultural and intercultural uses of popular music have enriched understanding of social context, reception and subject position. Popular genres as distinct as reggae, township, bhangra, and flamenco are features of a shrinking, transnational world. The series recognises and addresses the emergence of mixed genres and new global fusions, and utilises a wide range of theoretical models drawn from anthropology, sociology, psychoanalysis, media studies, semiotics, postcolonial studies, feminism, gender studies and queer studies.

Stan Hawkins, Professor of Popular Musicology, University of Oslo &
Derek B. Scott, Professor of Critical Musicology, University of Leeds

Acknowledgements

We would firstly like to thank all of our contributors who have worked tirelessly with us to bring this volume together.

Catherine would also like to thank the membership of IASPM-ANZ, Kirsten Mclean, Andrew Woolcock, her family and friends, and Barbara for being a fantastic co-editor.

Barbara would like to thank Catherine in return, Bruno Levasseur and her colleagues at Manchester.

Chapter 1

The Great Gig in the Sky: Exploring Popular Music and Death

Barbara Lebrun and Catherine Strong

Death and the Rock Star examines the ways in which the deaths of popular musicians trigger new affective, aesthetic and commercial responses to their life and work, focusing on a range of interested parties that includes fellow artists, industry professionals, the media, political representatives, fans and family members. Our curiosity in this topic stems from our common interest in artists who committed suicide, whose musical identities we have examined elsewhere – Kurt Cobain of the grunge group Nirvana (Strong, 2011), and the Franco-Egyptian pop singer Dalida (Lebrun, 2013). Beyond music genres and generations, as well as beyond gender and continents, these two deaths have tended to seal the identity of the singers as 'tragic', in line with the Western, romantic fascination with the figure of the doomed artist. The manner of their deaths and the way they were mediated have, then, considerably restricted the musical meanings of their outputs. Meanwhile, their deaths have also triggered touching displays of empathy among fans worldwide, and greatly expanded the commercial possibilities of their music thanks to posthumous releases, covers, tributes and other forms of memorial processes that generate new pathways for emotional attachment, and additional revenue. It is this paradoxical power of death, its capacity to simultaneously restrict and expand meaning and possibilities, that this book addresses.

This is not a radical or novel ambition. Rather modestly, this book seeks to complement and expand our understanding of the ways in which our societies respond to the death of music celebrities, and how an artist's death affects the promotion, mediation and reception of their music. It does so by inserting itself into the growing trend for the study of popular music and death, and of popular music and death-related topics such as illness and ageing (Bennett and Hodkinson, 2012; Forman and Fairley, 2012; Jennings and Gardner, 2012). Specifically, the majority of our contributors acknowledge their debt to the rich and lucid collection by Steve Jones and Joli Jensen, *Afterlife as Afterimage: Understanding Posthumous Fame* (2005), which was the first to deal in depth with the fact that death modifies the celebrity status of popular music artists and the reactions of their fans. The present collection is less based in fandom and celebrity studies, but adds to Jones and Jensen's volume by covering several disciplines ranging from sociology and ethnography to film studies, cultural studies, legal studies and musicology.

In doing so, this book addresses some of the important cultural and technological changes that have taken place since the publication of *Afterlife as Afterimage*.

Indeed, the last 10 years have seen the quick succession of high-profile deaths by artists such as Michael Jackson (2009), Amy Winehouse (2011), Whitney Houston, Donna Summer, Ravi Shankar and Robin Gibb of the Bee Gees (all 2012), Lou Reed and JJ Cale (2013) – several are discussed here. There have been key technological improvements allowing for the mock-resurrection of artists through audio-visual duets between the dead and the living. Social media platforms such as Twitter, which launched in 2006, have also allowed for new fan-driven mourning activity. Increasingly, too, local and national authorities have recognised the symbolic and commercial advantage of commemorating the death of popular music artists, whether by organising state funerals, sponsoring memorial monuments or dedicating key dates in the calendar to tributes.[1] All these new trends, alongside older ones, are addressed here.

These trends are also examined through case-studies of artists drawn from the broad genres of rock, rap, pop, disco, punk and Afrobeat (the 'rock star' part of this book's title must be taken loosely). The artists principally discussed are the British Freddie Mercury, Ian Curtis and Amy Winehouse; the Americans Whitney Houston, Donna Summer, Kurt Cobain, Michael Jackson, GG Allin, Elvis Presley, Nat 'King' Cole and Tupac Shakur; the Australians Paul Hester, Chrissy Amphlett and Rowland S. Howard; the Dutch André Hazes; and the Nigerian Fela Kuti. Beyond the diversity of their musical expression and their varying degrees of fame, these artists have in common the fact of being now dead, and the capacity of their death to infuse new meanings into their recorded outputs.

Before presenting the key themes, arguments and methods of each chapter, we provide some brief context on the intersection of popular music with death. Indeed, why death and popular music in the first place? What is the nature of the relationship between the biological reality of death and the artistic practice of popular music? Is popular music as a medium affected by death differently from other artistic expressions?

Death and Popular Music

Firstly, the definition of the term 'death' cannot be taken for granted. Pragmatically, 'death' is the cessation of life, the ending of vital functions in biological organisms. Beyond this simple definition, however, lurks a bundle of philosophical and

---

[1]   For example, a statue of Amy Winehouse (as shown on the front cover of this book) was erected in Camden, London, on the key date of her birthday in September 2014, having been authorised by the local council (Selby, 2014). The statue is now considered a worthy attraction benefiting local trade, as advertised on Camden's Stables Market website (http://www.camdenmarket.com/whatson/amy-winehouse-statue-unveiled-1100-14th-september-2014-stables-market/).

empirical paradoxes, which affect cultural production and the social meanings attached to it. For death is also, as perceptively explained by Vladimir Jankélévitch (1966), simultaneously banal and mysterious: banal because every human body undergoes this process following their birth; yet mysterious because it is intangible until it happens, and it only ever affects an individual once. Death is familiar, regulated, an administrative formality to be declared; yet someone's death is always unheard-of, a scandal, an extra-ordinary event. Death in that sense is 'an always new banality', a most profound metaphysical puzzle (Jankélévitch, 1966 pp. 6–8). Understandably, this puzzle has preoccupied human beings ever since they first comprehended their own mortality.

Attempting to define death thus involves thinking about the attitudes and behaviours of the living (Jankélévitch, 1966 p. 33), for only those who outlive the dead, who experience a person's death by proxy, continue to make sense of the dead person, of themselves and of the world around them. Put slightly differently, one person's death only takes on its meaning beyond itself, in the social practices of those around the dead, and these practices are, like all human behaviour, imbued with symbolism and belief (see Berridge, 2001 p. 268). It is the role of cultural activity, then, to deal with death, to explore and elucidate it, to confront and confound it, to forget and cheat it. It is even likely that, as Zygmunt Bauman suggests (1992 p. 31), our acute self-awareness as mortals explains all cultural activity in the first place: 'there would probably be no culture were humans unaware of their mortality; culture is an elaborate counter-mnemotechnic device to forget what they are aware of'. Thus, from humble daily objects to precious or large-scale sculptures, through to whole cities and empires, human activity and cultural production can be seen as an attempt to defy our mortal condition by creating something that outlives us. By having their portraits painted, their deeds recorded or simply their patronage noted, patrons of the arts have, likewise, strived for a piece of immortality (Assmann, 2011).

Music is one artistic practice that has served to explore our relationship with death, and although all arts have had a similar preoccupation, the musical works that deal with death have taken arresting and influential forms. In the (post-)Romantic compositions of the 1870s (Saint-Saëns's 'La Danse Macabre', 1874; Mussorgsky's 'Songs and Dances of Death', 1875–7), like in twentieth and twenty-first-century popular music, death has been a key theme in the lyrics and compositions of many artists. Today, entire genres of popular music either are, or are perceived to be, fixated on it, including goth (Hodkinson, 2002), emo (Thomas-Jones, 2008) and several revealingly named heavy metal sub-genres such as 'death metal' (Phillipov, 2012) and 'suicidal black metal' (Silk, 2013). But the relationship between death and popular music does not stop at thematic inspiration. It also encompasses material constraints and symbolic meanings which distinguish popular music from other art forms, and which arguably tighten its links to both the concept and the physical reality of death.

Firstly, music is, like film, an 'art of time' rather than of space, a medium that unfolds sequentially through, and is limited by, time (Elleström, 2010 p. 19).

This technical constraint means that a song always foretells an end, and always entails the metaphoric and symbolic death of a human voice. The French *chanson* theorist Stéphane Hirschi (2008 pp. 33–4), for instance, considers that interpreters and audiences are always aware of a song's imminent end, and describes each song as an 'agony' on one level.[2] By contrast, there is no 'end' to the still art forms of painting, sculpture and photography, and even a book, whose narrative does end after the last word, remains materially present. When a song reaches its end, however, it is gone. A song's recorded format and capacity to be played again and again actually heightens that impression, as we emphasise below.

Secondly, and even when visual identity and performance are inseparable from the medium, popular music remains a primarily sound-based art form, relying on musical instruments and a singer's voice to exist. A singing voice, as Barthes (1992 p. 251) has eloquently theorised, implicitly mobilises the whole body of the singer, by necessitating breathing and by making the singer's physiological, individual asperities to be heard. Therefore, singing specifically evokes a human's capacity to be alive, while foreshadowing their (symbolic) mortality due to its time constraint.

The impression that a singer is wholly 'alive' may be particularly poignant during an aptly named 'live' performance, as in dance and theatre, but the paradox that a song evokes the artist's capacity to be alive, or their 'liveness' (Auslander, 1999), and their mortality as well, is enhanced during audio-recording. Indeed, from its inception in the 1890s, the sound recording technique has had the capacity to 'freeze a moment in time and move it into the future' (Laing, 1991 p. 3), thereby allowing listeners to ignore the biological condition of the speaker and to engage with them regardless of whether they are actually alive or dead during the broadcast. Thus sound recording, in addition to producing a strikingly fleshed out form of aural intimacy with another human being, seemingly reverses mortality itself, forging the uncanny experience of simultaneous absence-presence (see Sterne, 2005). If popular music in general evokes human life (the voice we hear is unique, and moving through time), and foretells mortality (a song is about to finish), then recorded popular music in particular evokes death (the singer might as well be dead) while ignoring it (the singer's death is irrelevant since we can still hear them). The idea of death, then, is core to the conceptualisation and technical possibilities of popular music as a medium.

In addition, the physical reality of death is central to popular music as a practice due to its performative element, its physical embodiment in the gestures of singers and musicians. Indeed, popular music artists project their bodies in a presumably more wholesome, direct way than other performing artists whose art also unfolds sequentially, like screen and stage actors. While the latter follow scripts that are rarely self-penned, and knowingly create the illusion of identity through their role-playing, popular musicians and especially singer-songwriters are partly required,

---

[2]   Keith Negus (2012) expands the idea of popular music's temporal experience in a recent article.

and largely perceived, to transmit through their performance something of their 'real' emotional self (Weisethaunet and Lindberg, 2010). This corresponds to the imperative of 'authenticity', one of the most powerful conventions to have framed popular music since the Second World War, at least in the West, and whose prestige has been central to all the popular music genres since rock music. 'Authenticity' remains a key concept in music criticism and popular music scholarship today, despite significant reservations concerning its meaningfulness (Machin, 2010 pp. 14–18).

Nevertheless, this expected overlap between life and art in popular music explains that large segments of the audience frequently develop what they believe to be intimate connections with an artist, sensing that the artist's life unfolds in their creative works. As several of the following chapters demonstrate, audience members can find themselves profoundly lost when an artist dies, and this sentiment is particularly troubling, and sometimes perversely satisfying, when the artist displayed, during their lifetime, a creative interest in death. For instance, striking effects of 'authenticity' whereby life appears to imitate art occurred when the singer-songwriters Ian Curtis (1956–80) and Kurt Cobain (1967–94) committed suicide after composing songs with death-obsessed lyrics, including 'Existence, well what does it matter?' in Joy Division's 'Heart and Soul' (1980), and Nirvana's seemingly programmatic (but actually tongue-in-cheek) 'I Hate Myself and I Want To Die' (1994). Likewise, when the American gangsta rap artist Tupac Shakur, who often described and occasionally glorified gang violence in his lyrics, died in a shooting that many believe was caused by a gang feud, the connection between death and popular music took on a strikingly 'real' and sinister turn, which later artists have themselves enjoyed exploring (see Williams in this volume).

Lastly, the convergence between death and popular music is particularly striking in sociological terms. For instance, popular musicians tend to die sooner, more unexpectedly and more violently than other artists (and than the rest of us), due to the lifestyles they adopt and the risks they can face. In the UK and USA at least, 'famous' rock and pop stars have died younger than the general population and continue to do so until 25 years after they first become famous (Bellis et al., 2007). Similarly, Dianna Kenny (2014) has found that the lifespans of popular musicians were 'up to 25 years shorter than the comparable US population', and that '[a]ccidental death rates were between five and 10 times greater. Suicide rates were between two and seven times greater; and homicide rates were up to eight times greater than the US population'. Indeed, rock music has claimed young victims from its first days in the 1950s, when artists died violently in plane and car crashes, most famously the Big Bopper, Buddy Holly and Ritchie Valens who were all killed on the same flight, aged 29, 25 and just 17 respectively. Popular musicians have also frequently suffered from overdoses of various substances (Jim Morrison, Whitney Houston, Amy Winehouse), or died on and off-stage in sudden ways, from being electrocuted (Leslie Harvey of Stone the Crows), suffering a heart-attack (Mark Sandman of Morphine) or being shot by a crazed fan (John Lennon; Dimebag Darrell of Pantera). The coincidence that many died at the age of 27 has also given rise to one of the most popular conspiracy theories, that of the '27 Club' (see Bennett in this volume).

Thus it is that death, whether as an artistically fruitful theme, as a symbol embedded within audio-recording techniques, or as a physiological reality, has become a central element in popular music generally, and in the mediated 'star texts' (Dyer, 1998 p. 63) of popular singers and musicians specifically. Death can be, as in the examples explored in this collection, so intimately tied to an artist's songs, life and star image that it confers a heightened emotional charge to the discourses that surround them. Death can be particularly fundamental, as this book insists, in the meaning-making processes that the entourage of the dead engage in, whether these people are colleagues, fans, journalists or other parties. Examining these processes produces insights not only into how we understand these artists, but also into the ways in which our society relates to death itself.

To facilitate this exploration, this book is divided into four parts: 'Death and Taboo', 'Mediating the Dead', 'The Labouring Dead' and 'Resurrections', a grouping we discuss below. Beyond this practical divide, however, all the chapters share a number of similar arguments. In particular, all our authors demonstrate that, once an artist has died, the immediate overwhelming tendency is to pay homage to the dead, to express respect for the musical skills and the creative individuality of the artist, and to mourn through a vast range of new words, gestures, rituals and objects. These can be obituaries by press journalists (Hearsum; Fast), tweets by grieving fans (Miller), covers or new songs by fellow artists (Bennett; Madeley and Downes; Williams), including duets (Williams; Brunt; Arnold). They can be museum exhibitions and stage shows (Gardner), biopics and TV series (Spirou; Miller), memorial sites including street signs (Strong) and statues (Stengs), and of course eulogies and funerals (Dumbauld; Stengs; Miller). The vast majority of these memorialising practices are well-intentioned and generous, artistically inventive and even joyful. They can also be self-centred, however, as when an artist's death provides an opportunity for record producers and copyright holders to maximise profit (Madeley and Downes), or when fellow artists benefit from the dead's aura of prestige (Brunt; Williams). Typically, too, memorial practices appear restrictive in reducing the full complexity of an artist's life and work to a much smaller set of signs, with the tendency to ignore certain aspects and to essentialise others. This book's chapters develop this point with reference to very different artists.

Part I: Death and Taboo

For many centuries, at least in the West, humans have had a great physical proximity with death, as several generations usually lived together and family members died in the home. This, the cultural historian Philippe Ariès (1974 p. 544) has argued, led to a relationship with death that was relatively comfortable and familiar, as its reality was ever-present. This proximity unravelled progressively, however, first with new inheritance laws in the Early Modern period, then with advances in medicine and hygiene in the second half of the twentieth century. This resulted in the old and the sick dying predominantly in hospitals and care homes, only exceptionally at home, and in our contemporary lack of familiarity with death. Death turned into an 'unnameable thing', 'the principal taboo of the modern world' (Ariès, 1974 p. 553). Since the post-war period, this taboo has taken the form of an increased sanitisation, with death now placed in the hands of doctors and undertakers, and of an increased commoditisation as professionals vie for this most reliable of markets. Death is also taboo in the sense that the dying and the grieving alike are expected to display secrecy and self-control, to find 'the courage to be discreet' (Ariès, 1974 p. 544). Exuberance, noise and excessive bodily displays (tears, snot, jerky movements) are not in good taste around the dying and the dead.

The paradox is that, as our intimacy with the physical reality of the deaths of those we are close to has waned, so one's own death is more intimate than ever, a personal and lonely affair. And as the death of a known or loved one is no longer public, so the death of many more unknown individuals is increasingly mediatised. Indeed, since the post-war era and not coincidentally at around the same time that popular music became a major cultural form, death has re-emerged into the public eye in new ways fundamentally shaped by mediatisation, individualisation and capitalism. Theorists from Geoffrey Gorer (1960) to Margaret Gibson (2007a) have highlighted the increasingly explicit representations of death to be found throughout Western popular culture, whether fictionalised in violent movies or as representations of the 'real' in the news. The various examples of popular music artists fascinated with death mentioned above, and those (sometimes the same) whose deaths were heavily mediatised, further demonstrate this trend. In her study directly responding to Ariès's claim, subtitled 'The End of the Death Taboo', Kate Berridge (2001) has shown that the public and private spheres of identity have become increasingly blurred in relation to death and mourning, as intensely personal experiences of death (one's own or that of others) are offered for public consumption through artistic *mise-en-scène* and 'confessionals' of various sorts. This evolution does not, however, represent a return to an everyday and familiar relationship with death. On the contrary, Gibson (2007a) argues that mediated death may make individuals less able to deal with actual death when faced with it.

Thus, if death is simultaneously distant and close, common and impersonal, it remains conventionally framed, in our Western society, by avoidance, restraint and dignity. It is in this paradoxical context that popular musicians, as one kind of mediated celebrities, have sometimes challenged social conventions around death by displaying their physical vulnerability during performance, and by defiling and modifying their bodies in a manner that goes against the death taboos of discretion, health and self-control. In rock music in particular, the many unpredictable and messy ends of young stars 'choking to death in their own vomit' have confronted the ideal of dignified, sequestered death, and exemplified the ugliness of death

DEATH AND THE ROCK STAR

for fans and the general public. Rock star corpses not only make death visible and non-conformist, but also make its nature – universal, inevitable, irreversible – impossible to deny.

As Ben Dumbauld demonstrates, the American punk GG Allin built his career around such subversion as a sado-masochist with an interest in the macabre, and his funeral during which the public touched various parts of his unwashed and decomposing corpse was a moment of heightened negation of conventions, almost a return to a pre-Modern sensibility and a time when putrefaction, the horrors of physical death, were part and parcel of artistic expression (see Ariès, 1976 p. 41). In her chapter on the Dutch singer André Hazes, Irene Stengs also shows that artists who 'let themselves go', by drinking and smoking excessively for instance, imbue their performance with subversive value, and encourage the fans after their death to continue to challenge the social order, for instance by using the dead body in spectacular and intimate ways alike – not every singer has their ashes used for firework displays and tattoos. In a similar vein, in a thought-piece expanded from its original 2009 publication, Susan Fast argues that Michael Jackson's changing physical appearance during his lifetime, and his refusal to perform either masculinity or 'blackness' in line with societal norms, led to the public perception that he was somehow 'unnatural', going against conventions of decency and parenthood. When he died, obituaries and public reactions dwelled on these transgressions, and his body was presented as a site of abjection more significant to understanding his 'identity' than his musical skills.

In this way, the taboos that artists break during their lives can come to define them in their death, but to different ends. Hazes and Allin's taboo-breaking activity, their capacity to challenge conventions and to perform vulnerability, addiction or unhealthiness, has been celebrated by their fans in their memory. In the case of Jackson, however, his transgressions have been used to shore up the taboos he challenged and to reinforce conventions, even as his death elicited sympathy denied to him during the last years of his life.

Part II: Mediating the Dead

Since death is the affair of the living, all death is mediated somehow, in the sense of there being a human intermediary between the deceased and those who learn about that death, or who invest themselves in the dead person's life and work. Gibson (2007a p. 420) has argued that, as our everyday life is increasingly mediated and as new forms of media emerge, 'celebrity deaths have increasingly gained significance as the means through which collective and public forms of mourning are ritualised'. Celebrity deaths are thus given form and meaning through intermediaries that include relatives, colleagues, journalists, songwriters, producers, museum curators, commercial lobbies and town planners, as the chapters in this book all explore in varying degrees of detail. In this part, three chapters provide an in-depth analysis of the contemporary mediations of dead artists, focusing on the use of the social media Twitter by music fans as a grieving tool, and on new audio-visual creations like biopics and tribute acts to selectively re-invent aspects of the dead's identity.

Andy Bennett begins this part by considering that mediation, often in the form of televised concert footage, can create collective memories of a dead music star across space and time. Nonetheless, among a finite pool of available images, only a restricted number tends to re-circulate, with the consequence that the identity of the dead tends to be fixed, for the following generations, in an essentialised, even if sympathetic, manner. By contrast, with their at times unsettling simulation skills, tribute artists provide audiences with the experience of something approaching the 'authenticity' of an original show by John Lennon or Freddie Mercury, and can be more experimental than existing footage in their revisiting of the dead artists' performance – sometimes to the bewilderment of fans.

The notion that an artist's death influences posthumous representations is key in Penny Spirou's chapter, in which she demonstrates the growing popularity in biopics that focus on deceased popular musicians. Developing the examples of Kurt Cobain and Ian Curtis, who both killed themselves, she shows that the manner of their death is selectively handled by film-makers to suggest that suicide is the most important lens through which to interpret the artists' life and work. Her analysis of soundtrack and visual editing, alongside narrative connections to suicide stereotypes (for instance, the perception of the suicidal as isolated and withdrawn), ultimately frames suicide as inevitable. In turn, these films add to the already existing 'media texts' that define and limit the artists through their death.

In his chapter, Taylor Cole Miller analyses the tweets of Whitney Houston fans who mourned her passing, and proposes the concept of 'social sorrow' to explain their collective behaviour. While mass public displays of grief have occurred historically during the passing of religious, political and artistic figures,[3] with Twitter, a new social media launched in 2006, we witness instant, collective and global grief for the dead, in a display of social bond that cuts across absence (of the dead) and distance (between one another). Twitter's novelty lies in its instantaneity, global ubiquity and expressive constraint, and allows grieving to be fan-driven rather than organised by families and officials. In this, Twitter drastically updates the age-old practices of expressing compassion and sharing emotions in times of hardship.

---

[3] All echelons of the UK population grieved for days with the sudden passing of Princess Charlotte of Wales in 1817 (Williams, 2010); 2 million people attended the Paris funeral of novelist Victor Hugo in May 1885 (Bressant, 2008); and if only 1 million flocked to Westminster Abbey for the funeral of Princess Diana in September 1997, an estimated 2.5 billion watched the TV broadcast (Merrin, 1999).

Part III: The Labouring Dead

We outlined above the contemporary paradox that the death of close, 'real' ones is taboo while that of distant, unknown, 'famous' people is mediatised and exhibited. Another paradox outlined by Jason Stayek and Benjamin Piekut (2010 p. 16) is that, in our (post-)capitalist society, not only does death not mark the end of productivity or labour, but the living are also engaged in an 'intermundane' relationship with the dead, continuously 'rearticulating' them in various ways. This process is precisely observable in the tributes to dead artists orchestrated by the living for combined emotional, aesthetic and, not least, commercial purposes, for death can be a good opportunity for profit-making in the music industry (Jones and Jensen, 2005 p. 3). Anniversaries often become commercial opportunities of great scope; as Gibson (2007b p. 2) notes, 'the production of media archives of celebrities ensures that they never entirely disappear. Indeed, the anniversary becomes a commercial opportunity and deceased celebrities are resurrected year after year'. In this part, on mediation, all the chapters evaluate the discourses and intentions held by cultural gate-keepers who speak from a relative position of authority in society, creating meanings around dead artists that sometimes conflict with those from the bottom-up, from the fans and families. Importantly, these chapters show collectively that every new cultural item produced relating to dead musicians, including obituaries, biographies, exhibitions, movies and memorials, dialogues with a pre-existing world of meanings, and 'puts the dead to work' in order to serve the interests of the living (whether in terms of prestige, income or ideology).

In her chapter, Catherine Strong shows the activity of family members, fans, journalists and municipal leaders who decide to name Melbourne streets after dead artists. Often taking years to come into effect, with bureaucratic constraints to contend with, such memorialising processes only happen thanks to the energy, time and effort of interested parties whose lives are, within the remit of this specific goal, very much shaped by the dead. With the living's hope that a new street sign will enhance the memory and respect for an artist, the dead are certainly not 'permanently removed ... from the society of the living', but rather continue to have an 'impact on the lifeworld' (Howarth, 2007 p. 216). At the same time, however, these namings have multiple benefits for the living, for example through increased tourism for the city and higher cultural capital for both the city and the individuals involved.

In their two chapters, Paula Hearsum and Abigail Gardner examine the role of obituaries in honouring the dead, alongside the production of stage shows and exhibitions. Both demonstrate the biased nature of posthumous tributes, as the varied and often conflicting musical meanings of artists, during their lifetime, are reduced, when they die, to convenient labels tapping into gendered and racial stereotypes. Hearsum shows the emphasis on the trope of motherhood in obituaries of Amy Winehouse, Whitney Houston and Donna Summer. Gardner discusses the emphasis on sexuality and race in the case of Fela Kuti. Both underline that an artist's death, while generating a huge amount of 'living' activity, often works by essentialising and generalising identity, with potentially negative social consequences. Given that obituaries are often brief and quick responses to fast-moving news, fitting into pre-existing journalistic frames, they tend to put the dead to 'work' to stabilise the status quo.

Madeley and Downes identify a similar and much more deliberate process in what they call the 'transpropertisation' of dead musicians, specifically of Elvis Presley, whose songs and image have been recombined and channelled through a multitude of cultural objects and events. A dead artist of this scope requires a huge legal and commercial institution to control the uses of his 'identity', and the copyright holders of Elvis Presley's name, music and image only authorise the reproduction of certain songs and performances, setting out legal limitations on what constitute 'correct' posthumous tributes. In this case, we see attempts to control cultural meanings in order to protect commercial interests, and a narrow version of Elvis now 'works' to generate income for those who have legal ownership of him.

Part IV: Resurrections

Finally, if as Stayek and Piekut (2010 p. 14) argue, 'the living do not one-sidedly handle the dead, but participate in an inter-handling, a mutually effective co-laboring', then this pattern is most evident in the current trend for the 'resurrection' of dead artists, in the form of technologically enhanced posthumous duets between the living and the dead. This trend updates, to an extent, the human need to preserve and simulate the physical likeness of those who have died. In the thirteenth century, for example, stone and wood effigies adorned the tombs of the dead and reproduced their 'living' features in a manner as realistic as then possible (Ariès, 1976 p. 47). While this funeral art was intended as *memento mori* however, as objects reminding humans of their own mortality, the final three chapters question the contemporary needs and ethics for seemingly 'reviving' the dead in the first place.

Shelley D. Brunt reminds us that 'posthumous duets' first developed in the 1950s, as analogue recording enabled the voice of a dead artist to be taped and mixed alongside that of a living person. In the early twenty-first century, the fine-tuning of CGI techniques allows for complete audio-visual performances to be created that show dead artists as if alive. Brunt focuses on three instances of televised posthumous duets, demonstrating that invoking the dead in this way can be a source of entertainment for audiences, of distinction for performers, and of income for producers.

In her piece examining the much discussed duet between the living Snoop Dogg and the dead Tupac Shakur at the Coachella festival in April 2012, Regina Arnold questions the moral imperative behind the apparent 'resurrection' of the dead, suggesting that making artists participate in duets without their (impossible) consent is akin to a form of modern enslavement. She argues that Shakur's body, and the uses it was put to in this posthumous performance, became emblematic of the misuse of black bodies in US history, and more widely in post-colonial societies. She understands Shakur as a dead black man and a victim of racial violence who, in death, becomes a fetishised Other for the delight of a mostly white middle-class audience, in a depressing continuation of colonial power structures.

While both Arnold and Brunt examine the lack of agency of the dead, and question the moral imperative of the living to resurrect them, both Arnold and Justin A. Williams consider race an important element in the production of posthumous meanings. Indeed, by analysing the lyrics and compositional practices of US gangsta rap artists, including the California-based, black rapper The Game, Williams praises in the final chapter the inventiveness of posthumous voice sampling, and the important function that this technique plays in shaping prestige and lineage for the living. Drawing attention to the musical tradition of the lament and to the Christian overtones of African-American music culture, Williams also shows that commemorating the dead through voice sampling can reinforce, but also complicate, the place of violence in US hip-hop culture.

In summary, this volume expands research into the relationship between popular music and death, observing the impact of new technology and behaviours on existing debates revolving around the notions of agency, authenticity, ethics, prestige, gender, race and more. For all the numbing effects that death procures, it still does not mark the end of human activity, and in the case of popular musicians death can often be as much a beginning as an end.

Bibliography

Ariès, Philippe (1974 [1967]) 'The Reversal of Death: Changes in Attitudes toward Death in Western Societies', *American Quarterly*, 26 (5), pp. 536–60.
———— (1976) *Western Attitudes toward Death: From the Middle Ages to the Present*. Translated by Patricia M. Ranum. London and New York: Marion Boyars.
Assmann, Aleida (2011) *Cultural Memory and Western Civilisation: Functions, Media, Archives*. Cambridge: Cambridge University Press.
Auslander, Philip (1999) *Liveness: Performance in a Mediatized Culture*. Abingdon and New York: Routledge.
Barthes, Roland (1992 [1972]) *L'obvie et l'obtus. Essais critiques III*. Paris: Points.
Bauman, Zygmunt (1992) *Mortality, Immortality and Other Life Strategies*. Stanford, CA: Stanford University Press.
Bellis, Mark A., Tom Hennell, Clare Lushey, Karen Hughes, Karen Tocque and John R. Ashton (2007) 'Elvis to Eminem: Quantifying the Price of Fame through Early Mortality of European and North American Rock and Pop Stars', *Journal of Epidemiology and Community Health*, 61, pp. 896–901.

Bennett, Andy and Paul Hodkinson (2013) *Ageing and Youth Cultures: Music, Style and Identity*. London: Berg.

Berridge, Kate (2001) *Vigor Mortis: The End of the Death Taboo*. London: Profile Books.

Bressant, Marc (2008) *Les funérailles de Victor Hugo*. Paris: Michel de Maule.

Dyer, Richard (1998 [1979]) *Stars*. London: British Film Institute.

Elleström, Lars (2010) 'The Modalities of Media: A Model for Understanding Intermedial Relations', in Lars Elleström (ed.), *Media Borders, Multimodality and Intermediality*. Basingstoke and New York: Palgrave Macmillan, pp. 11–48.

Forman, Murray and Jan Fairley (eds) (2012) 'As Time Goes By: Music, Dance and Ageing', special issue of *Popular Music*, 31 (2).

Gibson, Margaret (2007a) 'Death and Mourning in Technologically Mediated Culture', *Health Sociology Review*, 16, pp. 415–24.

————— (2007b) 'Some Thoughts on Celebrity Deaths: Steve Irwin and the Issue of Public Mourning', *Mortality*, 12 (1), pp. 1–3.

Gorer, Geoffrey (1960) 'The Pornography of Death', in Maurice Stein, Arthur J. Vidich and David Manning White (eds), *Identity and Anxiety: Survival of the Person in Mass Society*. New York: The Free Press.

Hirschi, Stéphane (2008) *Chanson. L'art de fixer l'air du temps. De Béranger à Mano Solo*. Paris et Valenciennes: Les Belles Lettres/Presses Universitaires de Valenciennes.

Hodkinson, Paul (2002) *Goth: Identity, Style and Subculture*. Oxford: Berg.

Howarth, Glennys (2007) *Death and Dying: A Sociological Introduction*. Cambridge: Polity.

Jankélévitch, Vladimir (1966) *La mort*. Paris: Flammarion.

Jennings, Ros and Abigail Gardner (2012) *'Rock On': Women, Ageing and Popular Music*. Aldershot: Ashgate.

Jones, Steve (2005) 'Better off Dead: Or, Making it the Hard Way', in Steve Jones and Joli Jensen (eds), *Afterlife as Afterimage: Understanding Posthumous Fame*. New York: Peter Lang, pp. 1–16.

Jones, Steve and Joli Jensen (eds) (2005) *Afterlife as Afterimage: Understanding Posthumous Fame*. New York: Peter Lang.

Kenny, Dianna (2014) 'Stairway to Hell: Life and Death in the Pop Music Industry', *The Conversation*, 27 October, http://theconversation.com/stairway-to-hell-life-and-death-in-the-pop-music-industry-32735, accessed 27 October 2014.

Laing, Dave (1991) 'A Voice without a Face: Popular Music and the Phonograph in the 1890s', *Popular Music*, 10 (1), pp. 1–9.

Lebrun, Barbara (2013) 'Daughter of the Mediterranean, Docile European: Dalida in the 1950s', *Journal of European Popular Culture*, 4 (1), pp. 85–97.

Machin, David (2010) *Analysing Popular Music: Image, Sound, Text*. London, Thousand Oaks, CA, New Delhi and Singapore: Sage.

Merrin, William (1999) 'Crash, Bang, Wallop! What a Picture! The Death of Diana and the Media', *Mortality*, 4 (1), pp. 41–62.

Negus, Keith (2012) 'Narrative Time and the Popular Song', *Popular Music and Society*, 35 (4), pp. 483–500.

Phillipov, Michelle (2012) *Death Metal and Music Criticism: Analysis at the Limits*. Plymouth: Lexington.

Selby, Jenn (2014) 'Amy Winehouse Statue Unveiled in Camden', *The Independent*, 14 September, http://www.independent.co.uk/news/people/amy-winehouse-statue-unveiled-in-camden-9732038.html, accessed 31 October 2014.

Silk, Janet (2013) 'Open a Vein: Suicidal Black Metal and Enlightenment', *Helvete: A Journal of Black Metal Theory*, 1 (1), pp. 5–20.

Stayek, Jason and Benjamin Piekut (2010) 'Deadness: Technologies of the Intermundane', *The Drama Review*, 54 (1), pp. 14–38.

Sterne, Jonathan (2005) 'Dead Rock Stars 1900', in Steve Jones and Joli Jensen (eds), *Afterlife as Afterimage: Understanding Posthumous Fame*. New York: Peter Lang, pp. 253–68.

Strong, Catherine (2011) *Grunge: Music and Memory*. Farnham: Ashgate.

Thomas-Jones, Angela (2008) 'Emo is not the New Black: Current Affairs Journalism and the Marking of Popular Culture', *Metro Magazine: Media and Education Magazine*, 156, pp. 72–7.

Weisethaunet, Hans and Ulf Lindberg (2010) 'Authenticity Revisited: The Rock Critic and the Changing Real', *Popular Music and Society*, 33 (4), pp. 465–85.

Williams, Kate (2010) *Becoming Queen Victoria: The Tragic Death of Princess Charlotte and the Unexpected Rise of Britain's Greatest Monarch*. New York: Ballantine.

PART I
Death and Taboo

Chapter 2

The Afterlife of the People's Singer: Bodily Matters in a Dutch Sing-along Culture

Irene Stengs

One stereotypical way in which many people in the Netherlands like to think of 'the Dutch' is as a sober-minded, commonsensical people. This perception may explain the surprise, disdain and existential despair evoked by the nationwide media coverage and emotional responses to the death of Dutch 'songs of life' singer André Hazes (1951–2004). Most discussion was provoked by the free farewell concert organised by fellow singers and celebrity friends in the Amsterdam football stadium (Amsterdam ArenA), particularly because, unusually, the singer's body was present at the event. The farewell's live broadcast – on 27 September 2004, by state-funded broadcaster TROS – drew an audience of 5 million Dutch and 1 million Flemish (out of 16 million and 6 million respectively) from all echelons of society (see De Hart, 2005 pp. 32–3). Nearly 50,000 people attended the concert, entitled *André bedankt* (*Thank you, André*), including the singer's family.[1]

It seems a matter of course that extraordinary people require extraordinary farewell ceremonies. However, who is considered extraordinary changes over time, as do the celebrations. Moreover, as the André Hazes farewell demonstrated, such changes are not self-evident or uncontested. The way societies organise their celebrities' deaths, and the practices and places employed in commemoration, articulate some of the wider political and moral issues at stake. As we will see, the *André bedankt* farewell ceremony was only the beginning of an expanding and changing commemorative culture surrounding the deceased singer. To analyse this culture, I take the body and bodily matters as my central focus. Three empirical observations motivate this choice. First, Hazes's dead body remained active in the world of the living much longer than usual. Hazes's corpse belonged to the category of – in Verdery's (1999 p. 13) words – the 'named and famous', which partly explains the wider interest in and struggle over his body, and its resulting journeys. Yet, even for a celebrity, the amount of interest and struggle was extraordinary, at least in the Dutch context. To understand the specific ritual forms

---

[1] Part of the argument in this chapter was developed in Stengs (2009; 2010). I am indebted to the editors for their critical reading and suggestions, and to Jeroen Beets for his comments and for editing the text.

of the subsequent handlings of the body and its remains, Hazes's stardom – that is, the interconnectedness between 'Hazes' and the media – will prove to be central.

A second impetus for this bodily focus is Hazes's physical appearance. Bodily identification with the singer through ritualising his unhealthy habits (particularly drinking and smoking), mimicking his appearance, and singing along with his songs, are vital to the way the singer's hard-core fans remember their idol. Mary Douglas's perspective on the human body as an image for society helps to understand the significance of Hazes's actual physical appearance. The latter may be interpreted as a symbolic vehicle for a counter-model of society (Douglas, 1970). Moreover, following Scheper-Hughes and Lock (1987 pp. 23–4), I regard the relationship between individual and social bodies as one of power and control, or 'body politics'.

Hazes's multiple resurrections provide the third argument for taking the body as the core object of study. Hazes lives on in a variety of bodies, which all in their way 'alter the temporality associated with the person, bringing him into the realm of the timeless or the sacred, like an icon' (Verdery, 1999 p. 5). These resurrections include his statue, the look-alikes, his offspring performing in his style and, finally, his 'more real than life' impersonator in the successful musical on Hazes's life. Hazes's posthumous fame eventually reached dazzling heights in the Netherlands, a development that to my interpretation should be placed in the context of the current preoccupation with national identity in that country. However, understanding why Hazes became the object of such extensive interest and why his body is so significant in remembering him requires first an introduction to the phenomenon of Hazes during his life, and an explanation of how his music is embedded in Dutch society.

'The People's Singer'

André Hazes was one of the many performers of the sentimental Dutch music genre *levenslied*, literally 'song of life'. The genre's main characteristics are the use of specific idioms in the lyrics, addressing such topics as the love, hardship and loneliness of 'the ordinary person', and a strong opera- or operetta-like vibrato, the latter adding to the songs' sentimental or dramatic character. What distinguishes *levenslied* from other song genres (children songs, pop songs, opera) is its mainstream white, autochthonous, locally informed, 'adult' sing-along culture. Generally, these so-called 'sing-along songs' (*meezingers*) are simple in text and melody and known by heart by millions of Dutch. Whether during a night out in the pub, at family birthday parties, public feasts or in various work settings, *levenslied* songs may be sung out loud. I understand a sing-along culture as the practice of singing-along with the voices of singers, irrespective of whether these voices are live or recorded. Herewith, I distinguish sing-along culture from song-culture in general, in which, for instance, the singing of children's songs or participating in choirs can be included. Taking singing-along as a distinctive feature shifts the research focus from lyrics or melody (as in prevailing song research) to the performative dimensions of (joint) singing.

Hazes gave a new turn to *levenslied* by combining it with pop music elements to create *levenspop*. *Levenspop* became also known as *polder blues*, a label better resonating with Hazes's ambitions to become a blues singer, as he felt emotional affinity with the blues in the first place (Haagsma, 2004 p. 86). This increasing ambition explains his Blues Brothers-inspired outfit adopted in the later 1990s: black clothes, black hat, sunglasses and rock 'n' roll side-whiskers. The latter elements still inform look-alike practices in the Hazes commemorative culture. Hazes, in a sense, had initiated such practices himself. In 2002, for example, he had 20,000 Hazes hat-and-sunglasses packages made to sell during a concert.

Today, many Dutch celebrities are *levenslied*-cum-*levenspop* performers, their concerts attracting tens of thousands of people time and again. Yet, this development dates only from the 1990s and may be understood as a revaluation of Dutchness and 'all things Dutch' in response to globalisation and social tensions in an increasingly multi-ethnic society. Although *levenslied* is mainstream today, the genre is perceived as belonging to or originating from the urban lower class. Consequently, *levenslied* was – and in many respects still is – not taken seriously in the higher echelons of society. Strongly associated with 'lowbrow' tastes, the music was even banned from national radio stations until the 1980s (De Bruin and Grijp, 2006 p. 948; Klöters, 2006), and could only be heard on illegal channels, amateur or commercial, the so-called 'pirate broadcasters' (*etherpiraten*). These historically informed characteristics of 'lowbrow' tastes, illegality and anti-establishment are vital to an understanding of Hazes's position within *levenslied* popular culture. Although Hazes's life ended in stardom, it started in poverty and neglect, as recounted time and again in widely mediatised (auto)biographical texts and images. This explains why Hazes and his *levenspop* are strongly connected with places and occasions of 'ordinary people'. Upon asking, people will answer that it is the lyrics that captivate them: the fans recognise themselves and their own lives in Hazes's (un)happy moments and failures, his problems and loneliness. He was a man from a working-class background, singing about 'life as it really is for ordinary people' and therefore somebody with whom his fans could identify – and still do. This background enabled Hazes's image to develop into that of a man of 'exceptional ordinariness', as expressed in the epigraph on the statue unveiled one year after his death at the Amsterdam Albert Cuyp street market: 'Really special, really ordinary. Just a very special man'.[2] For a better understanding of this dimension, I will briefly recount the most important elements of his life story as it is generally told.

---

[2] 'Heel bijzonder, heel gewoon. Gewoon een heel bijzondere man'.

A Dramatic Life

The story of Hazes's life is a narration of a 'jack-of-all trades and master of none', gifted with a remarkable vocal talent from childhood on. Virtually all accounts start with the endearing anecdote of Hazes as a boy of eight, singing at the Albert Cuyp market to earn some money to buy a present for his mother. This account disseminates three important elements: first, it locates Hazes as an Amsterdam working-class lad; second, it testifies to Hazes's natural talent as a singer; and third, it gives proof of Hazes's sentimental and emotional personality. The last of these places him within a moral framework: he was poor but he had a heart of gold.[3]

Hazes's problematic youth is often mentioned as an important source for his sentimentality. Born as the fourth child of six in a poor family, he grew up without much warmth or security. Although his mother was good to her children, his father was an alcoholic, often unemployed, who beat his children. The combination of a sensitive nature, a simple background and hard youth usually accounts for Hazes's later excellent performance of the *levenslied*. Truly singing *levenslied* is considered to require such personal life experience: the singers should not just 'sing' but 'embody' *levenslied*. For the aficionados, the singers bring out their own real-life experiences – the difficulties, setbacks, sadness, love and happiness – so intensely that the sentiments that go with such experiences will simultaneously be felt by the listeners, who – in their turn – will recognise those feelings from their own real-life experiences.

Irrespective of his talents, Hazes's way to success was not easy. Leaving school early, he began his first job at the age of 14. Singing remained a hobby. After a range of jobs, Hazes finally became a bartender. No biography fails to mention how the singer gained local fame as 'the singing bartender'. The honorary nickname evokes a double-sidedness that still informs much of today's understanding of Hazes. The epithet 'singing' renders Hazes's existence as a singing being-in-the-world. As 'a natural talent', Hazes's singing usually needs no further explanation (see Rojek, 2001 pp. 29–30). In addition, the nickname shows Hazes as an ordinary man, a man from 'the people', working hard to earn a modest income. 'Bartender', however, also evokes the image of a life drenched in alcohol, an association that would gain in prominence over the years, and is recounted time and again in divergent media and cultural productions.

In present-day Western societies, the Netherlands included, where youth and health are highly valued, a self-destructive lifestyle such as Hazes's stands out as immoral (Mackenbach, 2010) and as in direct opposition to 'core cultural values [of] autonomy, toughness, competitiveness, youth and self-control' (Scheper-Hughes and Lock, 1987 p. 25). With its fat and unhealthy appearance, Hazes's body became a testimony of self-neglect and abuse. In particular, the documentary *Zij gelooft in mij* (*She Believes in Me*, dir. Appel, 1999), one of the most popular

---

[3] Compilation mainly based on Haagsma (2004), A. Hazes (1982; 2001), R. Hazes (2005).

Dutch documentaries ever made (Haagsma, 2004 p. 136), has fixed this perception.[4] The documentary made Hazes's physical disintegration painfully visible: his increasing hearing problems and the effects of his alcoholism specifically. Morning or evening, working or at leisure, Hazes always appears with a can of beer. Through the documentary, the acronym *BVO-tje* (*biertje voor onderweg*, 'a small beer for the road') made its entrée in Dutch parlance. Because the moviemaker also shows Hazes's vulnerable sides, such as his anxiety before each performance and the problematic relationship with his wife, the documentary – in its capacity as a high-end, intellectual product – reached people with a distaste for Hazes's music or for *levenslied* in general. At the same time, its success was partly based on the existing fascination with Hazes's physical appearance and 'lifestyle', an interest that may account for the documentary being made in the first place.

As Rojek has argued in his book *Celebrity* (2001), it is irrelevant whether an individual's status as a celebrity in the public sphere is derived from glamorous or notorious qualifications. Both enhance the social distance between star and audience, and allow for an enlargement of a celebrity's deeds or habits in the media. The only thing that matters in cases of celebrity is impact on the public consciousness. Catering to a general fascination with transgression and excess, *She Believes in Me* impacted the Dutch public consciousness. Indeed: Hazes and certain songs of his became, so to say, Dutch cultural heritage.[5] The *André bedankt* farewell ceremony and the massive interest in his death also testify to this impact. Returning to the ceremony, the next section will elaborate on the public interest in Hazes's death and the subsequent disposal of his body.

Presence through Disposal

The Amsterdam ArenA, home of the Amsterdam football team Ajax, is a multifunctional stadium with 50,000 seats, purposely designed to host mega-events that include football matches, but also concerts, dance events and festivals. As a singer, a football supporter and a football song composer, Hazes had a long-time connection with the stadium. In 2003, he celebrated his silver jubilee there with two concerts. His 1988 song 'We houden van Oranje' ('We Love Orange', 'Orange' referring to the national football team) instantly became a hit when *Oranje* won the European Championship that year, and has remained the national football anthem ever since. Furthermore, Hazes frequently performed in

---

[4] Hazes's 'Zij gelooft in mij' (1980) is a Dutch cover of Steve Gibb's 'She Believes in Me' (1978).

[5] Extraordinary numbers of people saw the documentary in cinemas, on national television or bought it on video or DVD (Haagsma, 2004 p. 136; http://www.beeldengeluidwiki.nl/index.php/John_Appel). Since Hazes's death, certain songs of his regularly appear in the Dutch hit parade, and specific songs are popular for funerals ('The Rose') or weddings ('She Believes in Me').

the stadium during the intervals of Ajax matches. No other location, therefore, could have better fit a farewell concert. World-famous football icon Johan Cruyff honoured Hazes with his presence at the concert and showed a clip of Hazes singing 'We houden van Oranje', with a compilation of remarkable goals showing in the background.

With the (closed) coffin containing Hazes's corpse on the centre point, the fans were offered a very concrete opportunity to bid 'André' farewell, whether watching television at home or in the stadium itself. The event basically resembled a funeral service, an association reinforced by the coffin arriving in the stadium in a black hearse preceded by an undertaker. However, different from funeral services, the event was not closed with a burial or cremation. Nor was the atmosphere one of mourning as we know it. The stadium resounded with football yells – *olé olé* – alternating with 'André slogans' – *André bedankt, André bedankt* – and cries for beer – *biertje, biertje* – referring to Hazes's appetite for the beverage. As during Hazes's concerts, people were waving scarves bearing his name, others were dressed as look-alikes. Some had brought banners and posters with the singer's image, or objects referring to his most popular songs. Many were rather cheerful, clearly having a good time and enjoying the event, and quite a few of them had a beer in their hands. Yet, this festive atmosphere was hard to reconcile with the real-life grief of the mourning family also in attendance, which made the event fascinating and embarrassing at the same time.

Elaborating on the general illusion that dead bodies have one meaning only – being single bodies with a single name – Verdery (1999) points to the significance of their materiality in this respect. The material presence of Hazes alluded to the idea that all – celebrities, singers, family members, fans – had come to say farewell to 'the people's singer', and by implication that Hazes meant 'the same thing to all those present, whereas in fact [he] may mean different things to each' (Verdery, 1999 p. 29). In fact, all that was shared was the recognition of this death as being of national importance in some way, somehow. But the different affective moods within the audience indicated differences in commitment and interests with regard to 'commemorating Hazes', a topic I return to below.

Hazes was cremated in private the day after the concert. The disposal of the ashes would only happen one year later, in a series of public commemorative events. The potential of ashes for, what I have called earlier, 'serial disposal' (see Stengs, 2009), holds for anybody's bodily remains, but may gain a specific currency if it comes from those of celebrities. Cremation transforms the larger singularity of the body into a multiplicity of small parts. Each particle of the ashes has the potential to represent the whole it once was part of, the deceased. This multiplicity allows for multiple disposals: a series of rituals, separate in space and time, with one body (see also Prendergast, Hockey and Kellaher, 2006). In the case of celebrities, whose identities are media constructions, each subsequent disposal ritual has the potential to generate its own, renewed media attention. Ashes, not unlike relics, possess a unique power of their own. Different from the powers attributed to the relics of medieval saints, this power is their media potential. The 'serial disposal' of a celebrity's ashes, one may say, fits the serialised nature of the attention media give to celebrities. Serial disposal may therefore be of great help in extending the media presence of a deceased celebrity. As is the case with more traditional relics, access to and power over (re)distribution or disposal is pivotal (see also Geary, 1986). In the case of Hazes, the ownership of his legacy – the ashes as well as the copyrights over his songs and image – basically all lie with his third and last wife, Rachel Hazes (Melvin Produkties BV). Hence, she was directing the major initiatives taken during the first year after his death.

This contribution leaves no space to address the series of Hazes disposal events in detail. I only briefly mention that small portions of ashes were used in tattoos, buried in the garden of the House of Blues in Orlando, Florida ('a favourite place of André'), and divided over personal urns; all these events were shared with the television public in a reality series featuring his wife and family, titled *On Behalf of André* (*Namens André*). Together, this all served as a build-up towards 'André Hazes Commemoration Day', taking place on the first anniversary of his death, 23 September 2005. That day, a sequence of events was planned: the unveiling of the statue of Hazes, in company of the Amsterdam mayor,[6] next a commemorative concert in Rotterdam, and as *grand finale* a closing performance at the beach during which the main part of Hazes's ashes – divided over 10 sky-rockets – were launched into air over the North Sea. The last of these had been an explicit wish of the singer. Both the concert and the rocketing of the ashes were broadcast in full on television, again by TROS. The broadcast was watched nationwide by 5 million people.

The After-life

On this culminating day of disposal, Hazes's after-life definitively took shape. As it turned out, from then onwards, the singer would be commemorated with concerts both on his days of death (23 September) and on his birthdays (30 June). The latter continues a tradition initiated by Hazes himself: he regularly marked his birthday with a concert. In addition, aficionados organise Hazes events throughout the year, such as Hazes Fan Days, Hazes Nights and Hazes Meetings – usually modest pub gatherings dedicated to Hazes and his songs. Such a continuous commemorative culture is by no means self-evident or traditionally Dutch: no other singer in the Netherlands is so extensively commemorated with annual commemorative concerts and other events.

---

[6] As part of this ceremony, Rachel Hazes presented the mayor with the first copy of her Hazes biography, *Typically André* (*Typisch André*).

24   DEATH AND THE ROCK STAR

Intermezzo, Part I: The 5 Years without André Hazes *commemoration ceremony,* **Amsterdam, 23 September 2009**

At around 2pm, approximately one hundred Hazes fans have gathered at the singer's statue at the Albert Cuyp Street Market. With their 'Hazes outfits' – black hats, sunglasses, black T-shirts with Hazes's image – and Hazes tattoos, they make it unmistakably clear who they are and why they are here: to commemorate their idol, André Hazes, 'the uncrowned king of the levenslied' *on the fifth anniversary of his death. From all over the Netherlands, and even from Belgium, fans have travelled to Amsterdam. At the statue, the number of flowers is increasing, as are other objects signifying Hazes (portraits), his songs (lyric quotes and kites)[7] and the way he lived (cigarettes, cans and bottles of Heineken beer). The fans, mainly men and women ranging from 30 to 60 years old, take photographs of each other posing with the statue. When a man wants to pay tribute through the placement of a can of coke, a woman with Hazes hat and Hazes tattoo shouts from behind the statue: 'Have you lost your mind? No Coke!' Startled, the man quickly removes his can. As if speaking to himself, I hear someone next to me softly repeating: 'No Coke! Has he lost his mind?'*

The ceremony starts with a brief speech by one of the organisers, addressing the collective pain of the loss of Hazes, who 'will always live on in our hearts, however'. Thereupon, two minutes of silence are held, for many the moment to light a cigarette or raise a hand with a glass of beer. The most emotional part of the ceremony, however, is the joint singing of several Hazes songs. For the occasion, the organisers – Stichting AndréHazesFan, a modest fan club – have arranged an amplifier, a microphone and a lead-singer. Again, during the singing many cigarettes and beer glasses are raised, the lead singer affectively stroking the statue. After the ceremony, a middle-aged woman climbs the pedestal, embraces Hazes and gives him a kiss. Apparently, she is not hindered by the plaster around her left lower leg, which, for the occasion, is painted yellow with a white top, to represent a glass of beer. To ascertain that the message will come across, the yellow part reads: BVO-tje, *'… a small beer for the road' (Figure 2.1). As every year, the gathering is continued at the nearby pub of Hazes's youth, the Eddy Bar. From there, at around 8pm all leave for the commemorative concert* 5 Years without André Hazes, *also organised by AndréHazesFan.*

---

[7]   Referring to his song 'The Kite' ('de Vlieger', 1977). Most Hazes songs address topics such as loneliness and broken hearts, and are less easy to capture in concrete objects.

Figure 2.1　A kiss for 'André' (23 September 2009 commemoration at the André Hazes statue, Albert Cuyp Street Market, Amsterdam)

Photo: Irene Stengs

The commemoration at the statue demonstrates the importance of fans' bodily identification with their idol by means of mimesis, following the urge 'to get hold of something by means of its likeness' (Taussig, 1993 p. 20). First of all, the fans mimic Hazes by wearing Hazes outfits. In addition to the outfits, almost all wear T-shirts with a Hazes portrait, and many have one or more visible Hazes tattoos (see Figure 2.2). The resulting impression may best be described as a living 'Droste-effect', the recursive appearance of smaller versions of a picture in itself: the fans are modest imitations of Hazes, wearing in their turn smaller Hazes images on the clothes and, smaller again, on their skins. The pivotal material substantiation of the Hazes commemorative culture is therefore the André Hazes portrait, whether that is in the form of bodies or images. The second form of bodily identification is drinking beer and smoking cigarettes, both habitual Hazes practices. Yet, within the context of the commemoration these habits are ritualised to accompany moments of heightened intensity. As rituals, the everyday practices of Hazes become charged with new meaning, articulating a social differentiation between 'fans' and 'others', for whom Hazes's body evokes aversion instead of identification.

For the fans, the wish to commemorate Hazes stems from their desire to 'keep Hazes alive', a desire which mimesis helps to fulfil. This 'capacity to Other' is carried both by imitation (*copy*) and by *contact*: 'a palpable, sensuous connection between the very body of the perceiver and the perceived' (Taussig, 1993 p. 21). However, the 'something' that the fans try to get hold of does not concern Hazes's own, physical body, but his social body. Through its unpolished appearance and way of being in the world, this body offers what I have called a counter-ideal of rough authenticity; an ideal that appeals to those who cannot or do not want to comply with the dominant societal ideals of youth, health and beauty (Stengs, 2009; 2010).

The third practice of bodily identification works through the collective singing-along. Of course, as so many other singers, Hazes lives on through his recorded voice, and through the voices of other singers who sing his repertoire. But Hazes comes best to life in the regular coming-together of his fans, singing his songs together or along with Hazes's voice. Whether at a modest gathering like the above commemoration or at any other concert, everybody present will be singing from the chest.

Figure 2.2   André Hazes fans at the commemorative ceremony of
23 September 2006 (Albert Cuyp Street Market, Amsterdam)
Photo: Irene Stengs

28   *DEATH AND THE ROCK STAR*

***Intermezzo, Part II: The* 5 Years without André Hazes *commemorative concert,
Amsterdam, 23 September 2009***
*Thanks to the efforts of the Stichting AndréHazesFan more than 10 more or
less well-known Hazes singers will perform this evening, including Hollywood
Boulevard – for many years Hazes's regular accompanying band. It goes without
saying that tonight only Hazes songs are programmed. The concert, announced as
'the musical tribute to André Hazes', has attracted a thousand people. Although the
hall is rather dark, I judge from the multitude of hats that most have come in Hazes
outfits. As soon as the concert starts, virtually everybody joins in the singing, the
spotlights alternating between the singer on the stage and those 'in the field'. When
the light switches away from the stage – basically during each refrain – the lead
singer usually stops to encourage the audience to join in ('now you!'), although
everybody knows very well that it will be 'their turn' now. In front of me, five men in
their early twenties are singing-along – deep from their chests – during the entire
concert. While singing, they look each other in the eyes. As so many others, they
sing 'in duet' or – maybe more accurately – 'in dialogue', as if the song were a
direct message towards one's counterpart(s). It is in this singing-along that the
distinction between 'true fans' and 'others' may become painfully visible: only 'true
fans' know the entire lyrics by heart.*

Intermezzo, Part II spotlights the ritualised forms in which much of the singing
takes place, structuring both interactions between performers and audience, and
between members of the audience themselves. These ritualised modes of singing-
along are characteristic of any Hazes concert, whether low-profile and modest, or
large-scale professional concerts organised by Hazes's heirs and their commercial
partners. Yet, what may differentiate these larger 'official' Hazes events is the
presence of a singing Hazes in the form of video footage.[8] The concert organised
in commemoration of Hazes's birthday in 2008, entitled *Together with Dré Live in
Concert* (*Samen met Dré Live in Concert*), was entirely organised to the formula
of celebrated *levenslied* performers singing their favourite André Hazes songs
alternating 'in duet with Dré/André' on the screen, and with the audience regularly
joining in.[9]

---

[8]   All copyright-protected material owned by Melvin Produkties BV, and hence not
accessible to other parties.

[9]   This concert, again in the Amsterdam ArenA, began with shots of Hazes entering
a white stretched limousine to be followed by the actual entrance of the same car into the
stadium, escorted by men in black. Although the escorts were security guards this time,
the scene closely paralleled the arrival of Hazes's body at the 2004 farewell concert. When
the doors opened, Hazes's children Roxeanne (b. 1993) and André Jr (b. 1994), stepped
out to open the concert with Hazes's song 'It is Cold Without You' ('Het is koud zonder
jou'). From a perspective of ritual, the opening scenes may be interpreted as an attempted
transference of Hazes's identity as 'the people's singer' to his children.

When all ingredients of Hazes commemorative concerts are in tune – Hazes's music, Hazes impersonators, Hazes look-alikes, ritualised modes of Hazes singing – these events powerfully work, in Connerton's words, through 'the rhetoric of re-enactment' (1989 p. 65), which may account for their persuasiveness. Evoking the experience of what is collectively imagined as an 'authentic' Hazes concert, such re-enactments directly tap into the fans' social memory, a shared body of memory that at the same time is shaped, conveyed and sustained in and through ceremonial gatherings (Connerton, 1989 p. 4). For the participants, whether they actually ever have been at a Hazes concert with Hazes performing or not, these events bring the past into the present. Social memory is thus, as Connerton argues, not only preserved and transferred in the collective recollection of words and images, but also by the repetitive performance of bodily practices. The Hazes fans, with their Hazes outfits and through their singing – the latter an example of bodily engagement par excellence – provide the habitual substrate that gives these commemorative ceremonies a persuasive power of their own.

Epilogue: 'We Believe in Hazes'

The opening night of *Hij gelooft in mij* (*He Believes in Me*), the long-awaited musical 'on the dramatic life of André Hazes', came on 11 November 2012. The musical is a coproduction of Melvin Produkties and Joop van den Ende Theaterproducties, one of the largest media-stakeholders in the Netherlands. *He Believes in Me* is basically a flat remediation of *She Believes in Me* (the documentary), emphasising Hazes's drinking problem and increasing deafness, but rather from the perspective of his wife (hence '*He Believes in Me*'). The stakes were high: 90,000 tickets were sold in advance. Its success was undeniable. All national newspapers gave the musical rave reviews, even those considered elite and intellectual – 'never was a musical rated with so many stars'[10] – and it has been endowed with four national musical awards. The lead singer Martijn Fischer, who in size, posture, general appearance and style of singing created an exact copy of Hazes, has become a national celebrity, a welcome guest in talk shows and even performing at occasions with more national allure, like Coronation Day (30 April 2013).

Paradoxically, the musical attracts both audiences who otherwise would never go to a Hazes (or *levenslied*) concert, and principal Hazes aficionados, many of whom otherwise would not go to a theatre. Yet, although the musical is carried by Hazes's songs, it offers a different experience from a Hazes concert. Rephrasing and recomposing have made singing-along impossible, a disappointment for many 'true' Hazes fans. Significantly, the musical has spurred other, widely promoted and mediatised Hazes initiatives: a 'people's singer' (*volkszanger*) talent scouting show titled *Blood, Sweat and Tears* (*Bloed, zweet en tranen*), named after Hazes's most

---

[10]   As advertised on the musical's website and posters.

30   *DEATH AND THE ROCK STAR*

celebrated song, and a series of concerts titled *Holland Sings Hazes* (*Holland zingt Hazes*), 'a tribute to the life and music of André Hazes'.[11] Organised and supported by the same stakeholders and media partners, these different initiatives work in tandem: one event offering publicity for the other and vice versa, with the lead singer from the musical and the winner of the talent show performing at 'Holland sings Hazes'. Catering to both 'loyal fans and the new generation ... the inimitable Hazes sensation will be revived'.[12] This begs the following question: why, these days, do so many Dutch 'believe in him'? To this question, no straightforward answer can be given. But in these new, applauded versions of Hazes – 'An icon! A people's hero! A legend!'[13] – his original, uneasy subversiveness seems to be largely annihilated. Instead, the audiences are promised an uncomplicated experience of something perceived as authentically Dutch.

Bibliography

Bruin, Martine de and Louis P. Grijp (2006) 'Van Levenslied tot Smartlap', in Louis P. Grijp (ed.), *Een muziekgeschiedenis der Nederlanden (Een vervolg 2000–2005)*. Amsterdam: Amsterdam University Press, pp. 947–53.

Connerton, Paul (1989) *How Societies Remember*. Cambridge: Cambridge University Press.

De Hart, Joep (2005) *Voorbeelden en nabeelden: Historische vergelijkingen naar aanleiding van de dood van Fortuyn en Hazes*. Den Haag: Sociaal en Cultureel Planbureau.

Douglas, Mary (1970) *Natural Symbols: Explorations in Cosmology*. New York: Vintage Books.

Geary, Patrick (1986) 'Sacred Commodities: The Circulation of Medieval Relics', in Arjun Appadurai (ed.), *The Social Life of Things*. Cambridge and New York: Cambridge University Press, pp. 169–91.

Haagsma, Robert (2004) *Hazes, 1951–2004*. Utrecht: Spectrum.

Hazes, André (1982) *Ik lach me kapot*. Amsterdam: Loeb, Tiebosch.

———— (2001) *Al mijn woorden* .... Utrecht, Antwerpen: Kosmos.

Hazes, Rachel (2005) *Typisch André*. Mijdrecht: Melvin Producties.

Klöters, Jacques (2006) 'Inleiding', in Jacques Klöters (ed.), *Zo de ouden zongen: De mooiste levensliedjes met bladmuziek*. Amsterdam: Nijgh en Van Ditmar, pp. 8–19.

Mackenbach, Johan (2010) *Ziekte in Nederland: Gezondheid tussen politiek en biologie*. Amsterdam: Elsevier Gezondheidszorg, Mouria.

---

[11]   Translated from http://delamar.nl/voorstellingen/2012-2013/hij-gelooft-in-mij/.
[12]   Translated from http://www.ziggodome.nl/event/402/Holland-zingt-Hazes.
[13]   Translated from http://hij-gelooft-in-mij.nl/#home.

Prendergast, David, Jenny Hockey and Leonie Kellaher (2006) 'Blowing in the Wind? Identity, Materiality and the Destinations of Human Ashes', *Journal of the Royal Anthropological Institute*, 12 (4), pp. 881–98.

Rojek, Chris (2001) *Celebrity*. London: Reaktion.

Scheper-Hughes, Nancy and Margaret M. Lock (1987) 'The Mindful Body: A Prolegomenon to Future Work in Medical Anthropology', *Medical Anthropology Quarterly*, 1 (1), pp. 6–41.

Stengs, Irene (2009) 'Death and Disposal of the People's Singer: The Body and Bodily Practices in Commemorative Ritual', *Mortality*, 14 (2), pp. 102–18.

———— (2010) 'Echt André. Belichaming en beleving van ruige authenticiteit onder André Hazesfans', *Sociologie*, 6 (2), pp. 50–70.

Taussig, Michael (1993) *Mimesis and Alterity: A Particular History of the Senses*. New York and London: Routledge.

Verdery, Katherine (1999) *The Political Lives of Dead Bodies: Reburial and Postsocialist Change*. New York: Columbia University Press.

Filmography

Zij gelooft in mij, dir. John Appel, Zeppers Film and TV, 1999.

Chapter 3

'I Don't Preach Premature Suicide': The Biopolitics of GG Allin

Ben Dumbauld

Thinking about the body can take place only between two paradigms: the body as a site of regulation, or as a site where hegemony is evaded and resisted.

Deborah Wong (2004)

My mind is a machine gun, my body the bullets, the audience the targets.

GG Allin (1991)

The Corpse

At his funeral in July 1993, punk rocker GG Allin was laid in an open coffin. As per request from his brother Merle, the body was displayed without any make-up or perfume and unwashed since the day he died, if not well before. During the wake, Allin's bloated body, veins once filled with heroin now with embalming fluid, was documented extensively by fans and friends, and narratives of the event soon disseminated to multiple underground punk zines. His unofficial biographer, Joe Coughlin, described the moment in one such publication:

> Now, we all knew [Allin] wasn't going to die of old age and we all knew it wouldn't be an ordinary service, but I wasn't quite prepared for what I saw. The band's drummer was drawing on GG's leg with a magic marker. The body was dressed in his leather jacket and a jockstrap that said 'Eat Me'. He held a microphone in one hand and a jug of Jim Beam in the other. Everyone was hammered. When the beer ran out, people wrenched the jug from his arms to swig from it. GG looked like hell. There were gouges and scars everywhere and he was discolored, and frankly, starting to go bad after five days ... One girl put her underwear on his face. Other people were putting stickers on the casket, pushing pills and liquor into GG's mouth, having their smiling pictures taken up by his face, taking his dick out and playing with it ... the works ... Most common phrase of the night had to be, 'He woulda wanted it this way'. (Coughlin, n.d.a)

Such a presentation of Allin's body served as a eulogy in itself. The roadmap of scars, the broken teeth, the whisky and microphone by his side, the jockstrap and leather jacket pronounced without an utterance the life Allin led: a life without boundaries or hierarchies, a life most appropriately mourned through the defiling of a body already defiled. In death, Allin was surrounded by that which he lived for and that which would kill him. His music bombarded the funeral home, his fans continued to abuse him, he continued to ingest drugs and alcohol. In the amateur video footage capturing the event, Allin's brother Merle tells the cameraman, 'I gave him his sip of Jim Beam, gave him his Valium, toasted him', giving one the impression that this was all that could be asked. Later, Merle would provide a final offering to the corpse of his brother: right before closing the coffin, he placed headphones on GG, connected them to a portable tape player, and played *The Suicide Sessions*, one of Allin's over 30 albums. Featuring songs such as 'Jailed Again', 'I Want to Burn', 'Drug Whore', 'I Will Not Act Civilized' and 'I'm Dying, I'm Dying, I'm Dead', the album acted as a second silent eulogy, travelling from Allin's disembodied voice to his dead ears.

In a certain way, there was sense of purity in such grotesque mourning practices. What was presented at the funeral was only the fact: a machine without a spirit, a corpse without artifice. Such an approach stands in stark contrast to what one has come to expect with the death of a rock star. Like countless popular musicians before and since, Allin died of a drug overdose. Yet his death brought no dawn-to-dusk media coverage, no anxious waiting for the coroner's report, no talk of missed opportunities for prevention, no psychoanalytic dissections, no passing blame to friends, family or the music industry. The funeral videotape shows if anything a grim acceptance – there was little illusion among the mourners that Allin the punk, the alcoholic, the drug user, the man who threatened to commit suicide on stage would live a long life. Nor was there pity for the life he chose to live.

Given this fact, it is perhaps wholly unsurprising that the funeral was marked by a general indulgence in the very substances that killed the singer. As Stengs notes on the death and mourning of singer André Hazes (this volume), embodied forms of mimesis are often one of the strongest vehicles for fans to commemorate their fallen idols. Moreover, the funeral gave mourners the opportunity to legitimate their own hardcore punk ethos in the presence of their fallen comrade – an ethos that often takes degradation and aggression as a foundational rallying point, and directly relates one's filth and destitution to anti-authoritarian ideals.[1] Such practices continued well after the interment, with fans honouring Allin's legacy not by leaving flowers on his grave, but empty alcohol bottles, urine and faeces. What better way to honour the man who embodied the pinnacle of hardcore purity?

---

[1] See, for instance, Fox's ethnography (1987) of the punk subculture in southwestern United States, where he observes that those considered the most 'Hardcore' in the community (that is, those possessing the most cultural capital) are usually unemployed, homeless and addicted to alcohol or cheap drugs like glue.

Without a doubt, everything about Allin's life and art, ranging from his music (loud, fast and careless) to his lyrics and song titles ('Watch Me Kill', 'My Sadistic Killing Spree', 'Bruise Me [I Want to Die]'), to his lifestyle was widely offensive to civil society. But little work has been done in analysing Allin's work and conceptualising his lasting legacy. Taking Thompson's (2004 p. 5) argument that punk performatives 'represent repressed cultural impulses and desires' as a starting point, in this chapter I will consider a simple question: what exactly are the 'repressed cultural impulses' embodied by GG Allin, both in life and death? Answering such a question sociologically (rather than psychoanalytically), I argue that Allin's performances serve most readily as mechanisms of counter-conduct – that is, mechanisms of power, often deployed at the social extremities, that serve as means to disrupt hegemonic notions of social organisation and the role of the citizen (Foucault, 2003 pp. 27–8). In particular, his transgressive performances and nomadic lifestyle both confronted and discounted the social construction of the body and its role in 'modern' society. In simple terms, Allin became a legend within hardcore punk because he was the antithesis to the model Western subject. Before discussing the particular trajectories through which Allin countered Western constructions of the body, however, it is first necessary to frame his work and lifestyle properly.

The Masochist

Hours before his death, Allin played what would become his last and perhaps greatest show. The performance occurred at the Gas Station, a club in the Lower East Side of New York City – a fitting place for Allin's swansong, given the neighbourhood's historic association with punk and hardcore culture.[2] In a fan-made video recording of the performance, we see a clearly inebriated and likely high Allin wearing military boots and women's underwear. Before the performance starts, Allin visibly ingests small white pills given to him by a fan, and then grabs and kisses a female audience member, who seemed not to have any objections. Once the music begins, Allin quickly strips naked and starts lunging violently at the audience, at multiple points throwing and receiving punches with the various fans that dare approach him. After only two songs, the sound crew cuts the power, effectively cancelling the show (not a rare occurrence given Allin's penchant for destroying audio equipment while performing). The inability to perform quickly leads Allin into a violent frenzy: he smashes a glass window with his fist, slams an empty beer can violently against his head multiple times, and defecates on stage. After multiple failed requests by the audience to return power to the microphone, Allin eventually leaves the club and walks onto the streets naked and covered in blood, dirt and faeces. The crowd follows him, chanting: 'G-G, G-G ...'.

---

[2]   See McNeil and McCain (1997) and Blush (2010) for detailed accounts on the development of punk and hardcore subcultures (respectively) in the neighbourhood.

In the background of the video, we hear sounds of broken glass, sirens, screeching tyres, police yelling through the distortion of a megaphone. The film quickly blurs as the camera man starts running. At the end of the video, we can clearly hear the voice of an unnamed fan: 'that was one of the greatest shows of all time'. Less than 24 hours later, Allin would be found dead in a Lower East Side apartment.

Such a performance perhaps serves as a fitting conclusion to Allin's life. In his final show, the space dedicated to physically containing and socially relegating the chaos of a GG Allin concert cracked, leaking onto the otherwise ordered and stratified city streets of New York City. Such a viewpoint, however, threatens to imply that it was only through performance that such an event could take place – that the riot demanded as its foundation the inherent liminality of the initial concert. Perhaps this was indeed the case for the audience, who might not have violently acted out if it were not for the concert. But for Allin, transgressive and dangerous acts were never exclusively confined to particular performance spaces; they were as much a part of his private life as they were his public. As Coughlin argues, 'no other artist's life and work are so consistently true to each other' (n.d.b).

That Allin's lifestyle was, as another journalist penned, 'worse offstage than onstage', greatly complicates the idea that Allin was merely a showman, being shocking or transgressive only before an audience (R.M., 1993). Instead, Allin enacted violence and aggression as much in private as in public. But such acts of violence, regardless of setting, were framed around the same circumstances – circumstances that I would argue were inherently masochistic.[3] In 'Coldness and Cruelty' (1989), Deleuze differentiates sadistic violence from masochistic violence by noting that while sadism is inherently demonstrative – that pleasure is derived by the sadist demonstrating their power over the victim by force – masochism is dialectical, involving the establishment of a contract between the participants which frames and regulates the violent event. In examining accounts of Allin's actions both in public and in private, we immediately find a trend in which both Allin and the 'victim' of his violence enter a contractual agreement in which both willingly accept that abuse may occur. Such forms of contractual aggression are pervasive in hardcore culture, perhaps most apparent in the associated dance styles of moshing and slamdancing, which are violent but nonetheless rely on an explicit code of ethics (Tsitsos, 1999; Blush, 2010).

At concerts, such a contract often began at the door of the venue, where there were posted 'enter at your own risk' type disclaimers at Allin's request (Coughlin, n.d.b). Such notices, coupled with Allin's notorious reputation as a performer, served to filter out possible unwilling or unprepared audience members. But even attending a show was not enough to become implicated in Allin's violent performances – one had to almost request it. In his memoir *I Was a Murder Junkie*, author Evan Cohen, who accompanied Allin on his final tour, describes the demographics of the typical GG Allin audience:

---

[3] See also Bloustein (2003), who describes masochistic characteristics of punk fashion and style.

There were several classes of people that came to see him. The first group saw GG because they had heard about his wild and crazy stage show. They showed up at the club to see if it was for real or not, and stood in the back ... The second group was a bit more daring. They tried to get as close to GG as possible during the show, but ran like hell whenever he came near them. They wanted near the flaming car wreck, but they didn't want to get burned.

The third level was the scariest and most dangerous one of the bunch. It was comprised of the tried and true GG Allin fanatics. They enjoyed getting beat up by him, and getting his shit on their bodies. They would stay up front no matter what happened. They would take all the abuse and more, and thank him afterwards. I wouldn't have believed it if I hadn't seen it over and over again. (Cohen, 1999 pp. 30–31)

Much of Evan's book is sprinkled with accounts of such 'tried and true' fans thanking Allin for his abuse after a performance, asking for more abuse, or bragging about the scars and bruises inflicted upon their bodies by their idol.

In private, Allin's violent activity was carried out on a similar contractual basis, often utilising methods common to bondage, dominance and sadomasochist (BDSM) sexual practice. As described by Cohen, interestingly enough Allin more often chose to play a submissive role in sexual encounters, asking female fans to demean him in various ways while he masturbated. Rarely, at least according to Cohen, did such encounters result in actual intercourse.

That those most abused by Allin were also his biggest fans complicates the image of the performer as a criminal aggressor – an image that was promoted largely by Allin himself. Thus, in spite of his hyperbolic song titles and lyrics ('I'm Gonna Rape You', 'Legalize Murder', 'I Wanna Kill You'), actual self-proclaimed 'victims' of his performances were in fact very hard to find. A case in point is Allin's criminal record: outside of a litany of misdemeanours related to public indecency, intoxication or destruction of property, Allin's only felony indictment involved the abuse of a fan who, in addition to prosecuting Allin, wrote him love letters and marriage proposals. At the trial the possible masochistic nature of the abuse was heavily considered, and at the verdict the judge, conceding that 'there are lifestyles which this court does not understand', convicted Allin only on the grounds that he pled no contest to the charges. In this way, any discussion of the victim's possible complicity in the abuse was sidestepped (Fertig, 1989; Reynolds, 1989; State of Michigan Circuit Court Case number 89–24090 FH). The judge sentenced Allin to two years at an Ann Arbor penitentiary.

Ultimately, Allin's rock 'n' roll reputation for danger and chaos was then not built via physical violence purposefully levelled upon the unsuspecting 'mainstream' masses. On the contrary, Allin's violent performances were contractual and consciously framed by singer and his most diehard fans. His legacy for controversy was rather solidified because he embodied, as I will argue, the antithesis to the model Western subject as constructed by Western governmentality.

The Sovereign

In volume one of *The History of Sexuality*, Foucault describes the process by which Western conceptions and regulations of the human body have evolved since the Roman Empire. Historically, he writes, people were regulated primarily via mechanisms of deduction, in which the sovereign would take from its subjects a certain amount of labour, time, goods or services in return for protection of their respective territory. In the most extreme cases, the sovereign is granted the right to deduct life itself from its subjects, killing them under the assumption that such an act is necessary to protect the stability of the rest of the populace (Foucault, 1990 p. 136). Gradually, such deductive mechanisms faded from being the primary strategy for regulation to becoming but one of a number of strategies aimed less at dealing death to subversive elements and more on administering life to such an extent as to minimise the possibility of subversive action altogether. This new set of strategies incorporated two mechanisms of bodily regulation: the first being the 'anatamo-politics' of the individual body, or the 'body as a machine: its disciplining, the optimisation of its capabilities, the extortion of its forces'; the second, 'bio-politics', which takes as its object the administration of the population, incorporating issues of longevity, mortality and family planning (Foucault, 1990 p. 139). Both forms are deployed in order to maintain a primary conceptualisation of the body in society, one tightly integrated with capitalist production (Foucault, 2003 p. 31). In short, in the history of Western civilisation, a gradual change in the idealisation of the subject occurred, moving from being fundamentally *loyal and strong* (in order to protect one's territory and sovereign) to being *productive and healthy* (in order to protect one's national economy).

In terms of Allin's life and work, it becomes quickly apparent that the singer embodied the complete rejection of the latter ideals of productivity and health, while idiosyncratically deploying the former, loyalty and strength. While there is no doubt that Allin was prolific in regard to artistic output, his lifestyle as an often homeless addict was far from the (particularly American) ideal of the middle-class homeowner with some disposable income. In terms of health, Allin's broken teeth, alcoholism and drug abuse, and multiple bouts of blood poisoning (a probable consequence for artists who simultaneously work with their own blood and faeces) serve as testament enough to his priorities in terms of maintaining any semblance of a healthy lifestyle. Rather, Allin purposely injured himself and made himself sick because he privileged the experiences of such embodied states more than he privileged maintaining a healthy, beautiful body. 'I've done things to my body that most can't or wouldn't do', he once said, 'but it's good for me to have experienced pain because it makes me much stronger' (Anon., 1992). Stronger, I would argue, not biologically or aesthetically, but because each instance of transgression or masochism further empowered his sense of radical individuality and anti-authoritarian resolve. Through masochistic performance Allin both refutes the ideal of a healthy constitution while at the same time reasserting a sovereign right to physically enact violence upon the body – both acts a direct confrontation with contemporary biopolitical ideals.

Perhaps the most illuminating aspect to Allin's use of his own body, however, was his views on suicide. In 1988, Allin published a letter in the underground zine *MaximumRocknRoll* promising to kill himself on stage on Halloween the following year. Due to his aforementioned arrest and imprisonment in Ann Arbor that year, Allin could not live up to his promise, frustrating many of his admiring fans and journalists who continued to ask whether he would carry through with his plan, when, and where. While in prison, he responded to such questions (in addition to others) through a series of written correspondences with fans and supporters. In discussing his intention for suicide, he responded in one letter:

> I have lived on stage and that is where I will die. I will commit suicide at the peak of my life ... Death is the most important event in your life, your last final thrill and adventure. Don't waste it by dying a meaningless death. You must control the moment. (Allin, 1992)

This public stance towards suicide serves as perhaps his greatest affront to Western biopolitics – greater than his masochistic tendencies and transgressive performances. Foucault (2003 p. 248) writes:

> Now that power is decreasingly the power of the right to take life, and increasingly the right to make live ... death becomes, insofar as it is the end of life, the term, the limit, or the end of power too. Death is outside the power relationship ... And to that extent, it is only natural that death should now be privatized, and should become the most private thing of all. In the right of sovereignty, death was a moment of the most obvious and spectacular manifestation of the absolute power of the sovereign; death now becomes, in contrast, a moment when the individual escapes all power, falls back on himself and retreats, so to speak, into his own privacy. Power no longer recognizes death. Power literally ignores death.

By proclaiming that he would commit suicide in public at a concert, Allin remade death into spectacle, thus reclaiming the sovereign's right to take life, which in an interesting turn, happened to be his own.

The Nomad

As modes of governmentality gradually shifted from privileging the nation state (*raison d'état*) to privileging the market, so too the strategies whereby the body of the citizenry was regulated changed.[4] Thanks largely to the Enlightenment, notions of individual liberty and governmental non-intervention grew to become the new administrative ideals for the 'modern' nation-state – but only insofar

---

[4] See particularly Foucault (2007; 2008) in which he traces the genealogy of 'governmentality' roughly from the Medieval Age to the present.

40   *DEATH AND THE ROCK STAR*

as they protected and nurtured the citizen as an economic unit (Foucault, 2008 p. 252). The entire system of regulation and administration thus began to rely almost entirely on the construction of the citizen as a unit of the nation's economy, a 'man of enterprise and production' (Foucault, 2008 p. 147). Economic policy was then gradually overlaid upon all aspects of population control and regulation, which consequently led to the citizen ceasing to be conceptualised as an individual being to be governed, but merely one component out of many that either added to or detracted from the overall profitability of the nation, whether in terms of health, safety or economy (Foucault, 2008 p. 45).

If there is at all an underlying, consistent impetus running throughout Allin's career, it would be the direct confrontation with such a *homo economicus* ideal. Indeed, for the past few decades scholars have illuminated the myriad of methods in which punk rock cultural workers have countered the prevailing 'mainstream' model of musical commodification (Goshert, 2000; Davies, 1996; James, 1988–1989; Moore, 2004; 2007; O'Hara, 1999; Thompson, 2004; Hebdige, 1979; Willis, 1993). One way in which this counter-conduct occurs is through privileging the body as a producer of affect rather than the body as a producer of labour. As Thompson (2004, p. 123) explains in discussing punk rock's priorities in producing records and touring:

> [in] the privileging of shows over recordings and raw over clean production, punks valorize modes of punk commodities that they take to represent affect rather than professionalization, because the latter category denotes economics in ways that the former does not. Affect connotes emotion and the body, as the bearer of emotion, both of which punks place at a greater remove from economics than professionalization, a term that suggests the erasure of the body. The body is literally absent in recordings but not during shows, while in cleanly produced music the body's signifiers – such as coughs, the squeak of fingers shifting on strings, stage banter, etc. – disappear.

Allin embodied the temporality of the moving, affective body more than any other hardcore musician or group. A self-proclaimed 'Gypsy Motherfucker', Allin's approach to touring was beyond simply a way to prove his anti-mainstream position as a musician, but a consistent lifestyle. During the peak of his career Allin was essentially homeless, his only possessions the clothes on his back and sleeping in cheap hotels, the homes of his fans, or in hospitals and prisons. While a shameless self-promoter, his artistic output was not particularly strategic economically: rather than creating a steady stream of definitive works, Allin's oeuvre consists of a myriad of often poorly-produced albums, EPs, compilations and live recordings through over 20 different underground labels.[5] Moreover, concerts did not provide

---

    [5]   Given this kind of output, it is nearly impossible to provide a definitive discography for Allin, let alone sales figures. As an estimate, the website discogs.com currently lists 59

Allin much economic capital either, due to the fact that, as zine editor Al Quint noted, 'he rarely played 'cause he got banned everywhere' (Blush, 2010 p. 280).

Allin's model of musical performance thus runs contrary to the *homo economicus* construction of the modern citizen. Rather than building relationships in order to broaden one's marketability, Allin left each venue he played in ashes, grabbing what he could to survive before quickly fleeing furious venue owners and fans who, more often than we might expect, were upset that Allin was not as transgressive and violent as they imagined. Despite such an economically inconsistent touring practice, Allin's dedication to such a lifestyle remained strong. In an interview with *MaximumRocknRoll*, for instance, journalist Jay Sosnicki asks Allin what he would do if he ever made a significant income from his music career:

> Maybe I could fly somewhere, instead of taking a Greyhound. Wouldn't matter – I'm still gonna have my own seat because I'm still gonna stink if you sit beside me. I'd take the money, probably get a higher class bunch of hookers, that's all, or maybe a better set of drugs. I might even give some of it away. I don't give a fuck .... (Sosnicki, 1993)

Nowhere in the above quote do we see the image of a musician suffering through tours with the hopes of the subsequent payoff of 'making it' one day, a strategy much more compatible to economy-based modes of governmentality. A financial windfall would not change Allin's lifestyle, but would rather be consumed, burned or forgotten.

Perhaps more than most performers, Allin's performances and lifestyle placed him in close alignment with Deleuze and Guattari's image of the *nomad* and Foucault's image of the *barbarian*. For Deleuze and Guattari (1987 pp. 380, 400), the nomad is one for whom 'every point is a relay and only exists as a relay', a 'war machine' whose weapon is affect, 'which relate[s] only to the moving body in itself, to speeds and compositions of speed among elements'. Foucault (2003 p. 195) paints a similar picture in describing the figure of the barbarian:

> The barbarian is always the man who stalks the frontiers of the States, the man who stumbles into city walls ... He appears only when civilization already exists, and only when he is in conflict with it. He does not make his entrance into history by founding a society, but by penetrating a civilization, setting it ablaze and destroying it. There can be no barbarian without pre-existing history: the history of the civilization he sets ablaze.

Both the barbarian and the nomad are figures that represent the antithesis of the modern 'proper' citizen who positions him or herself within fairly strict spatial

---

GG Allin releases in total, not including 'unofficial' recordings, bootlegs, appearances on compilation albums and so on.

hierarchies, repeating the same paths between various points in order to contribute to the economic stability or productivity of the state. As an almost constantly touring musician with a reputation for destruction (whether directed at himself, his fans or the venue's sound equipment), Allin the nomad and barbarian operates in a different space, continually relaying between various points of civilisation, staying only long enough to violently disrupt them.

Failed Martyr, Reluctant Rock Star

GG Allin was born Jesus Christ Allin, a name given to him by his antisocial and highly religious father. And even though this name was later changed by his mother, the appeal of martyrdom remained with him throughout his life. Indeed, within Allin's numerous, often contradictory interviews in print and broadcast, his expressed ultimate goal remained remarkably consistent: to destroy rock 'n' roll in order to revive its dangerous, transgressive roots. Yet despite the constant discourse invoking 'hate' and 'lawlessness' perpetuated both by the media and by the singer himself, such a goal was actually not pursued via uninhibited malice or unchecked aggression towards his audiences. In truth, Allin's violent performances and actions followed a fairly strict – one may even argue ethical – set of rules and boundaries. Much like his namesake, then, Allin's radical goals were primarily pursued via the re-interpretation of his own physical body – the practices inflicted upon it or enacted through it.

With the growth of the capitalist system, there has developed the idea that it is both the individual's and the state's priority to keep the physical body relatively clean, healthy and productive. Such a concept has embedded itself so deeply into Western culture that one can rarely turn on the evening news without hearing at least one story dedicated to breakthroughs in medical research, debate over federal health programmes, or new safety concerns related to specific products, practices or natural phenomena. For better or worse, Allin achieved cult status because he rejected such ideals. For him, the fundamental goals of life did not encapsulate bodily, economic and spatial stability. Rather, Allin's life and work privileged instability, movement, brutal experience and, ultimately, the sovereign right to control one's individual body in whatever way one sees fit.

Taken to its logical conclusion, this dedication to countering the ideal of the healthy, productive body in increasingly violent ways could only lead to an early death. This was something everybody expected. Thus for many fans it was not Allin dying early that was truly the disappointment, but the way he died. As one fan I spoke to expressed, 'he [Allin] could have died a legend, but he died a rock star', afterwards miming the act of injecting heroin and passing out. Indeed, for many hardcore fans, the biggest failure in what was conceived as an otherwise brilliant career was that Allin died like the very rock stars he spent his life critiquing. In their view, Allin did not live up to his promise: he did not kill himself on stage, spectacularly in public – but privately, quietly, slipping away from overdose.

Despite this, he remains to many the most comprehensive embodiment of hardcore ethos, and thus a complete rejection of Western governmental and economic ideals.

*   *   *

Special thanks to Diana Taylor for advice on an early draft of this paper, and to Phil Lentz and Justin Melkman of World War IX for their insights.

Bibliography

Allin, GG (1991) 'Mission Statement', http://ggallinonline.com/mission.php, accessed 5 August 2013.
———— (1992) 'Correspondence Letter', http://www.oocities.org/ekx001/MG/MI1992MG.html, accessed 23 April 2013.
Anonymous (1992) 'Punks over 30', *MaximumRocknRoll*, http://www.oocities.org/ekx001/MG/MRR110MG.html, accessed 23 April 2013.
Bloustein, David (2003) '"Oh Bondage, Up Yours!" Or Here's Three Chords, Now Form a Band: Punk, Masochism, Skin, Anaclisis, Defacement', in David Muggleton and Rupert Weinzierl (eds), *The Post-Subcultures Reader*. Oxford and New York: Berg, pp. 51–64.
Blush, Steve (2010) *American Hardcore: A Tribal History*. Port Townshead, WA: Feral House.
Cohen, Evan (1999) *I Was a Murder Junkie: The Last Days of GG Allin*. Torrance, CA: Recess Records.
Coughlin, Joe (n.d.a) 'G.G. Allin's Funeral', *ABUSE* 4, http://www.heathenworld.com/music/ggallin.aspx, accessed 16 May 2012.
———— (n.d.b) 'GG Allin, the First Amendment, and the Law', *Gray Areas*, http://www.grayarea.com/ggallin.htm, accessed 23 April 2013.
Davies, Jude (1996) 'The Future of "No Future": Punk Rock and Postmodern Theory', *Journal of Popular Culture*, 29 (4), pp. 3–25.
Deleuze, Gilles (1989) 'Coldness and Cruelty', in *Masochism*. New York: Zone Books, pp. 9–142.
Deleuze, Gilles and Félix Guattari (1987) *A Thousand Plateaus: Capitalism and Schizophrenia*. Minneapolis, MN: University of Minnesota Press.
Fertig, Beth (1989) 'Horror Story Shocks World: Girl Tells, "I Almost Married GG Allin!"' *Boston Rock*, http://www.oocities.org/ekx001/MG/BR1989MG.html, accessed 18 May 2013.
Foucault, Michel (1990) *The History of Sexuality: Volume 1: An Introduction*. New York: Vintage Books.
———— (2003) *'Society Must be Defended': Lectures at the Collége de France, 1975–76*. New York: Picador.

44   DEATH AND THE ROCK STAR

——— (2007) *Security, Territory, Population: Lectures at the Collége de France, 1977–78*. New York: Picador.

——— (2008) *The Birth of Biopolitics: Lectures at the Collége de France, 1978–79*. New York: Picador.

Fox, Kathryn Joan (1987) 'Real Punks and Pretenders: The Social Organization of a Counterculture', *Journal of Contemporary Ethnography*, 16, pp. 344–70.

Goshert, John Charles (2000) '"Punk" after the Pistols: American Music, Economics, and Politics in the 1980s and 1990s', *Popular Music and Society*, 24 (1), pp. 85–106.

Hebdige, Dick (1979) *Subculture: The Meaning of Style*. London: Routledge.

James, David (1988–1989) 'Hardcore: Cultural Resistance in the Postmodern', *Film Quarterly*, 42 (2), pp. 31–9.

McNeil, Legs and Gillian McCain (1997) *Please Kill Me: The Uncensored Oral History of Punk*. New York: Penguin Books.

Moore, Ryan (2004) 'Postmodernism and Punk Subculture: Cultures of Authenticity and Deconstruction', *The Communication Review*, 7, pp. 305–27.

——— (2007) 'Friends Don't Let Friends Listen to Corporate Rock: Punk and a Field of Cultural Production', *Journal of Contemporary Ethnography*, 36 (4), pp. 438–74.

O'Hara, Craig (1999) *The Philosophy of Punk: More than Noise!* London: AK Press.

Reynolds, Roy T. (1989) 'Musician Sentenced to Assault', *Ann Arbor News*, 25 December.

R.M. (1993) 'G.G. Allin', AW #32, 5 May, http://www.oocities.org/ekx001/MG/AW050593MG.html, accessed 30 April 2015.

Sosnicki, Jay (1993) 'Maximum GG Allin', *MaximumRockNRoll*, 124, http://www.oocities.org/ekx001/MG/MRR124MG.html, accessed 24 November 2013.

State of Michigan Circuit Court Case number 89-24090 FH.

Thompson, Stacy (2004) *Punk Productions: Unfinished Business*. Albany, NY: State University of New York Press.

Tsitsos, William (1999) 'Rules of Rebellion: Slamdancing, Moshing, and the American Alternative Scene', *Popular Music*, 18 (3), pp. 397–414.

Willis, Susan (1993) 'Hardcore: Subculture American Style', *Critical Inquiry*, 19 (2), pp. 365–83.

Wong, Deborah (2004) *Speak it Louder: Asian Americans Making Music*. New York: Routledge.

Chapter 4

Difference that Exceeded Understanding: Remembering Michael Jackson (Redux)

Susan Fast

In the fall of 2009, as Stan Hawkins and I were editing a special issue of *Popular Music and Society* on Michael Jackson, Gary Burns, the editor of that journal, asked me to write an obituary on the artist.[1] The immediate aftermath of Michael Jackson's death in June of that year was chaotic and frenzied: websites and search engines crashed (including, among others, Google, Twitter, AOL Messenger, *The Los Angeles Times*) as people scrambled to reconnect with an artist who had long been relegated to a freaky sideshow by all but his most ardent fans. Some estimates put an increase in Internet traffic worldwide as high as 20 per cent, leading AOL to call it a 'seminal moment in Internet history' (Rawlinson and Hunt, 2009; also Shiels, 2009). An estimated 31 million people watched his Staples Center memorial on television (Nielsen, 2009), and he became the best-selling artist of 2009 with 35 million records sold worldwide (Anon., 2010). Over a million of those were downloaded in the week following his death in the US alone (Caulfield, 2009). At the same time, closely-guarded information about his personal life was disclosed that worked to temper – or perhaps, just further complicate – his social legibility: information about his skin condition, his life as a father/mother, his intimate relationships, and his hodgepodge network of unlikely but supportive friends. In death, Jackson and his art began to be excavated from the ruins of his difficult public life; pathologising his differences gave way, in small measure at least, to an interest in understanding them as, in the words of James Baldwin (1985 p. 690), 'echoes of our own terrors and desires'. It was in this context that I wrote the obituary, which, in addition to covering milestones in Jackson's life and career, also reflected on how he was scorned and reviled for his differences, from his looks to his ways of living and how those of us who think and write about popular music were negligent in allowing not only the media hype, but Jackson's astonishing body of work to go unexamined; it took his death for us to sit up and notice. That piece is reprinted here. It is followed by some thoughts, written on the eve of the fifth anniversary of his death, about how his work and life have been taken up since that time.

---

[1] Parts of this chapter originally appeared in *Popular Music and Society*, 33 (2), 2010.

October 2009

Following Michael Jackson's tragic and untimely death on 25 June 2009, I began to listen and watch again. Like millions of others who were suddenly buying up his records in vast quantities, putting him on top of the charts for the first time in years, I wanted once again to be mesmerised, enchanted, and moved to tears by his brilliant singularity as a singer, songwriter, dancer and choreographer, and I was. His difference as a performer is what made people around the globe flock to him from the time he was a little boy, what eventually gave him the biggest-selling record of all time (*Thriller*), what made us call him a genius. 'In the world of pop music', wrote Jon Pareles (1984) of the *New York Times*, 'there is Michael Jackson and then there is everybody else'. The sounds he could make with his voice and the movements he could call up out of his body were like those of no one else, but this part of his difference, while incomprehensible, was embraceable. It was magic. Until his death, for all but his fans (not an insubstantial population), this difference seemed to have been forgotten, taken for granted, or overshadowed by his other, less embraceable differences.

For months after his death, the only recordings, DVDs and old VHS tapes that made their way into my various players were his. I listened to his exquisite voice wring a song from some unfathomable depth of his being, belting the blues as a very young boy with the Jackson 5 ('Who's Loving You'), trembling about the loss of romantic love ('She's Out of My Life'), taking us to church ('Man in the Mirror') or grinding out distorted funk (the sexy 'She Drives Me Wild'). I listened to this voice make a point about global warming (the beautiful 'Earth Song', which some find far too sappy – I love this side of him) and race relations ('Black or White', 'They Don't Really Care about Us'). I listened to the performances he gave on record that are among the most beautiful in pop music ('Human Nature', 'Speechless'), many of which were shaped with the help of producer Quincy Jones, but some of them with later collaborators such as Teddy Riley. No one was more emotionally invested in the performance of a song than Jackson (he is at some emotional breaking point on 'Jam', and exploding with anger on '2 Bad'). He sang with technical perfection, too. His voice was pitch-perfect, vibrato-infused, clear, impossibly high, but the range of qualities he could elicit from this instrument was equally impressive: the increasingly deep use of distortion, the exploration of a lower range ('Get on the Floor') and, of course, his incredible command of rhythm, demonstrated not only in his staccato melodies and punctuations thereof, but in his grooves, which he often created or contributed to through beat-boxing. The different vocal qualities he could summon were irreconcilable; he could sound dirtier than James Brown on one track and smooth as silk, like Smokey Robinson or Barbra Streisand, on the next.

I watched again and again all his brilliant short films (he didn't like to call them 'videos'), pieces that for all intents and purposes defined the new medium of music video in the 1980s and which are still of incomparable quality: 'Thriller', 'Beat It', 'Billie Jean', the long version of 'Bad' directed by Martin Scorsese

DIFFERENCE THAT EXCEEDED UNDERSTANDING

(he always collaborated with people at the top of their game), 'Smooth Criminal', 'Black or White', with the remarkable and controversial solo dance sequence at the end – the list goes on. His were the first videos by a black artist to be put in rotation on MTV (there is controversy concerning how this came to be, but it nevertheless happened). This was part of his important legacy as an African-American performer who pushed through racial barriers – in fact the first one to do it on such a global scale. I revisited the performance he gave on the Motown 25 television special in 1983, where he showed the world the moonwalk, a moment of singular significance in the history of popular music. His dancing made Jackie Wilson, Fred Astaire and the Electric Boogaloos improbable companions (more irreconcilability), to say nothing of the debt he owed James Brown, whose singular stylings were often on full display during Jackson's live shows. The choreographer Michael Peters, with whom Jackson worked, remarked how effortlessly Jackson learned and executed dance moves and routines – much more so than many dancers with extensive formal training, of which he had none. This is especially evident in the stylised ensemble dancing, which Jackson practically invented for pop music, where even next to highly skilled professional dancers he manages to look more graceful and at ease while performing the same moves. I watched the 1993 Super Bowl halftime show, the first time a superstar of his magnitude performed solo at that event, establishing a trend that continues today. I took in the jaw-dropping *Michael Jackson Live from Bucharest: The Dangerous Tour*, originally broadcast live on HBO in 1992 (it garnered HBO its largest audience to that date). The concert begins with Jackson being propelled into the air from underneath the stage on an elevator platform that 'toasts' him, after which he stands motionless for a full three minutes. He is an extraordinary vision in his trademark military style gold jacket, long black curls and aviator shades, gold sparks cascading behind him. When he finally removes his sunglasses, the revelation of his sculpted, made-up face only deepens the mystery. It is surely one of the most arresting and powerful ways an arena concert has begun in the history of the genre. This glitzy spectacle might be cheesy if it weren't followed by two and a half hours of non-stop, spectacular dancing and singing that somehow justifies his self-deification at the beginning. King of Pop indeed.

I listened. I watched. This is how I wanted to remember Michael Jackson's difference, as a virtuoso musician and dancer. As Madonna put it in her moving tribute to him at the MTV Video Music Awards in September 2009, he was a 'magnificent creature [who] once set the world on fire'.[2] But it is not possible to remember Michael Jackson's difference as an artist without also remembering all the pain and controversy that surrounded him and how so much of this must also be understood as the result of his difference, difference much less easy, if not impossible, to embrace, so unsettling to the hegemonic order that it had to be contained through ridicule, misinterpretation, sensationalism and finally criminal indictment. Michael Jackson's subjectivity off the stage was disquieting.

---

[2]   See https://www.youtube.com/watch?v=U4aQatsyz-Q.

He was unknowable. He was impossible to 'figure out'. While some of this difference was demonstrated through what was viewed in the mass media as 'eccentric' behaviour (the presence of his companion Bubbles the chimp, the black surgical masks, the rumour that he wanted to buy the Elephant Man's bones, some of this surely calculated to attract attention), it was really his more substantive, underlying differences that were most troubling – racial, gendered, able-bodied/disabled, child/teenager/adult, adult man who loved children, father/mother. These differences were impenetrable, uncontainable, and they created enormous anxiety. Please be black, Michael, or white, or gay or straight, father or mother, father to children, not a child yourself, so we at least know how to direct our liberal (in)tolerance. And try not to confuse all the codes simultaneously. Jackson tested the boundaries of subjectivity, not with the ironic distance of his contemporaries, Madonna and Prince, but with his heart on his sleeve, and he eventually lost. On those rare occasions when he tried to explain himself, he seemed instead to dig a deeper hole. Many remained sceptical; too many normative social codes were in flux, and none were ever neatly put back in the container (again, unlike Madonna and Prince, who were both eventually domesticated in 'normal' ways).

Perhaps the only controversial element of Jackson's biography that was widely accepted and sympathetically received was that he was beaten and teased by his father, literally whipped into shape as a performer from the age of five, when he started singing with his brothers in the Jackson 5. In fact, it was this piece of information that was used to contextualise and pathologise some of his later 'eccentricities', including the (ostensibly)[3] vast amount of plastic surgery he underwent to alter his appearance (some said [for example, Taraborrelli, 2009] that he did this to look as little like his father as possible), and his desire to reclaim a childhood he said he never had because he spent his working, and under terrible conditions. Not only was he physically abused but, according to his biographer Randy Taraborrelli (2009 p. 96), he also suffered through his older brothers having sex with girls while he tried to sleep in hotel rooms that he shared with them as a child.[4] Joe Jackson booked the group into a night-club in their hometown of Gary, Indiana, before they signed with Motown when Michael was nine years old, so that he could make steady money off his sons; there, and in the various other places the group performed, Jackson witnessed all manner of adult sexual and other behaviour. In his autobiography, Michael Jackson (2009 p. 39) tells of watching a transvestite stripper in one of these clubs and follows this by writing: 'As I said, I received quite an education as a child. More than most. Perhaps this freed me to concentrate on other aspects of my life as an adult'.

Whatever he may have meant by this, it did not really matter to the mass media. That he wanted to spend his time with kids, while seeming to be uninterested in

---

[3] I say 'ostensibly' because some scholars question that his surgeries were that extensive. His vitiligo and lupus may have played a greater role in his changing appearance than has previously been taken into account (see Stillwater, 2014).

[4] Taraborrelli's book is not authorised and dwells on the sensational.

or incompetent with women, began to shape narratives about his gendered and sexualised self: that he was gay, or 'asexual'. These claims were fuelled by his surgeries, which made him look increasingly androgynous. He married twice, but these were short-lived relationships that the media found laughable.[5] He eventually had three children of his own and parented them himself, wives and mothers seemingly superfluous. When Jackson's skin began getting lighter there was speculation that he wanted to 'be white' and not African-American; the surgeries seemed to erase his black facial features as well. He tried to explain (vaguely) to Oprah Winfrey in 1993 that he suffered from vitiligo, but this was met with scepticism; it was a rare skin disease that few had ever heard of at that time. And shortly after this interview with Oprah, the bombshell exploded: he was accused of child sexual molestation. His practice of opening up the gates of Neverland Ranch, his home that included an amusement park, zoos and unlimited quantities of candy, to thousands of mostly disadvantaged children, and giving them the run of the place, including his bedroom, opened the door for disaster. He was accused twice, the first time allegedly paying his accuser in excess of $20 million to settle out of court, the second time resulting in a criminal trial (he claimed that he gave in not because he was guilty, but because he just wanted the episode behind him – see Taraborrelli, 2009). The trial, held in 2005, was a media circus, and according to friends it broke his spirit, even though he was acquitted on all counts.[6]

Sadly, it is only in the wake of Jackson's death that counter-narratives concerning his difference might be possible. Sudden and tragic death is sobering; initially, at least, it softens us, making it possible to re-examine someone's life in more sympathetic terms, allowing a fuller, richer account to penetrate the noise of negative judgment. If ever anyone needed to be viewed a little more softly, it is Michael Jackson. While we do not want to wipe away whatever pain this man might have suffered, or whatever questionable judgment he might have exercised, or oversimplify a profoundly complex life, we need to make room for other stories about him, especially in scholarly writing where he has been relatively neglected.

What might these counter-narratives look like? Some who were close to Jackson have opened up since his death and at least some in the media seem more willing to listen now. The autopsy results, his dermatologist Arnold Klein, and his long-time friend Deepak Chopra all confirmed that he did, indeed, have vitiligo, and that, according to the dermatologist, the de-pigmentation of his skin was so profound that it became too difficult to use darker make-up to cover it up (this had

---

[5] Since I first wrote this piece in 2009, it has come to light that Jackson's relationship with Lisa Marie Presley was not short-lived. After they divorced, they continued to try to reconcile until after 2000 (see Lisa Marie Presley's interview with Oprah Winfrey, aired on 21 October 2010).

[6] Jackson effectively went into exile after the trial, moving first to Bahrain and then Ireland, finally coming back to the US in 2006, where he rented a house in Las Vegas. These final, lonely years are recounted by the two men who served as his security guards from 2006–9 (see Whitfield, Beard and Colby, 2014).

been said before, by him, among others, but not really heard). Scholars who have written about Jackson's change in skin colour, including Awkward (1995), Fuchs (1995) and Yuan (1996), have done so in a way that suggests he had control over it. Even if they mention the possibility of vitiligo, the question of 'but what if he didn't?' casts a shadow over what they write. Some have already suggested that his white skin forces the question about what it means to be African-American, which it surely does. Despite his skin colour, Jackson claimed he was proud of his black heritage and his friend Gotham Chopra has recently said that he always identified as African-American (in Messer, 2009). What might he have meant by this? How might the discourse around Jackson's shifting skin colour change if his vitiligo is taken as fact? Might it have been a painful loss to him and if so, might it have influenced the direction he took with his plastic surgeries, or the way he eventually played with his skin colour, sometimes making it clown white, sometimes more bronze as Yuan (1996) has pointed out? Should his condition be viewed as a disability?

While the world has mostly looked at Jackson's facial transformations as pathological, a combination of deep-seated hatred of his appearance with a desire to remain forever impossibly young, it is interesting to note that, after his death, his dermatologist commented that Jackson thought of his own face as a work of art. Perhaps this was a feeble attempt to cast a more positive light on the matter, but perhaps we should contemplate this idea further: if Jackson's plastic surgery were re-contextualised as a form of performance art, such as that by Orlan (whose 1990s 'The Reincarnation of Saint-Orlan' involved a series of plastic surgeries), would we be celebrating him as 'avant-garde' instead of 'troubled'? A few scholars, including Mercer (1986), Awkward (1995) and Yuan (1996), have offered readings of Jackson's facial transformations that move in this direction, not quite calling it 'art' but suggesting that his face became a constantly changing mask, a surface on which he wrote his celebrity in ways that went far beyond what would have been necessary to understand him as white (see also Fast, 2014).

Scholars barely scratched the surface of these issues and they stopped writing about them long before Jackson's death; the last decade or so of his life has not been considered at all. His marriage to Lisa Marie Presley in 1994 was widely thought to be a publicity stunt, a means through which to repair the bruising his image took after he was accused of childhood sexual molestation in 1993 and to neutralise rumours that he was gay. But when Jackson died, Presley once again stated how much she had loved him and how difficult the decision had been to leave him (she left because she felt she was losing her identity in his and she disliked the people he surrounded himself with). The incredulity that Jackson could be an object of sexual desire, especially heterosexual desire, would be equally unbelievable to millions of his fans who regularly gush on the Internet about what a sexy guy he was, even in his final years. One wonders why the opinions of these fans have not been more seriously studied, or taken into account at all in the media coverage of him (save to acknowledge the general hysteria that always surrounded him), except that it is probably too threatening to conventional masculinity; how much of the virulent press on Jackson has come from those (men?) who felt fearful about his unknowability as a gendered and sexual being? In an article on the film *Farinelli* (dir. Gérard Corbiau, 1994), about the eighteenth-century Italian castrato singer who reportedly drove women wild with his brilliant singing and virtuosic love-making, musicologist Harris (1997) briefly draws a comparison with Michael Jackson; this comparison suggests a potentially 'dangerous', 'exotic' sexuality, a menace perhaps even more threatening than if he were openly gay. That Jackson produced a profoundly erotic body on stage is indisputable, although many critics simply will not acknowledge it, or dismiss it because they think the heterosexual frame he put around this body is a lie.

This erotic body was also problematic from the point of view of those who were never quite able to accept Jackson as an adult, sexualised being. Had he only maintained the same sweetness as an adult that he displayed as a child (in the way that, say, Donny Osmond managed to do), all would have been well. But a body that moved like his on stage and in videos like 'Black or White' and 'In the Closet', and the expression of adult sentiments about race and other subjects that were sometimes angry, was unsettling. His entire 'adult' output (*Dangerous*, *HIStory*, *Blood on the Dance Floor*, *Invincible*) is sometimes dismissed, I believe, for this very reason (they are surely among the most underrated records in pop music). The prudish response to his crotch-grabbing has precluded any serious and sophisticated analysis of this gesture; and that is only the tip of the erotic iceberg in his performances. One of the few scholars to address the subject of his sexuality is Cynthia Fuchs (1995), but her essay was published two decades ago. As far as his biography is concerned, that Jackson had few public love affairs does not rule out him having had private ones, but, perhaps more interestingly, the fact that he was rarely seen with a lover in public is itself quite extraordinary. As one critic put it, a man whose focus is not on sex is as revolutionary as a woman, like Madonna, whose is. Could it be that his early childhood experiences really did make him want to focus his adult energies elsewhere? And in a world where there is an unrelenting focus on sex, could we view his lack of engagement with it in the public eye as enlightened instead of tragic, or his love of 'elementary things', as he says in the song 'Childhood', as refreshing?

We also learned in the wake of his death that he was a devoted and loving father/mother to his three children. Home video broadcast on American network television showed the usually glitzy King of Pop doing something as mundane as wiping his son's nose (in full make-up, mind you), cleaning up a puzzle while singing with his two oldest children, teaching them to dance 'The Wiggle', and telling his son on his birthday that he could be anything he wanted to be in his life. Friends and associates gave testimony concerning how good he was at parenting, how well-behaved and loving his children were. There is a rumour that he is not the biological father of these children because some feel they do not look enough like him (meaning, as far as I can tell, that they are not black enough), but perhaps this is just a way to further emasculate someone whose masculinity has always been viewed as problematic. Even though some men are more involved in childcare in the West than they were previously, it is still unusual for a man to be the sole parent to children, especially by choice – single women have babies, yes, single men not so much. After his divorce from Presley, when his dreams of having children seemed shattered, he claims to have been so devastated that he would walk around his house cradling baby dolls. What man wants the experience of fatherhood this much? This is, in fact, the behaviour of a mother; if he had been a woman who wanted children this much, there would have been widespread sympathy for this desire and praise for his efforts as a single parent. And what if, just what if he loved to be around kids, loved to help those who were sick or poor (the extent of his charitable work with children is unparalleled by any other celebrity), and act like a kid himself, without hurting anyone in the process? Both times Jackson was accused of molesting a child, the evidence of wrongdoing was slim (and in some cases downright ludicrous), while evidence that he was being extorted for money was strong. Journalist Aphrodite Jones, who began reporting the 2005 trial convinced of Jackson's guilt and ready to hang him, ended up, along with many other reporters who sat through the trial, convinced of his innocence instead. Jones (2007) reviews the events of the trial in her book *Michael Jackson Conspiracy*. The money to be made from reporting salacious details that painted Jackson as (more of) a freak, to say nothing of what a guilty verdict would have brought, kept the press from giving any kind of balanced view of the trial. It is also uncertain whether race may have played a role in Jackson's indictment, but he was certainly not wrong when he said in an interview with Jessie Jackson (2005) that the accusation of the innocent is 'a pattern among black luminaries in [the United States]'.[7] Jones (2007), who was granted access to court documents after the trial in order to write her book, reports not only the wildly inconsistent testimony of the accuser and his family, most of it contradicted by other witnesses, but also that of other kids who hung out at Jackson's house, who describe a child's paradise: play with great toys, and your hero Michael Jackson, until you drop somewhere and sleep off the fun.

Finally, let me return to the work. When Jackson died, he was in the final stages of preparing a new live show, a comeback after 12 years of being away from the stage. He had sold out 50 shows at London's O2 arena, testimony to how much people still cared about him as a performer (newspapers reported that 2 million people tried to buy pre-sale tickets in less than a day). Rehearsals for these shows were filmed and four months after his death the documentary *Michael Jackson's This is It*, pieced together from this footage, was released in movie theatres around the world. The film was critically acclaimed and widely viewed, taking in more than $200 million in the first two weeks it was screened. It depicts a vibrant Jackson, rehearsing some of his best-known songs, the splendid voice in fine form, the 50-year-old body executing the choreography with the same ease and grace as it had 20 or even 30 years earlier (like absolutely everything else in Jackson's life,

---

[7] The complete interview is available here: https://www.youtube.com/watch?v=pawGvkUF0-I.

this film is not without controversy, some feeling that the representation of him as healthy was manipulated, but it is difficult to argue with his performance in the film, or how happy he looks to be doing it again). What's more, we see Jackson, who rarely spoke to his audiences, or in interviews, giving directions to his musicians, interacting with them and his dancers in a gentle, respectful and sometimes endearingly funny manner, similar to the way his many collaborators over the years say he engaged with them. The film, and the return to his audio and video recordings by so many, is working to balance the media sensationalism, bringing the focus back to his brilliance as a musician and performer.

Viewing the film and immersing myself in his life's work forces me to ask why so precious little of quality has been written about him – there is not even a decent critical biography, let alone very many penetrating analyses of his work (none that deal with sound). In her MTV tribute of 2009, Madonna also said, with her characteristic directness, that as the 'witch hunt' against Jackson by the media and others unfolded, 'we abandoned him'. As a scholar of popular music, I feel part of that 'we'. Michael Jackson's death presents an opportunity to reflect on why we allow some very important artists to become invisible while we give so much attention to others, why we do not challenge more fiercely, and with compassion, media representations of popular music artists who are hated for their difference. We need to put our considerable skills to work in the analysis both of Jackson's life and his important body of work and in the process consider how much of our apathy toward it has stemmed from our own discomfort with his difference.

June 2014

There are perhaps five major strands to Michael Jackson's public afterlife: the continued re-discovery and appreciation of his artistic works that ignited after his death; the continued tabloid silliness; corporate exploitation; small voices that continue to ask for the truth of what happened when he died to be exposed; and a growing body of scholarship that is, indeed, trying to tell new stories about Michael Jackson. This is not so different from the afterlife of many rock stars, except perhaps in scale and in the continued difficulty to shift the narrative.

In May 2014, Sony, with, of course, the blessing of the Michael Jackson Estate, released the second posthumous Michael Jackson solo record. Called *Xscape* – a clever marketing strategy that links it to the Sony Xperia mobile phone (you get a free copy of the album with purchase of the phone) – it offers 'contemporised' versions of demo recordings made by Jackson over a number of years, going back to 1983, with production overseen by L.A. Reid. Sony has marketed the record aggressively, at least in the US: the lead single 'Love Never Felt So Good' can be heard everywhere, from radio stations to the American television show *Dancing with the Stars* to your local grocery store. In the 'making of' documentary that accompanies the deluxe edition of the album, Reid comments that his motivation for becoming involved in the project was to 'make a difference': Michael 'tapped us on the shoulder and said "Would you just do me one small favour and remind people why I'm the greatest" and we all said "yes"'.

A more disingenuous comment is difficult to imagine. If we want to be reminded of Jackson's greatness, we can go back to the remarkable body of work he produced when he was alive, work that was created with a precision and desire for perfection that Reid and the other producers who worked on *Xscape* have no idea how to achieve; the problem with that, however, is that it wouldn't line Reid's pockets, nor, apparently, would it generate quite enough income for everyone else involved. In the years since Jackson's death, the Estate, in collaboration with Sony (a company that Jackson reviled) and Cirque du Soleil, has not only wiped out the artist's considerable debt, but also generated staggering profits by reworking, releasing and re-releasing material under Jackson's name, including the film *This Is It*. A book entitled *Michael Jackson Inc.*, also released in May 2014, lists Jackson's posthumous earnings, from the time of his death in 2009 to 2013, as $710 million. To contextualise this, it is instructive to go back a few years: between 2006 and the first half of 2009, Jackson generated a mere $60 million (O'Malley Greenburg, 2014 p. 251). The quality of the Cirque du Soleil shows and solo albums is questionable; one cannot imagine Michael Jackson sanctioning any of it.

If he had not died a broken man, this might be less grotesque. But the evidence is mounting that in the final years of his life, after the 2005 trial and culminating in the enormous stress of preparations for his comeback concerts, he was lonely and, in the end, sick and exhausted. When I commented in 2009 that in *This Is It*, Jackson looked 'vibrant ... the splendid voice in fine form, the 50-year-old body executing the choreography with the same ease and grace as it had 20 or even 30 years earlier', these words were echoed many times by those working for the Estate, Sony and AEG Live, the companies financing the posthumous shows. I am beginning to believe, however, that I was complicit in a lie. In the months after Jackson's death, many wanted to hold on to the idea that he would have made a stunning comeback. Accounts to the contrary were not only bad for possible law suits against AEG, they were bad for the world's collective psyche when it came to Michael Jackson. One of the lone voices desperately still trying to get the story of Jackson's final days across is Karen Faye, who served as his make-up artist and hair stylist for about 30 years. Insisting that she does not want to profit from her years with Jackson by publishing a tell-all story, she has taken to Twitter to stay in touch with fans.[8] The week before the fifth anniversary of Jackson's death, she tweeted a chilling day-by-day account of the events leading up to his death. Although she is a controversial figure and many fans are suspicious of her, there is little reason to believe that she would fabricate her account of how sick and tired Jackson was, how little control he had over the comeback, and how ruthless those around him were, including threatening to take away his children if he did not perform.

---

[8] She tweets as @wingheart.

There are also the voices of those scholars who have begun to publish 'different stories' about his work since his death, something I hoped would happen. Joseph Vogel was near the end of writing his book *Man in the Music* when Jackson died. With his album-by-album, track-by-track analysis of Jackson's solo works, Vogel (2011) has laid a foundation for the study of Jackson's music and short films that was sorely missing when I wrote my remembrance. Both the *Journal of Popular Music Studies* and *Popular Music and Society* have produced special issues devoted to Jackson's work (respectively in March 2011 and May 2012). Harriet Manning (2013) has written an interesting study that situates Jackson's dancing, in particular, in the context of black minstrelsy.[9] The blog *Dancing with the Elephant: Conversations about Michael Jackson, His Art, and Social Justice*, has also produced three years' worth of bi-weekly posts that have taken up a wide range of songs, videos and issues in a substantial way.[10] Several US institutions, including Duke University and my own, McMaster, have offered courses on Jackson, revisiting some of the important literature by black scholars that was written about him in the late 1980s and 1990s, but somehow forgotten (work by Mercer, 1986; Awkward, 1995; Dyson, 1993; and Wallace, 1990). Despite this, the sensationalist tabloid stories and the deeply entrenched ideas about Jackson continue; the circulation of scholarly work and alternative points of view is not nearly wide enough. On the fifth anniversary of his death, journalist Tanner Colby (2014) published an article in *Slate* magazine regretting the lack of empathy with which most authors had discussed Jackson, subtitling his own piece 'Five years after his death, we've done little to locate the man beneath the tabloid caricature'. This is remarkably true.

Bibliography

Anonymous (2010) 'Jackson Sells 35 Million Albums since Death', *Today: Access Hollywood*, 27 June, http://www.today.com/id/37957972/ns/today-entertainment/#.U67c5KiWRJE, accessed 1 October 2014.

Awkward, Michael (1995) *Negotiating Difference: Race, Gender and the Politics of Positionality*. Chicago, IL: University of Chicago Press.

Baldwin, James (1985) *The Price of the Ticket: Collected Non-Fiction 1948–1987*. New York: St Martin's.

Caulfield, Keith (2009) 'Michael Jackson Sells 1.1 Million Albums in One Week', *Billboard*, 8 July, http://www.nielsen.com/us/en/newswire/2009/31-million-watch-michael-jackson-memorial-service-on-tv.html, accessed 29 September 2014.

---

[9] A bibliography of serious writings about Jackson's life and works is found at http://www.joevogel.net/mj-studies.

[10] See http://dancingwiththeelephant.wordpress.com/.

56 DEATH AND THE ROCK STAR

Colby, Tanner (2014) 'The Radical Notion of Michael Jackson's Humanity', *Slate*, 24 June, http://www.slate.com/articles/arts/culturebox/2014/06/michael_jackson_death_anniversary_we_recall_thriller_and_bad_but_what_about.html, accessed 29 September 2014.

Dyson, Michael Eric (1993) *Reflecting Black: African-American Cultural Criticism*. Minneapolis, MN: University of Minnesota Press.

Fast, Susan (2014) *Michael Jackson's Dangerous*. New York: Bloomsbury.

Fuchs, Cynthia J. (1995) 'Michael Jackson's Penis', in Sue-Ellen Case, Philip Brett and Susan Leigh Foster (eds), *Cruising the Performative: Interventions into the Representation of Ethnicity, Nationality, and Sexuality*. Bloomington, Indianapolis, IN: Indiana University Press, pp. 13–33.

Harris, Ellen T. (1997) 'Twentieth-Century Farinelli', *The Musical Quarterly*, 81, pp. 180–89.

Jackson, Michael (2009 [1988]) *Moonwalk*. New York: Doubleday.

Jones, Aphrodite (2007) *Michael Jackson Conspiracy*. Bloomington, IN: iUniverse.

Manning, Harriet (2013) *Michael Jackson and the Blackface Mask*. Farnham and Burlington, VT: Ashgate.

Mercer, Kobena (1986) 'Monster Metaphors: Notes on Michael Jackson's *Thriller*', *Screen*, 27 (1), pp. 26–43.

Messer, Lesley (2009) 'Deepak Chopra: Michael Jackson Had Lupus', *People Magazine*, 27 June, http://www.people.com/people/package/article/0,20287787_20288162,00.html, accessed 29 September 2014.

Nielsen (2009) '31+ Million Watch Michael Jackson Memorial Service on TV in U.S.', 8 July, http://www.nielsen.com/us/en/newswire/2009/31-million-watch-michael-jackson-memorial-service-on-tv.html, accessed 1 October 2014.

O'Malley Greenburg, Zack (2014) *Michael Jackson, Inc.: The Rise, Fall and Rebirth of a Billion Dollar Empire*. New York: Atria.

Pareles, Jon (1984) 'Michael Jackson at 25: A Musical Phenomenon', *The New York Times*, 14 January, http://www.nytimes.com/1984/01/14/arts/michael-jackson-at-25-a-musical-phenomenon.html?scp.2&sq.michael%20jackson%20at%2025:%20a%20musical%20phenomenon&st.cse, accessed 29 September 2014.

Rawlinson, Limmie and Nick Hunt (2009) 'Jackson Dies, Almost Takes Internet with Him', CNN.com [Technology], 26 June, http://www.cnn.com/2009/TECH/06/26/michael.jackson.internet/index.html?eref=ib_us, accessed 14 February 2014.

Shiels, Maggie (2009) 'Web Slows after Jackson's Death', *BBC News*, 26 June, http://news.bbc.co.uk/2/hi/technology/8120324.stm, accessed 13 July 2014.

Stillwater, Willa (2014) 'Monsters, Witches and Michael Jackson's *Ghosts*', *Popular Musicology Online*, 2, http://www.popular-musicology-online.com/issues/02/stillwater.html, accessed 1 July 2015.

Taraborrelli, Randy (2009) *Michael Jackson: The Magic, the Madness, the Whole Story, 1958–2009*. New York: Grand Central Publishing.

Vogel, Joseph (2011) *Man in the Music: The Creative Life and Work of Michael Jackson*. New York: Sterling.

Wallace, Michele (1990) *Invisibility Blues: From Pop to Theory*. London and New York: Verso.

Whitfield, Bill and Javon Beard with Tanner Colby (2014) *Remember the Time: Protecting Michael Jackson in His Final Days*. New York: Random House.

Yuan, David (1996) 'The Celebrity Freak: Michael Jackson's Grotesque Glory', in Rosemarie Garland Thomson (ed.), *Freakery: Cultural Spectacles of the Extraordinary Body*. New York: New York University Press, pp. 368–84.

PART II
Mediating the Dead

Chapter 5

Mediation, Generational Memory and the Dead Music Icon

Andy Bennett

Rock stars cast an iconic presence over society, a quality that persists even in death. The earliest examples of the 'rock casualty', notably Buddy Holly, have demonstrated the propensity for a key music icon's death to elicit generational grief and mourning on a global scale. Similarly, in their account of the global media's response to the death of Elvis Presley following a drugs overdose in August 1977, Gregory and Gregory (1997) note that the rapid and overwhelming response of the global media was interwoven with the world-wide mourning that followed. They further observe how the media's role in the public enshrinement of Elvis evokes another critical element in the mourning of the popular music icon, generational memory: 'Even for those who had not really thought about Elvis for years, there was a great feeling that something had changed. A whole generation felt middle aged; a part of their youth was gone' (Gregory and Gregory, 1997 p. 227). Equally significant, however, is the way that, through the process of mediation, dead rock icons continue to 'live on', through their music, words (sung and spoken) and images. Exuding a truly 'beyond the grave' quality, dead rock stars continue to 'speak' to their audience in a way rarely achieved by those working in other idioms (with the possible exception of a small number of movie stars, such as James Dean). This chapter examines the phenomenon of the dead music icon using the related concepts of mediation and generational memory in order to understand the ongoing importance and sense of connect that these icons continue to have with their audience (and indeed with new audiences born years, and increasingly decades, later). In addition to considering the importance of textual and media artefacts in the collective remembering of dead music icons, the chapter will also examine another increasingly important medium through which they continue to be celebrated, the tribute band.

Recorded Music and the Mediation of the Dead

It is an interesting, not to say sometimes ethereal, experience to watch film and video recordings of deceased rock and pop artists engaging in performances that have now come to be regarded as seminal moments in their respective careers. Examples that immediately spring to mind here are Jimi Hendrix's performance of the American National Anthem, 'The Star Spangled Banner', in the film *Woodstock: The Movie* (see Bennett, 2004; Moore, 2004; Whiteley, 2004), John Lennon and George Harrison performing in the very last live appearance of the Beatles during the infamous concert on the roof of the Apple Building in the proto-rockumentary *Let It Be*, and Freddie Mercury's celebrated performance with Queen at Live Aid in 1985 (see Fast, 2006). Each of these performances has become a historic 'moment' but also, due to the way they have been captured on film and subject to continual replay, they appear to be suspended in time, reaching out to audiences and fuelling their memories of the particular time and era in which the performances took place. That audiences are able to relate to music icons in this way has much to do with the mode through which such icons are presented to and connect with their audience. Indeed, as Frith (1988), among others, has observed, an integral aspect of popular music since its mass industrialisation during the 1950s has been its mediation. Thus, rock and pop artists from the 1950s onwards, whether they are today living or dead, have been experienced primarily as mediations – as images on a screen, as sounds and voices on a vinyl album or CD, as figures on a stage whose music is conveyed electronically through amplification and PA (public address) systems.

Clearly, however, this aspect of the way audiences have experienced, and continue to experience, rock and pop icons has not prevented them from forming what they perceive as *personal* bonds with those icons. In relation to this, Frith (1987) argues that audiences claim 'ownership' of artists and their music, feeling a sense of connection with them that extends to few other forms of popular culture with the possible exception of sport. Thus, even as the primary means through which an audience connects with a particular music artist is through the mediated forms in which that artist is presented to them, a sense of loss is nevertheless deeply felt when the artist in question dies. Indeed, in many ways, the process of mediation can be said to accentuate this phenomenon. As noted above, following the death of Elvis, the media coverage including the many tributes that were broadcast on television and radio elevated Elvis's passing to a global and generational level of grief and mourning. Since the emergence of the Internet during the early 1990s, the ease with which audiences can engage in such processes of global, generational mourning has increased. For example, in her study of webshrines, Andsager (2005 p. 19) observes:

> Tribute pages for dead celebrities contain many of the elements of traditional mourning rituals: memorial items – those that perpetuate the memory – and ritualistic items – those described for use in the ritualized etiquette of mourning ... Memorial items on webshrines include biographies, disc- or filmographies, audio clips and photos. Birth and death dates under a favorite photo, fans' eulogies and poems, and photos or tombstones exemplify reverential references to dead celebrities.

As Andsager's account begins to illustrate, through their creation of such tribute pages, followers of particular celebrities – including rock and pop icons – do not only engage in patterns of online mourning (Moss, 2004), they also extend the characteristics of 'ownership' noted by Frith (1987) to a shaping of the ways in which the death and remembering of particular music artists should be recorded, represented and understood.

In a very clear sense, then, the mediation of the rock and pop icon is something that holds critical currency for the way that we understand their cultural significance in life *and* in death. Following the death of particular music artists, their ongoing mediation to audiences often assumes accentuated qualities in terms of how such artists are remembered and celebrated. This is particularly so in the cases where an artist's music has 'spoken' to fans in significantly forceful or meaningful ways. Notable examples here include John Lennon and Kurt Cobain (of the seminal grunge band Nirvana), whose political and ideological views were frequently expressed in their musical output (see Elliot, 1999; Strong, 2011). In this context, it is not difficult to see why songs such as Lennon's 'Imagine' and Nirvana's 'Smells Like Teen Spirit' continue to receive considerable radio airplay.

In recent years, the concepts of cultural and mediated memory have been increasingly applied by writers such as Huyssen (2000) as a means of conceptualising the ways in which the shared memories between particular social groups, including those bonded by generational aesthetics and affect, are underpinned and articulated through the various forms of media – including film, television, radio and so on – that they are collectively exposed to. Relating this directly to popular music, Bennett suggests that 'the collective cultural memories often built around popular music have functioned as an important generational steer, providing particular generations with an ongoing sense of themselves and their developing collective cultural identities' (2010 p. 248). It follows that the sense of loss experienced by fans following the death of a generational icon can be, and often is, highly pronounced. An additional important factor here is that many rock and pop artists have experienced untimely deaths, leaving fans not only in a severe sense of collective shock, but also with the shared feeling that a significant void has been created in their lives – one that feels impossible to fill. This is illustrated in the following extract taken from an interview conducted by the author with a British fan, then in his sixties, of Buddy Holly[1] (Holly died in a plane crash in February 1959):

> AB: … you said that you felt – your generation felt cheated by [the death of Buddy Holly]?

---

[1] This interview is part of a large-scale research project called Popular Music and Cultural Memory: Localised Popular Music Histories and their Significance for National Music Industries, funded under the Australian Research Council's (ARC) Discovery Project scheme for three years (2010–2012, DP1092910). Chief Investigators on the project were Andy Bennett (Griffith University), Shane Homan (Monash University), Sarah Baker (Griffith University) and Peter Doyle (Macquarie University), with Research Fellow Alison Huber (Griffith University) and Research Associate Ian Rogers (now at RMIT University).

PD: Yeah, because we were just getting used to having him around, and he'd just done – I think he'd done a concert in London not very long before that [February 1959], I think in November or December, I'm not sure – um, and we, we just loved his music so much. He was – he was better than Elvis Presley. He was much better regarded in Britain than Elvis Presley was at that time, and, um, I know, you know, my feeling, my personal feeling, as I said before, is [that] he's my all-time favourite of any of them, with Chuck Berry just a little bit behind, but he's a different style of music. But, ah, Buddy Holly was just so – and his name – it just lends itself to a brilliant performer, too. Okay, it was Charles Harden, born, but you know, Holly, such a brilliant name, you know, and, um, I just feel that, ah, well he'd be 75 now I think, wouldn't he, if he was still alive, something like that, so he'd be challenging Jerry Lee, he'd still be doing something, but, you know, we did – we felt cheated. We felt that we hadn't got what we wanted out of that …

In this account, a deep sense of connection with Buddy Holly is articulated in which Holly's perceived significance as a generational spokesperson and role model is contextualised within a description of the high degree of sorrow and loss experienced following Holly's death. Viewed in this context, it becomes easy to see why fans seek ways of 'reviving' the lives of their favourite icons, and indeed putting such revived lives on permanent hold.

A useful conceptual model for exploring this issue is cultural memory. As Huyssen (2000) notes, cultural memory serves as a means through which generations of individuals reproduce themselves, their shared identities and their collective values over time. A major dependent factor in this respect is the ability to keep in touch with those objects and images that underpin and fuel such memories. A further tantalising aspect of this as it plays out in the *replay and hold* aspect of mediated music artists is that they remain very much in the moment of their 'former glory' – forever young, cheating age and bodily decay in ways that give them an additional level of aura and charismatic appeal. Indeed, even in cases where alternative representations of particular artists exist, it is clear that fans often prefer, and choose to replay, and relive, the glory moments of an artist's life. This is illustrated by the release, barely a month after an ambitious tribute concert held in Queen singer Freddie Mercury's honour in April 1992 by the three surviving members the band and a host of celebrity guests, of the full concert-length version of Queen's performance at Wembley Stadium in July 1986. One of the very last live appearances of Mercury, this concert is considered by many to show Queen at the very height of their live performing career and its commercial release on video (and subsequently DVD) was warmly welcomed by fans around the world. Although Mercury continued to appear in promotional videos made by the group until several months before his death from an AIDS-related illness in November 1991, Queen fans are far more likely to cite the Wembley Stadium concert or Mercury's highly dynamic performances at Live Aid as the signature moments through which they typically choose to remember him.

Posthumous 'Iconic' Careers

> A truism of the music business is that death is a 'good career move'. Sales figures bear this out: rarely does any performer with the slightest bit of popularity fail to increase sales figures immediately after death, and often those who only have the slightest bit of popularity are the ones whose sales benefit most. (Jones, 2005 p. 3)

There is by now a shrewd and highly developed understanding of the marketability of the dead rock or pop star from a music industry perspective. Aligned with this are layers of mythology, suspicion and, in some cases, conspiracy theories around the deaths of particular rock stars (see, for example, Redding and Appleby, 1990). One intriguing example is what has come to be popularly known as the '27 Club', a reference to the fact that a number of famous pop and rock musicians, among them Brian Jones of the Rolling Stones, Jimi Hendrix, Janis Joplin, Jim Morrison and, more recently Kurt Cobain and Amy Winehouse, have all died at the age of 27. Although an official cause of death has been recorded in each case, this apparently strange co-incidence has fuelled a number of conspiracy theories over the years, sometimes linked back to the aforementioned fact that death can significantly increase record sales in the aftermath of an artist's passing and, in some cases, for several years after the fact.[2]

However, the posthumous career of the dead music artist cannot be cast in purely economic terms. Rather, there are important cultural dimensions to such 'careers'. At several points in this chapter, the term 'icon' has been used as this typically informs the way that many of the most successful rock and pop musicians are viewed by their fans, both in life and in death. In saying this, it could, however, be argued that in death the iconicity associated with rock and pop stars assumes significant new dimensions, becoming not merely a focus for the collective celebration of an individual artist and their work, but also a means through which the collective memory of a generation and the received memories of subsequent generations of fans are channelled. Bartmanski and Alexander (2012) have observed how the symbolic inscription of iconicity in the objects, images and texts of consumerism lifts them beyond their commercial value through the affordance of emotional power. In death, the iconicity attached to an artist becomes, in effect, hyper-present in the way that fans – and indeed the music industry – position them. No longer subject to the waxing and waning of creative urge and performative ability, dead rock and pop icons become enshrined within an aura of perpetual mastery and brilliance. This last point is borne out in the way that the iconic status of many artists has become increasingly magnified in the

---

[2]   The precise origins of the term '27 Club' are unclear but it is now frequently cited in music media and press publications (for example, see Sounes, 2013). Although often associated with more contemporary music artists, it should be noted that earlier artists included in the '27 Club' are, for example, ragtime musician Louis Chauvin and legendary blues singer and guitarist Robert Johnson.

decades following their death. Indeed, it should be remembered that a number of these artists, including Brian Jones, Jimi Hendrix, Janis Joplin and Jim Morrison, had relatively short careers in comparison to other artists of their generation who continue to make records and tour. Although each of them were certainly well established at the time of their deaths (although it has also been suggested that the creativity of Jones, Hendrix and Morrison was in decline at that time), how they are currently represented and regarded has much to do with the way that their music and images have been circulated since the time of their respective deaths, and how critical opinion has built accordingly on a global scale.

The mediation of selective, dominant material about these and other artists has enabled them to attract successive generations of fans, admirers and emulators. For such 'new' audiences, many of whom were born well after the deaths of the rock and pop icons they admire, the wholly mediated nature of their interaction with musicians takes on a heightened level of significance. Thus, the way that such artists are positioned in the global circulation of popular culture as perpetually 'young', vibrant and essentially cutting-edge (see Bennett, 2008) ensures that they are also interpreted as such by successive generations of youth audiences, with the effect that, despite having now been dead for several decades, they are assured a status as youth icons for many more years – and possibly centuries – to come. Evidence of this trend is seen in the following account offered by a participant in the aforementioned popular music and cultural memory project. It regards the contribution of former AC/DC vocalist Bon Scott (who died at the age of 33 in February 1980 due to excessive drinking and alcohol poisoning) to the group's ongoing appeal and the appeal of rock music in general:

> Yeah, interesting thing – when AC/DC went to London, 76–77, I think, you know, Bon Scott got asked the question, 'are you a punk band', and he said, 'no, we're a straight rock and roll band', and as Clinton Walker[3] put it in his book about Bon Scott, straight rock and roll bands are the best rock and roll bands, and I agree with that. Um, AC/DC were massive, I mean they haven't really made a great record, ah, since *Back in Black*.[4] They've been really treading water since then, making the same record, but not as good, for 30 years … I didn't – I have never seen AC/DC live, and I will go to my grave regretting it. I didn't get tickets to the last, to the last show, and I'm still bitter about it. Um, as a live act, though, the fact that they sold that many tickets, that fast, they're still unimpeachable.

---

[3]   Clinton Walker is an Australian writer with an interest in popular music and popular/ grass-roots culture. His books on music include *Highway to Hell: The Life and Times of AC/ DC Legend Bonn Scott* (1994) and, more recently, *History is Made at Night* (2012).

[4]   Released in July 1980 *Back in Black* was the first AC/DC album to be recorded following the death of Bon Scott. Dedicated to Scott's memory, the album features English-born vocalist Brian Johnson (formerly of the band Geordie) who has remained with AC/DC ever since.

> They're a phenomenon. Like the Beatles, there is something about them that has
> crossed generational, and crossed cultural appeal.

For this particular interviewee, although Bon Scott has been dead for over three decades, his presence continues to permeate AC/DC and to play a significant part in the band's continuing global success. However, it is not merely artists who have achieved global success that are ascribed such hyper-present iconic status. Through the work of what Bennett (2009) has referred to as DIY (do-it-yourself) popular music preservationists, a number of artists who were relatively obscure at the time of their deaths have also achieved this form of hyper-present iconic status. One notable example is Nick Drake, an English singer-songwriter whose career was cut short after three albums when he died of a drug overdose in 1974. Having remained something of a footnote in British popular music for a number of years, since the acclaim of musicians such as Robert Smith (of The Cure) and David Sylvian (formerly lead singer with Japan and now a solo artist) and the emergence of neo-folk music in the UK during the early 1990s, Drake posthumously found a new audience and is now acknowledged as a seminal figure in the British acoustic-folk and folk-rock of the 1970s alongside other artists such as the Incredible String Band, Pentangle and John Martyn.

Death, Generational Memory and the Tribute Band

Another way in which the iconic presence of rock and pop stars continues to be felt many years after their death is in the form of the tribute band – or tribute artist – show. As Bennett (2006 pp. 19–20) has observed:

> ... tribute bands respond to a range of mundane, everyday desires exhibited by audiences: to relive a particular moment in their youth; to experience again their personal icons in a live setting (and perhaps take their children along too); to engage in the rapport between performer and audience deemed integral to the communicative power of popular music.

In 2002, the author attended a concert by popular Beatles tribute band the Bootleg Beatles. One of the songs featured in the set was the John Lennon composition 'A Day in the Life'. Watching bootleg 'John' in his pale green Sergeant Pepper uniform seated at a white grand piano (a simulacrum of the pianos played by John Lennon on 'I am the Walrus' in the Beatles' television film *Magical Mystery Tour* and later on the promotional film for his post-Beatles hit 'Imagine'), it was apparent that both visually and musically the performance took aspects of the Beatles' history and reassembled them in an intriguingly postmodern way. Thus, while some of the songs performed earlier in the Bootleg Beatles' set had been based on actual live performances by the Beatles during previous moments in their career, here was a song that had not been designed to be played lived and, thus, depicted a performance that never actually took place. The Beatles officially retired from live performance following their 1966 tour of the US and *Sergeant Pepper's Lonely Hearts Club Band*, from which 'A Day in the Life' is the closing track, was released some time later, in June 1967. Moreover, at the point when this particular Bootleg Beatles concert took place, John Lennon was the only Beatle to have died (having been murdered by a deranged fan in New York City in December 1980). These factors created a surreal experience, with the spotlighted figure on the stage seeming to reach out to his audience of fans from beyond death, presenting for them a vision of Lennon at the peak of his creativity in a performance many wished could have taken place, either during the Beatles' career or during an oft-mooted, but never realised, Beatles re-union concert. This was apparently a feeling shared by many members of the audience for that particular Bootleg Beatles performance who maintained a respectful silence during the song (see also Bennett, 2006).

The tribute band phenomenon has been in motion for a number of decades (see Homan, 2006). Indeed, it has been mooted that as increasing numbers of established rock and pop artists retire from live performance and/or pass away, the tribute band performance will – like the classical and jazz music performance – be a place where fans and followers can come together to share in and celebrate the 'great' music and music artists of past eras. In the case of rock and pop, however, there is another critical dimension to consider – that is, the physical image of the artist or artists performing the music. In this respect, the tribute band takes on a further significant mediating role. Thus, ever since the emergence of early tribute bands such as the aforementioned Bootleg Beatles, ABBA tribute band Björn Again and the Counterfeit Stones, through to more recent examples such as No Way Sis (covering the songs of Oasis), visual emulation of the tributed group or artist has been as critical to the spectacle of the tribute band as its musical emulation. Moreover, visual emulation has often meant capturing the image of the tributed artist at a critical point in their career, usually that point during which they were at both their most creative and their most youthful. This relates back to the point made above regarding the freeze-frame quality of the way that audiences collectively wish to remember their favourite rock and pop icons. Indeed, the transition from original to tribute artist is a relatively small one in this respect. In each case, what the audience is presented with is a spectacle on a stage – a figure or series of figures dressed in stage costumes, bathed in stage lighting, engaged in a musical performance accentuated by special effects and powered by amplification. It is thus but a small leap of faith for an audience, for example at a Queen tribute band performance, to believe that what they are experiencing is a *real* Queen performance with the *real* Freddie Mercury powering through his trademark songs and on-stage antics including the legendary audience participation routines that were typically part of a Queen concert. Postings on YouTube regarding Australian Queen tribute band Killer Queen are an interesting case in point, with several fans describing their visual and musical depiction of classic Queen songs as like watching the real Queen in action. Similar endorsements exist for LA-based Doors tribute band Wild Child, with one fan writing that the lead singer, Dave Brock, bears such a visual and aural resemblance to original Doors singer Jim Morrison that they must be related.

In a very clear sense, then, the tribute band is also playing an important part in facilitating the process of mediation between a dead artist's output and the audience. However, the critical point of departure for the tribute band is the way it brings into play a perfect, or near perfect, simulacrum of the flesh and blood experience that audiences read into the live performance over the watching and re-watching of live concert footage on privately owned pre-recorded videos and DVDs (and increasingly also on YouTube, Apple TV and other online media). Since the emergence of rock and roll in the 1950s and the excitement it created among youth audiences (see Bradley, 1992), popular music has been regarded as a primarily live music. Although the recent, tribute-band inspired forms of popular music performance, such as 'Classic Albums Live', have focused on the reproduction of studio-crafted albums in a live context (see Bennett, 2008; 2009), the live concert has been, and continues to be, regarded as a place where the mere production of the music is transcended, providing an opportunity for new workings of songs that bring them closer to the audience. Again, this is a point of importance in relation to the tribute band, particularly where they revive highly treasured moments from the live performance legacy of particular artists, including perhaps especially, those who have died. The tendency of Queen tribute bands to feature Freddie Mercury and Brian May's acoustic re-working of the song 'Love of my Life' (from the group's 1975 breakthrough album *A Night at the Opera*) is an illustrative case in point. Originally recorded as a piano-based ballad in the studio, the live version substituted Mercury's piano for a new musical interpretation provided by May playing a finger-picked 12-string acoustic guitar. This allowed Mercury to concentrate fully on the vocal delivery of the song and to engage the audience in participation. Such reinvigoration of this and other treasured moments from audience's concert-going memories – or indeed from seeing these moments play out in recorded form on video and DVD – is integral to the importance of the tribute band as a medium for the replaying of memories – or received memories – of dead rock and pop stars.

Conclusion

As this chapter has illustrated, the iconic presence of the rock and pop star is as potent in death as it is in life. Although the passing of a globally established and widely respected popular music artist typically registers as a tragic moment for fans around the world, the artistic and charismatic legacy of that artist often lives on. Indeed, and as this chapter has endeavoured to show, capacity for such a preservation of legacy is, at many levels, rooted in the same processes of mediation that gave rise to the global popularity of such artists while alive but shifts to a new level whereby mediation ensures hyper-present iconicity for these artists as an untouchable, and thus untaintable, presence. If the celebrated rock

70   *DEATH AND THE ROCK STAR*

or pop icon lives their celebrity life as a mediated presence, then, equally, their mediated presence continues to circulate long after that particular artist has died. As rock and pop become an increasingly established part of contemporary culture, debates are beginning to emerge concerning the legitimacy of critically acclaimed artists, albums, venues, performances and so on as aspects of cultural heritage (see, for example, Schmutz, 2005; Bennett, 2009). At the same time, debates continue regarding the status of the ageing rock star in a sphere of popular culture that has conventionally been associated with youthfulness and cultural rebellion and innovation (see Bennett, 2013). While a case can certainly be made for the reassessment of rock and pop's cultural status given its age and longevity, the oft-preferred representation of the dead rock or pop icon in full generational bloom is perhaps a telling reminder that popular music and generational memory remain closely tied in both tangible and intangible fashions.

Bibliography

Andsager, Julie L. (2005) 'Altered Sites: Celebrity Webshrines as Shared Mourning', in Steven Jones and Joli Jensen (eds), *Afterlife as Afterimage: Understanding Posthumous Fame*. New York: Peter Lang Publishing, pp. 17–29.

Bartmanski, Dominik and Jeffrey C. Alexander (2012) 'Materiality and Meaning in Social Life: Toward an Iconic Turn in Cultural Sociology', in Jeffrey C. Alexander, Dominik Bartmanski and Bernhard Giesen (eds), *Iconic Power: Materiality and Meaning in Social Life*. New York: Palgrave Macmillan, pp. 1–14.

Bennett, Andy (ed.) (2004) *Remembering Woodstock*. Aldershot: Ashgate.

———— (2006) 'Even Better than the Real Thing? Understanding the Tribute Band Phenomenon', in Shane Homan (ed.), *Access All Eras: Tribute Bands and Global Pop Culture*. Buckingham: Open University Press, pp. 19–31.

———— (2008) '"Things They Do Look Awful Cool": Ageing Rock Icons and Contemporary Youth Audiences', *Leisure/Loisir*, 32 (1), pp. 259–78.

———— (2009) '"Heritage Rock": Rock Music, Re-presentation and Heritage Discourse', *Poetics*, 37 (5–6), pp. 474–89.

———— (2010) 'Popular Music, Cultural Memory and Everyday Aesthetics', in Eduardo De La Fuente and Peter Murphy (eds), *Philosophical and Cultural Theories of Music*. Leiden: Brill, pp. 243–62.

———— (2013) *Music, Style and Aging: Growing Old Disgracefully?* Philadelphia, PA: Temple University Press.

Bradley, Dick (1992) *Understanding Rock 'n' Roll: Popular Music in Britain 1955–1964*. Buckingham: Open University Press.

Elliott, Anthony (1999) *The Mourning of John Lennon*. Berkeley and Los Angeles, CA: University of California Press.

Fast, Susan (2006) 'Popular Music Performance and Cultural Memory. Queen: Live Aid, Wembley Stadium, London, July 13, 1985', in Ian Inglis (ed.), *Popular Music and Performance: History, Place and Time*. Aldershot: Ashgate, pp. 138–54.

Frith, Simon (1987) 'Towards an Aesthetic of Popular Music', in Richard Leppert and Susan McClary (eds), *Music and Society: The Politics of Composition, Performance and Reception*. Cambridge: Cambridge University Press, pp. 133–49.

——— (1988) *Music for Pleasure: Essays in the Sociology of Pop*. Oxford: Polity Press.

Gregory, Neil and Gregory, Janice (1997) 'When Elvis Died: Enshrining a Legend', in Vernon Chadwick (ed.), *In Search of Elvis: Music, Race, Art, Religion*. Boulder, CO: Westview Press, pp. 225–41.

Homan, Shane (ed.) (2006) *Access All Eras: Tribute Bands and Global Pop Culture*. Buckingham: Open University Press.

Huyssen, Andreas (2000) 'Present Pasts: Media, Politics, Amnesia', *Public Culture*, 12 (1), pp. 21–38.

Jones, Steve (2005) 'Better Off Dead: Or, Making It the Hard Way', in Steve Jones and Joli Jensen (eds), *Afterlife as Afterimage: Understanding Posthumous Fame*. New York: Peter Lang Publishing, pp. 1–15.

Moore, Allan, F. (2004) 'The Contradictory Aesthetics of Woodstock', in Andy Bennett (ed.), *Remembering Woodstock*. Aldershot: Ashgate, pp. 43–54.

Moss, Miriam (2004) 'Grief on the Web', *Journal of Death and Dying*, 49 (1), pp. 77–81.

Redding, Noel and Carol Appleby (1990) *Are You Experienced? The Inside Story of the Jimi Hendrix Experience*. London: Picador/Pan.

Schmutz, Vaughn (2005) 'Retrospective Cultural Consecration in Popular Music', *American Behavioral Scientist*, 48 (11), pp. 1510–23.

Sounes, Howard (2013) 'A Brief History of the 27 Club', *Rolling Stone*, November 12, http://www.rollingstone.com/music/pictures/a-brief-history-of-the-27-club-20131112, accessed 18 September 2014.

Strong, Catherine (2011) *Grunge: Music and Memory*. Aldershot: Ashgate.

Walker, Clinton (1994) *Highway to Hell: The Life and Times of AC/DC Legend Bon Scott*. Sydney: Pan Macmillan.

——— (2012) *History is Made at Night*. Sydney: Currency House.

Whiteley, Sheila (2004) '"1, 2, 3 What Are We Fighting For?" Music, Meaning and the "Star Spangled Banner"', in Andy Bennett (ed.), *Remembering Woodstock*. Aldershot: Ashgate, pp. 18–28.

Chapter 6
'From Death to Birth':
Suicide and Stardom in the Musical Biopic

Penny Spirou

A biopic, short for biographical picture (sometimes referred to as biofilm), is an artistic interpretation of an actual person's life through the medium of the feature-length film, whether that person is dead or alive (see Custen, 1992 p. 5). The individual in question can be from virtually any background including sport (*Moneyball*, dir. Miller, 2011; *The Fighter*, dir. Russell, 2010), politics (*The Iron Lady*, dir. Lloyd, 2011; *Lincoln*, dir. Spielberg, 2012), business (*The Social Network*, dir. Fincher, 2010; *The Wolf of Wall Street*, dir. Scorsese, 2013) or even crime (*Capote*, dir. Miller, 2005; *Monster*, dir. Jenkins, 2003). The chosen protagonist of the biopic can and often does influence the style and genre of the film, and so scholars and film critics alike will categorise biopics depending on the career path of the lead character. The biopic can connect to death in a number of ways, dependent on the actual person in focus. Marshall and Kongsgaard (2012 p. 358) consider that when the subject of the biopic has died, '[r]ather than enabling the subject to live on screen, the biopic affirms their death'. Biopics thus explore life narratives, and do so even more powerfully when the actual person they focus on is no longer living during film production or theatrical release.

The musical biopic has been a prevalent way of representing music artists in popular music history (see Custen, 1992; Bingham, 2010). Of late, there has been a renaissance of the Hollywood or classical narrative-style musical biopic, with 22 theatrical releases in an eight-year period (2002–2010), at least in the UK and USA.[1] One of the most intriguing aspects of these musical biopics is that only a handful of the music stars were alive while the films were made and released, approximately 90 per cent having died either before film production or just before its completion.[2] Musical biopics thus tend to concentrate particularly on death as film directors are likely to shoot their films once an artist has died, reinforcing the importance of death in the public narrative of a rock star. To better understand this trend, this chapter will explore the role of death in film narratives when the music star has committed suicide, with reference to two films, *Last Days*

---

[1] For an extensive analysis of the contemporary musical biopic, see Spirou (2011).

[2] In the case of *Walk the Line* (2005) and *Ray* (2004), Johnny Cash and Ray Charles respectively were notified of the films based on their musical lives while in the process of production, but both had passed away before the theatrical release of the films.

(dir. Van Sant, 2005) which is inspired by the final moments of Kurt Cobain, the American singer and guitarist for the 1990s grunge group Nirvana, and *Control* (dir. Corbijn, 2007), which focuses on Ian Curtis, the lead singer of the Manchester-based 1980s rock group Joy Division. The two overarching themes found within these biopics are struggles between personal and public identity, and isolation, and this chapter observes the ways in which the films' narratives, soundtracks and visual imagery work together to project suicide as the most significant aspect of the artists' life trajectories.

Suicide, Stardom and Musical Biopics

In the classical Hollywood film, narratives tend to focus on a protagonist who struggles to solve a problem or attain a goal; the story ends with either a victory or defeat, following the achievement or non-achievement of the protagonist's goals (Bordwell, 1986 p. 18). In musical biopics where suicide marks the story's end, the individual's struggle is usually to achieve success in the music industry (either as an artist or producer), or when this cannot be achieved (or perhaps when this time is over), to move on to the new goal of taking their own life (see Babington and Evans, 1985 p. 120, for an outline of the basic narrative structure of the Hollywood-era musical biopic). Narrative conflicts are particularly attached to the artists' relationships with colleagues, family and close friends (internal), or music professionals (external), and conclude with a relative victory from the perspective of the protagonist as committing suicide appears to reflect their choice, their power and their control over their life. The nature of classical film narrative is to have a beginning, conflict and resolution, and musical biopics often construct suicide as the resolution (typically matching the pre-existing knowledge of the film audience), and make all the film's components, including other life events, themes, music and character, converge towards the inevitable suicide.

Using the framework of celebrity consumption, Sean Redmond (2006) examines the relationship between fame and the 'damaged' star. He suggests that fame is seen as temporary and that monetary success can ruin the star. Stardom isolates and alienates the star, turning them to substance abuse, and even suicide, in order to 'escape':

> Fame is said to offer the star or celebrity too much of everything that is vacuous and surface level, and very little of the intimate, the psychologically deep, or the long-lasting, and this destroys their ability to be happy and contented. While the damaged star or celebrity is as much a construction as the replenished figure of fame, their identity crisis resonates in ways that signify beyond the discourse that they are made up in. (Redmond, 2006 p. 41)

These tragedies regarding the temporality of fame, wealth and success and their links to isolation and loneliness appear, in some shape or form, in the musical biopics analysed here, where suicide is considered to be the only way out. In these cases, the filmmakers suggest that for these stars to maintain their standing in music history, it is better to die rather than to just quit. If they quit, fans will be likely to simply forget them, whereas the finality and dramatic nature of suicide will secure their place in popular music history and public memory.

The clash between personal and public identity, and the pressures of fame, are recurring themes in the lives and biopics of the individuals under consideration, themselves fitting into broader trends in musical biopics dealing with suicide, as also seen in *What We Do Is Secret* (dir. Grossman, 2007), on The Germs' lead singer Darby Crash, and *Telstar: The Joe Meek Story* (dir. Moran, 2008). Although not shown in *Last Days*, Cobain's actual suicide note states that it is 'better to burn out than just fade away' (cited in Whiteley, 2003 p. 150). Deborah Curtis, wife of the Joy Division frontman, recalled Ian Curtis stating he did not want to live beyond his twenties and idolised musicians who died young including Jim Morrison (Curtis, 1995 p. 15). Ian Curtis's own fandom is reflected in early scenes in *Control*, where he appears in his bedroom, covered with music posters, playing records and even imitating artists he admires. In *Telstar: The Joe Meek Story*, record producer Joe Meek's lack of success and wealth after he has acquired taste for it ultimately ends in his death. Towards the end of the film, Meek questions what happens to people in situations like his, who gain a temporary fame and spend their lives trying to reach it again. Through dialogue, he exhibits concerns about being forgotten. Lastly, lead singer of The Germs, Darby Crash, was seemingly aware in *What We Do Is Secret* that fame is only short-lived and intended on committing suicide within five years of recruiting individuals to make up his punk band.

While the pressures of fame are not everyday concerns for most people, the theme of isolation reflects a more universal factor in suicide. According to the World Health Organization, suicide is one of the three leading causes of death in people from 15 to 44 years old. Approximately one million people commit suicide (successfully killing themselves) every year in the world (WHO, 2009). In the UK and USA, studies show that more males in every age group commit suicide than females (WHO UK, 2009; WHO USA, 2005), even though females have higher rates of mental illness and suicide ideation.[3] ABC reports that the reason why more males commit suicide is because they are less likely to ask for help (White, 2013). In an empirical study of suicide, psychologists suggest that social isolation is the largest predictor of suicidal ideation, among a sample varying in nationality and age (Van Orden et al., 2010 p. 579). These studies suggest that the most common cause of suicide (commencing with some form of ideation) is the social withdrawal from peers, family and friends. This, as we shall see, is a core aspect of the narrated lives of Cobain and Curtis.

Indeed, in *Last Days*, the character Blake (inspired by Kurt Cobain) is completely withdrawn from all friends and colleagues and finally dies in the greenhouse near

---

[3] 'Suicide ideation' is a term that is used in the field of psychology to define thoughts of committing suicide.

76   DEATH AND THE ROCK STAR

his home. This is evident from the opening scenes where Blake staggers across the land near his home. The song 'La Guerre' (discussed below) opens and closes the film, representing Blake's inability to communicate effectively with others, leading him to disconnect completely. In *Control*, Ian Curtis removes himself from his bandmates and family. He states through voice-over that he does not want to be in the band anymore, and in a scene featuring the couple walking down their street, he tells his wife Deborah that he does not love her anymore. Like Blake, then, he withdraws from everyone who is or could be close to him. The Joy Division song 'Atmosphere' plays after Deborah discovers that her husband has committed suicide in the concluding scene of *Control*. Described in greater detail below, the lyrics of this song emphasise the impact of Curtis's self-imposed isolation, leading to his suicide.

Given the profession of the protagonists in musical biopics, music tracks are particularly essential and directly linked to the artists portrayed. Much of the music featured in the films is written and/or performed by that individual, or had a very direct impact on their life and career. Because of this, the way music is incorporated into the visual storytelling contributes to the film audience's understanding of the star. Over the past decades, there has been substantial study of film soundtracks (Kassabian, 2000; Donnelly, 2001; Inglis, 2003; Reay, 2004; Larsen, 2007). In her study, Kassabian (2000 p. 11) suggests that music has relationship to other music in the film, to the narrative (diegesis) and to other elements including visual imagery, dialogue and sound effects. This intertextuality is particularly powerful when utilised to tell the story of a music star on screen.

Kurt Cobain (1967–94) and Ian Curtis (1956–80)

Kurt Cobain is a music artist known as the lead singer of Nirvana, referred to as a grunge, punk, post-punk and indie rock band (Erlewine, 2014). Formed in Aberdeen, Washington and based in Seattle (USA), Nirvana banded in 1987 and released their debut studio album *Bleach* in 1989 (Sub Pop) followed by *Nevermind* (1991, DGC) and *In Utero* (1993, DGC), after which they disbanded in 1994. The final line-up consisted of Kurt Cobain (lead vocals and guitar), Krist Novoselic (bass guitar) and Dave Grohl (drums, backing vocals). *Nevermind* achieved considerable commercial success (Railton and Watson, 2011 p. 72), particularly with the song 'Smells Like Teen Spirit'; however, it was during the same time that Cobain developed an addiction to heroin. In 1992, Cobain married Courtney Love, the front woman of rock band Hole, and had a daughter, Frances Bean Cobain, that same year (Prato, 2009). According to official reports, on 5 April 1994 Cobain committed suicide and died from a self-inflicted shotgun wound (although some fans have speculated that this may not have been the case).

At 19 years old, Ian Curtis married his girlfriend Deborah Woodruff, and by the time he was 22 the couple had a child, Natalie. In 1976, he formed a rock band in Salford, Greater Manchester, with Bernard Sumner (keyboards and guitar),

Peter Hook (backing vocals and bass guitar) and Stephen Morris (percussion and drums) named Warsaw, which became Joy Division after signing with Factory Records (Hook, 2012). During their career, from 1976 to 1980, the band released *An Ideal for Living* (1978), *Unknown Pleasures* (1979) and *Closer* (1980). Curtis suffered from epilepsy, and was prone to seizures which occurred spontaneously including on-stage, mid-performance. He struggled to maintain the personae that his friends, family and fans expected of him throughout his short career (and life), and finally committed suicide at the age of 23 by hanging himself on the clothesline in his kitchen on 18 May 1980, the eve of Joy Division's first tour of the USA. *Closer* was released posthumously and the single 'Love Will Tear Us Apart' became Joy Division's highest charting release (Ott, 2004).

Last Days (2005, Gus Van Sant) and *Control* (2007, Anton Corbijn)

Last Days is part of what is commonly referred to as the 'death trilogy' (Cotterink, 2010; Gonçalves, 2009), Gus Van Sant's trio of films inspired by media representations of true events. Van Sant's first feature in this series is *Gerry* (2002), based on the death of David Coughlin who was murdered by hiking partner and best friend Raffi Kodikian, when reaching Rattlesnake Canyon in New Mexico. The second film, *Elephant* (2003), is inspired by the 1999 Columbine High School massacre. The final feature of the death trilogy, *Last Days*, is a suggestive art-house film requiring the film audience to ascertain their own meanings from audio-visual representations. Scholars have adopted different methods, including anthropological and philosophical studies (Rogers, 2013) and multisensory studies (Antunes, 2012), to analyse what is clearly a minimalist style of film-making (Alberhasky, 2006).

The central protagonist of *Last Days*, called Blake and played by Michael Pitt, is based on Kurt Cobain, and *Last Days* is carefully marketed as a product bridging fact and fiction. Its Press Kit (2006 p. 9) states that this is 'a film designed for individual interpretation … an intimate meditation on isolation, death and loss. It is a requiem and a remembrance', and that 'although this film is inspired by the last days of Kurt Cobain, it is a work of fiction and the characters and events portrayed in the film are also fictional'. Similarly worded end-titles appear, followed by the final note 'In memory of Kurt Cobain 1967–1994'. *Last Days*, then, is not simply a 'musical biopic'. It plays out similar to other 'inspired by' films such as Todd Haynes' *I'm Not There* (USA, 2007), where six characters play different personae of Bob Dylan (see Spirou, 2010). Yet, much like other biopics, it represents the life and death of a music star who really existed. Director Gus Van Sant discloses that 'the inspiration for *Last Days* was not so much the immediate event [Cobain's suicide], but the intense fascination with these last days from seemingly the entire world … where were they and what were their last moments?' (Press Kit, 2006 p. 10). Much like Bob Dylan's elusive persona evoked in *I'm Not There*, the final days of Kurt Cobain's life (including his suicide)

78   DEATH AND THE ROCK STAR

are still the subject of speculation since he passed away in 1994, and therefore *Last Days* embraces this ambiguity, withholding the finer details of the characters, their pasts and even their futures.

The struggle to understand one's own identity, a core theme in *Last Days*, is also found in *Control*. The film is a black and white feature chronicling the second half of Ian Curtis's life. In *Control*, after an initial failed suicide attempt by Curtis, there is a voice-over where his character (played by Sam Riley) discloses:

> I don't want to be in the band anymore. *Unknown Pleasures* was it. I was happy. I never meant for it to grow like this. When I'm up there, singing, they don't understand how much I give and how it affects me. Now they want more and they expect me to give more. I don't know if I can. It's like, it's not happening to me but someone pretending to be me. Someone dressed in my skin. And now we're going to America. I've got no control anymore. I don't know what to do. (00:85:00)

The concerns of Curtis here link with Redmond's (2006) analysis of the star's identity crisis. Curtis is unsure of who he is as a private and public persona (if they are to be seen as two different identities) and cannot deal with the expectations that stardom brings. As White (2013) suggests, males considering suicide find it difficult to speak to others. It is appropriate here that the expression is in voice-over, implying an internal monologue for the benefit of the film audience only, and not for the other characters in the diegesis. Like Blake in *Last Days*, then, Curtis withdraws from family, friends and bandmates, suffering through the same self-imposed emotional isolation.

The Sound of Isolation

In *Last Days*, Blake spends most of the film completely alone, and when in the presence of others, he appears completely disengaged. He then dies (ambiguously), alone, in a greenhouse near the house he had lived in. In this last scene, a gardener walks by and finds Blake's lifeless body, before the police arrive. In a shot positioned just outside the greenhouse, looking in, Blake's spirit or ghost (a naked and transparent Blake) steps out of his body and carefully walks up a ladder that continues beyond the film frame. A static wide shot at the body closes the film as a song, discussed below, plays and continues to do so to the end credits. Most individuals in this final scene are back to camera and the shot is distanced, giving them a sense of anonymity. Blake's character is thus more than the body that remains, his moving ghost and the lingering music optimistic symbols that his star status will continue after his death – much like Kurt Cobain whose body was discovered days after his death.

Last Days opens and closes with 'La Guerre', a song by The King Singers which gives the film a full-circle, cohesive feel. Gus Van Sant explains:

It's a quintet of voices singing in a kind of nonsensical way, which is how Mike [Pitt] is speaking. In the song, the vocals create sound effects that resemble war, cannon-fire and horses. It's great. I used it at the beginning and the end of the movie, less as bookends than something that is unexpected. (Press Kit, 2006 p. 26)

As Van Sant intended, the music in the initial 40 seconds of the film reflects Blake's voice (and attempts at communication), which are difficult to understand. This is evident in his interactions with friends in the house and also with people who stop by (including a salesman who attempts to talk with Blake at 00:18:38). 'La Guerre', in effect, exemplifies Blake's isolation (a large predictor of suicide ideation, as noted above) as his voice and words, much like the song, are unintelligible. The lack of effective communication distances Blake from others within the diegesis of the film and hence potentially the film audience as well. The upbeat tune is also juxtaposed against the quiet nature of Blake's monotonous everyday life, where activities include grumbling, spending days at a time in the bushlands that surround his house and staring into space for extended periods of time. In the opening sequence, a long shot features Blake vomiting in an open forest, as a figure with a white T-shirt and red track pants stumbles across the landscape. The music stops as, in a new long shot, Blake walks down to a flowing river and the diegetic sound of the water replaces the non-diegetic music. Throughout the river scene, Blake is silent, while taking off his clothes, swimming in the river, emerging on the other side and standing up to urinate into the running water. This opening sequence introduces his character as isolated from human contact by choice.

In *Control*, during his voice-over, Ian Curtis is driven to a gig where he refuses to perform. He (and we) can hear the crowd shout his name and boo when another singer replaces him. Even though the sounds of the crowd are supportive and encouraging, Curtis isolates himself (physically and emotionally) from the situation, staying backstage, away from the audible screams and shouts of the fans. A riot breaks out amongst audience members and the band, marking the end of the scene. It appears at this point that Curtis has given up, has done all that he has set out to do and is considering a way out, much like Kurt Cobain, who did not have the desire to perform anymore.[4]

Repetition of Music and Imagery

Last Days is repetitive in the physical movement of Blake's character, which is slow and monotonous, and in the music utilised, particularly with 'La Guerre' opening and closing the film. Like in *Last Days*, shot composition is vital in *Control*, particularly due to the fact that its director, Anton Corbijn, is a photographer

---

[4] A copy of Kurt Cobain's suicide note can be found here: http://kurtcobainssuicidenote. com/kurt_cobains_suicide_note_scan.html (accessed 28 October 2013).

who actually spent time photographing Joy Division in 1979 (Whittaker, 2009). Of particular note is the repetition of shots of the kitchen clothesline that Curtis utilises to commit suicide. Shots of this clothesline are placed sporadically throughout the film, to highlight the looming conclusion to his life and also the film itself. The first shot (00:12:00) appears as Deborah innocently hangs up the washing. With a point-of-view shot (00:54:00), Ian then sees baby clothes hanging on the line. Later on, when a bandmate who is letting Ian stay in his home hypnotises him, there is a flash to the clothesline (00:94:00). The clothesline gets rolled up in this scene and then drops dramatically. It acts as a peek into the future and plays on audience awareness. Indeed, in the final film sequence, after waking up from a seizure he had alone in his home, Curtis looks at the clothesline in his kitchen, pulls it up, the screen turns black and all is heard is a thud (01:48:00). The last two shots do not visually show but imply the act of the self-hanging. One scene frames Curtis, visibly distraught, looking down at the rope and the second is that of the rope tightening around the lever attached to the ceiling. Then Deborah is seen driving back home, walking into the house while the shot remains outside (again, as the audience is aware of what happened and is not required to see the aftermath). She screams and stumbles back outside, in frame again. The Joy Division track 'Atmosphere' begins to play, which brings closure to the film as each shot focuses on the reactions of Curtis's friends, family and love, Annik Honoré.

Exactly like 'La Guerre' closes *Last Days*, so 'Atmosphere' continues to play non-diegetically in *Control*, its final verse being heard through the end credits. The recurring words in its lyrics are 'silence' and 'walk'/'walking away', which reflect the theme of isolation and underscore Ian Curtis's emotional disconnect from the people around him. Additionally, the repeated lyric 'Don't walk away in silence' reflects the idea of not being forgotten, and being launched into stardom through suicide.

Musical Contexts

An unexpected sentimental pop ballad plays in *Last Days* when Blake, at home, turns on the television where the music video 'On Bended Knee' by Boyz II Men is playing (00:28:00). This sequence is told from two different points of view, that of Blake and a random girlfriend (living in the house) who discovers him on the floor. According to Van Sant:

> I thought it [the song] was interesting because it was random. It doesn't really necessarily fit in that house, as the type of music that they would be listening to if it just happened to come on this channel that Blake is watching. Plus, it was kind of the flip side of his music – instead of the white boy rock band singing loud and dark songs, it's the black boy band singing light love songs. (Press Kit, 2006 p. 27)

The juxtaposition highlights that Blake's isolation has an effect on his psychological state. Instead of engaging with the music video playing on the television (in either a positive way by singing, dancing or watching, or negatively by heckling, leaving the room or even turning the TV off), Blake appears completely disconnected, slowly dropping on the floor, his body apparently lifeless. While this scene could suggest that life will still continue without the music star, it also highlights Blake's disconnect and isolation, core factors in studies of suicide ideation and in Redmond's (2006) analysis of fame and damaged stars.

In a study of the soundtracks in the films of Gus Van Sant, Kulezic-Wilson (2012) argues that *Last Days* emphasises the ways in which characters engage with music. Examples of this include the static camera shot while a character sings 'Venus in Furs' by The Velvet Underground, and the scene when Blake 'performs his own music while a camera positioned outside the window retreats slowly in a four-and-a-half-minute-long tracking shot that gradually expands its frame to reveal an image of the whole house with its surroundings' (Kulezic-Wilson, 2012 p. 83). Here, in a room where he and his bandmates are staying (at 00:71:00), Blake accompanies himself on the guitar and sings 'From Death to Birth'. This song was written by the actor-singer Michael Pitt who is, outside the film, the vocalist and guitarist for the band Pagoda – 'From Death to Birth' appears on their self-titled album, released in 2007. This music number is shot entirely in a static wide shot, which frames the room (the rehearsal studio of the house) with Blake positioned off-side, hair covering his face for the duration of the song. This composition creates a sense of anonymity, where the actor Michael Pitt, his character Blake and the inspiration Kurt Cobain all become interchangeable, yet forging one entity. The song's chorus, which states 'It's a long lonely journey from death till birth', is an appropriate summation of *Last Days* and Blake's internal thoughts. The idea of inverting the normal life cycle, from death to birth, enforces the significance of death. It assists the audience in understanding the life of the music artist and perhaps provides an opportunity, through feature film, to evaluate their music retrospectively.

Control explores the way that, during his high school years, Curtis developed an interest in musicians who died at a young age. Musicians such as Jim Morrison and Janis Joplin became inspiration for Curtis to end his own life in his twenties. As Deborah Curtis recounts, 'Anyone who had been involved in the young, arty medium of any form of show-business and found an early grave was of interest to him. When he told me that he had no intention of living beyond his early twenties, I took it with a pinch of salt' (1995 p. 15). These musical influences are featured in *Control* when, pre-Joy Division, Curtis attends a Sex Pistols gig which he seemingly enjoys. Sid Vicious, the bass player of the punk band, died of a heroin overdose in 1979 at 21 years old (the same year Joy Division released *Unknown Pleasures*). During the early scenes in the film, in the stages of character introduction and development, Curtis spends most of his time alone in his bedroom listening to the music of these artists, with posters of Jim Morrison, David Bowie and Iggy Pop covering his walls. He lays on his bed, smoking a cigarette, listening to a David Bowie record. He puts make-up on while staring into the mirror, to replicate Bowie, and even when there are friends in his room, he sits silently, smoking and watching them. When they leave, he returns to his bed and continues to stare at the ceiling. His reclusiveness is evident from this early narrative stage and a signifier of the later scenes of the film, where he returns to isolation. In a subsequent scene he poses in front of his mirror in his bedroom and sings Bowie's 'The Jean Genie'. The song's lyrics are said to have been inspired by Iggy Pop (Perone, 2007 p. 37). The musical inspiration of Bowie's song reaches a full-circle conclusion when Ian Curtis puts on the Iggy Pop record, *The Idiot* (1977), at home and listens to it while hanging himself on the kitchen clothesline. These scenes contextualise Curtis's suicide, showing how his life experiences, musical inspiration and career fit into popular music history. As well as the individual life histories of these music stars, Curtis admired their eclectic music style which carried on into his own musical creativity.

Conclusion

As demonstrated in this chapter, death is often a crucial element of the musical biopic. Most of the music stars featured in these films had either died before production or before the release of the film. However, when suicide is the reason for death, the musical biopic is guided by this significant part of the life narrative. It becomes the basis for, and the focus of, the film as the music star has made the conscious and meticulously planned decision to end their lives at a certain point in their career. Rather than just slowly leaving public memory, suicide pushes the music artist to new levels of fame. The musical biopic, in this case, addresses the audience's fascination with its own mortality through the display of that of others in tandem with validating the raised status of the music star.

Last Days demonstrates how music stardom can drive a character like Blake to withdraw from everyone and utilise suicide as an escape from fame. Ian Curtis's concern is the lack of control over his life, as per the film's title, also escaping public and personal circumstances through suicide. The key theme that runs through these films is identity and the difficulty for the music star to maintain a sense of self. The protagonists struggle with how to deal with stardom. Committing suicide is an escape from the pressures that stardom brings while at the same time securing them an enduring star status.

Not only are these films about Kurt Cobain and Ian Curtis, they also refer to other music stars who died at a young age, reflecting larger issues surrounding music stardom. Whether with posters on walls, attending their concerts, speaking about them or listening to their records, these musical biopics use one individual in order to personify broader issues. The musical biopic also suggests that the death of the artist does not mean the death of the music.

Bibliography

Alberhasky, Matthew John (2006) 'Minimalism and Art-cinema Narration in Gus Van Sant's *Gerry, Elephant,* and *Last Days*', *Retrospective Theses and Dissertations*. Paper 117. http://lib.dr.iastate.edu/rtd/117, accessed 30 April 2015.

Antunes, Luis Rocha (2012) 'The Vestibular in Film: Orientation and Balance in Gus Van Sant's Cinema of Walking', *Essays in Philosophy*, 13 (2), pp. 522–49.

Babington, Bruce and Peter William Evans (1985) *Blue Skies and Silver Linings: Aspects of the Hollywood Musical.* Dover, NH: Manchester University Press.

Bingham, Dennis (2010) *Whose Lives Are They Anyway? The Biopic as Contemporary Film Genre.* New Brunswick, NJ: Rutgers University Press.

Bordwell, David (1986) 'Classical Hollywood Cinema: Narrational Principles and Procedures', in Philip Rosen (ed.), *Narrative, Apparatus, Ideology: A Film Theory Reader.* New York: Columbia University Press, pp. 17–34.

Cotterink, Michel (2010) 'See for Yourself: A Rhetoric of Ambiguity in Gus Van Sant's Death Trilogy'. Masters Thesis. Universiteit Utrecht. March 2010.

Curtis, Deborah (2007 [1995]) *Touching from a Distance: Ian Curtis and Joy Division.* London: Faber and Faber.

Custen, George Frederick (1992) *Bio/pics: How Hollywood Constructed Public History.* New Brunswick, NJ: Rutgers University Press.

Donnelly, Kevin (2001) *Film Music: Critical Approaches.* Edinburgh: Edinburgh University Press.

Erlewine, Stephen Thomas (2014) 'Nirvana: Artist Biography', *AllMusic*, accessed 15 January 2014, www.allmusic.com/artist/nirvana-mn0000357406/ biography, accessed 15 January 2014.

Gonçalves, Helder Filipe (2009) 'Musical Signification and the Definition of Cinematic "Spaces": Gus Van Sant's "Death Trilogy"', *artciencia.com*, 4 (10), pp. 1–14.

Hook, Peter (2012) *Unknown Pleasures: Inside Joy Division.* London: Simon & Schuster.

Inglis, Ian (ed.) (2003) *Popular Music and Film.* London: Wallflower Press.

Kassabian, Anahid (2000) *Hearing Film: Tracking Identifications in Contemporary Hollywood Film Music.* New York: Routledge.

Kulezic-Wilson, Danijela (2012) 'Gus Van Sant's Soundwalks and Audio-Visual', in James Wierzbicki (ed.), *Musique Concrète, Music, Sound and Filmmakers: Sonic Style in Cinema.* London and New York: Routledge, pp. 76–88.

Larsen, Peter (2007) *Film Music.* London: Reaktion Books.

Marshall, Lee and Isabel Kongsgaard (2012) 'Representing Popular Music Stardom on Screen: The Popular Music Biopic', *Celebrity Studies*, 3 (3), pp. 346–61.

Ott, Chris (2004) *Joy Division's Unknown Pleasures.* London and New York: Bloomsbury Publishing.

Perone, James E. (2007) *The Words and Music of David Bowie.* Westport, CT: Praeger Publishers.

Prato, Greg (2009) *Grunge is Dead: The Oral History of Seattle Rock Music*. Toronto: ECW Press.

Press Kit (2006) *Production Notes: Last Days, a Film by Gus Van Sant*. Australian Film, Television and Radio School (16 February).

Railton, Diane and Paul Watson (2011) *Music Video and the Politics of Representation*. Edinburgh: Edinburgh University Press.

Reay, Pauline (2004) *Music in Film: Soundtracks and Synergy*. London: Wallflower Press.

Redmond, Sean (2006) 'Intimate Fame Everywhere', in Su Holmes and Sean Redmond (eds), *Framing Celebrity: New Directions in Celebrity Culture*. New York: Routledge, pp. 27–43.

Rogers, Anna Backman (2013) 'The Body of Dissolution: Becoming-imperceptible in Gus Van Sant's *Last Days* (2004)', *European Journal of American Culture*, 32 (1), pp. 25–41.

Spirou, Penny (2010) '"I'm Not There": The Future of the Musical Biopic', *Metro Magazine: Media & Education Magazine*, 165, p. 116.

——— (2011) 'The Musical Biopic: Representing the Lives of Music Artists in Twenty-First Century Cinema'. PhD thesis. Macquarie University, Australia.

Van Orden, Kimberly, Kelly C. Cukrowicz, Tracy K. Witte, Scott R. Braithwaite, Edward A. Selby, Thomas E. Joiner Jr. (2010) 'The Interpersonal Theory of Suicide', *Psychological Review*, 117 (2), pp. 575–600.

White, Cassie (2013) 'Boys Don't Cry: Young Men and Suicide', *ABC: Health and Wellbeing*, www.abc.net.au/health/features/stories/2013/06/13/3781044.htm, accessed 13 January 2014.

Whiteley, Sheila (2003) *Too Much too Young: Popular Music, Age and Gender*. London: Routledge.

Whittaker, Tom (2009) 'Frozen Soundscapes in *Control* and *Radio On*', *Journal of British Cinema and Television*, 6 (3), pp. 424–36.

World Health Organization (2009) 'Suicide One of Three Leading Causes of Death for Young People, Says WHO', *Pan American Health Organisation*, www.paho.org/hq/index.php?option=com_content&view=article&id=1761%3Asuicide-prevention-day-2009&catid=1443%3Anews-front-page-items&lang=en&itemid=1926, accessed 13 January 2014.

World Health Organization UK (2009) 'Number of Suicides by Age Group and Gender. United Kingdom of Great Britain and North Ireland, 2009', www.who.int/mental_health/media/unitkingd.pdf, accessed 13 January 2014.

World Health Organization USA (2005) 'Number of Suicides by Age Group and Gender. United States of America, 2005', www.who.int/mental_health/media/unitstates.pdf, accessed 13 January 2014.

Filmography

Capote, dir. Bennett Miller, MGM, 2005.

Control, dir. Anton Corbijn, The Weinstein Company/UK, 2007.

Elephant, dir. Gus Van Sant, HBO Films/USA, 2003.

Gerry, dir. Gus Van Sant, Miramax Films/USA, 2002.

I'm Not There, dir. Todd Haynes, The Weinstein Company/USA, 2007.

Last Days, dir. Gus Van Sant, HBO Films/USA, 2005.

Lincoln, dir. Steven Spielberg, Touchstone Pictures/USA, 2012.

Moneyball, dir. Bennett Miller, Sony Pictures/USA, 2011.

Monster, dir. Patty Jenkins, Media 8 Entertainment/USA, 2003.

Ray, dir. Taylor Hackford, Universal Pictures/USA, 2004.

Telstar: The Joe Meek Story, dir. Nick Moran, G2 Pictures/UK, 2008.

The Iron Lady, dir. Phyllida Lloyd, Twentieth Century Fox/USA and France, 2011.

The Fighter, dir. David O. Russell, Paramount Pictures/USA, 2010.

The Social Network, dir. David Fincher, Columbia Pictures/USA, 2010.

The Wolf of Wall Street, dir. Martin Scorsese, Paramount Pictures/USA, 2013.

Walk the Line, dir. James Mangold, Twentieth Century Fox Film Corporation/ USA, 2005.

What We Do Is Secret, dir. Rodger Grossman, Vitagraph Films/USA, 2007.

Chapter 7

Social Sorrow: Tweeting the Mourning of Whitney Houston

Taylor Cole Miller

Press'd by the load of life, the weary mind
Surveys the general toil of human kind;
With cool submission joins the labouring train,
And social sorrow loses half its pain.

Samuel Johnson (1811)

Whitney Houston's sister-in-law, best friend and long-time manager, Pat Houston, walked slowly and cautiously down the hallway of the Beverly Hills Hilton toward screams emanating from Houston's room. Inside, Whitney's body lay cold and wet on the bathroom floor as her bodyguard rocked on his knees failing to revive her (*Oprah's Next Chapter*, 2012). Meanwhile, the star's hairstylist dropped to the floor in shock, calming herself long enough to send a text message to her niece, who would become the first person in the world to publicly and declaratively announce Houston's death and the details surrounding it through Twitter: 'omgg, my aunt tiffany who work for whitney houston just found whitney houston dead in the tub . such ashame & sad :-('.[1] In a simple tweet of 120 characters, Aja Dior Mintz established her credibility and delivered the news, framed in a display of emotional tribute. Throughout the hour that followed on 11 February 2012 – the eve of the Grammy Awards – nearly two and a half million Twitter users shared word of Houston's death in a display of solidarity that carried the tributary hashtag #ReTweetforRespect (Flemings, 2012).

Houston's suffering was as legendary as her voice. Her relationship to pain and the struggles of excess – of wealth and celebrity, of addiction and abuse – tied her to a pantheon of divas gone-too-soon. At her peak she was an American icon, credited more than once for unifying the nation during times of war, connecting a people through her vocal virtuosity. At her low she was an American embarrassment, hers a cautionary tale of the ravages of drug abuse, spectacle and fame. It was this public suffering that enamoured her to her most loyal fans, making space for them to identify with her turmoil and connect to her community of followers.

---

[1]   Twitter user @BarBeeBritt tweeted 13 minutes before with 'Is Whitney Houston Really Dead?', but Mintz was the first to confirm (ajadiornavy). 11 Feb. 2012, 4:15 pm PST.

Music is extraordinary in its ability to make us feel. All music lovers have had the experience – especially during an emotional moment – of closing their eyes and feeling a kind of swelling of the soul while they listen, a spiritual experience. Trying to describe such moments demonstrates how words fail us; we may say we are 'moved', that we have 'chills', or that we have 'lost ourselves' in the harmonies. Fans of divas like Houston experience something similar during the belted melodies of their songs. Drawing them out like mariners to a Siren, a diva's voice carries her followers out of isolation and holds them together if only for a moment. Though only one body, she contains their multitudes, wrapping her fans in a world of collective strength and collective struggle, delivering them, as in the words of Samuel Johnson's poem, onto a 'labouring train', on which their 'social sorrow' can be shared, endured and processed – together.

Just as moving as the experience of listening to her music, a diva's death can also produce a powerful affective response, one just as complex and difficult to put into words. In an online social media sphere where the injunction is always to produce more and more 'knowledge' about oneself and one's feelings, the limits of language can be increasingly difficult to manoeuvre. This is even more pronounced with services like Twitter, an online social-networking site that enables users to read and send text messages, because it limits each post to a maximum of 140 characters. Twitter users can broadcast others' tweets (re-tweeting) or they can make use of hashtags – words or phrases prefixed with a # sign that group posts together by topics or types in an incredibly efficient manner, the most popular of which are called 'Trending Topics'. But because of its limitations, Twitter users so routinely employ specific tactics to articulate their feelings and emotions that they have almost become generic conventions. The certainty of those tactics, why they are employed, and how they are commodified by various industries are what I explore within this chapter.

In the days following Houston's death, among Twitter's worldwide trending topics were #IWillAlwaysLoveYou and #whitneytributes, leading to some more specific questions this chapter addresses. What does it mean to 'pay tribute' in today's convergent media landscape and how do social media allow users to create a space in which they can mourn? How does the musicality or virtuosity of the rock star amplify the mourning experience and how does it relate to the way people turn to Twitter as a tool to process and articulate their grief in '140 characters or less'? Using the death of Whitney Houston as a case study, this chapter interrogates the ways in which Twitter users articulate their emotions during moments of grief and sorrow when words seemingly fail them.

When Houston died suddenly, fans mourned not only for the loss of her body but for the connective potential of her voice. In what follows, I contribute to existing scholarship on affect theory, diva fandom and critical cultural audience studies to map out the aftermath of a star's death in different degrees of immediacy: within an hour, within a week (her memorial), and within two months (a special tribute episode on the American television program, *Glee*). I suggest that social media tools like Twitter act as a liminal mourning space in which users pool their tributes and remembrances to grieve socially rather than individually. Much like a wake, a funeral or a memorial, tweeting tributes breaks down private and public spheres in order to help users ameliorate their own suffering or alienation in the same way the diva's music has often done: through the adulation of a star and the resulting sense of intimate connection.

First, I explore Houston's cultural impact and the ways in which her star text worked to endear her to her fans not only through her voice but also through her hardships. In her, they found an apparatus through which to articulate their own adversities and connect with one another, using her music as a soundtrack for their lives. Second, I probe publicly-tweeted memorials and tributes as users responded prolifically to word of her death and her funeral. And third, I interrogate how tweeting the fallen star as a form of reparative cultural labour was modelled and exploited by the producers of *Glee* in a special tribute episode for Houston (2012). Overall, this chapter proposes the phrase 'social sorrow' to identify the ways in which devotees use social media sites like Twitter to fashion collective mourning spaces, mediating their grief and thus lightening its burdens through shared, semi-permanent virtual tributes that often take on formulaic and conforming dimensions.

The Diva's Voice and the Diva's Death

Whitney Houston's successes are staggering: she is the most-awarded female act of all time (Jackson, 2009 p. 460), with over 200 million records sold worldwide, alongside two Emmys, seven Grammys (including a Grammy Hall of Fame Award), and 22 American Music Awards (more than any other female artist). But 'The Voice', as Oprah Winfrey coined her, cemented her place in American cultural history with her 1991 rendition of the national anthem for Super Bowl XXV. Houston later released 'The Star Spangled Banner' as a charity single to raise funds for American soldiers and their families during the Persian Gulf War, donating all her proceeds to the American Red Cross. To date, hers is the only rendition to turn the US national anthem into a Top 20 hit, a feat she accomplished twice when it was re-released shortly after 11 September 2001 (Reid, 2001). Her voice was more powerful than her body, becoming itself 'patriotic': a mascot of the national anthem and a signifier of Americana. She corralled a sensitive people into a strengthened unity at two vulnerable moments in the nation's history, mediating their sorrow. 'The voice is a meeting of body and discourse', Albright (1997 p. 106) writes, '[y]et that voice is not an exclusively private or internal calling. Swelling far beyond the body that produces it, the voice emanates into the public'.

In a commercially-released video of Houston's Star Spangled Banner performance, the mother of a Persian Gulf War soldier, Martha Weaver, remembered the following about Houston's performance:

> I keep pride inside when I think about the day that I saw Whitney Houston singing the national anthem when our son was so far away. Pride that he was part of what

she was singing about: freedom for our nation. And not only for our nation, but, our nation helping other people who are in need. (*The Star Spangled Banner*, 1991)

Some years later, Winfrey described the moment as a spiritual experience, 'where the spirit hits and everybody has it. That old Hallelujah moment' (*The Oprah Winfrey Show*, 2006). Weaver's words continue the sentiment: 'It was an overwhelming feeling, kind of like there was a rainbow connecting us' (*The Star Spangled Banner*, 1991).

These sentiments illustrate the transportive capabilities of a diva's voice, breaking down bodily boundaries and allowing her listeners to conform along each other's contours and feel 'at one' in a collective skin. As Zakreski writes (2006 p. 176), the diva 'uses music to investigate what it means for a woman to have a voice; [she] explores the possibility of a transcendent artistic space in which the woman's voice can be free of both the constraining force of bourgeois constructions of morality and the degrading influence of the capitalist marketplace'. A diva's voice challenges our conception of a self-contained body because the musical voice cannot be seen or contained but expands ever-further like fog. It moves beyond the body and enters all bodies; it thus becomes a part of its listeners as long as its notes linger in the ears, and still long after as a record in the neural juke-box.

Brett Farmer (2005) has called this extracorporeal affect 'sublimity'. In science, sublimation describes the volatilisation of a solid into a gas without passing through a liquid state, a metaphor for the feeling of self-expansion and connection during such an experience which, as Weaver claimed, can be figured as expanding along the rays of a rainbow. Farmer argues that sublimity also comes bound in religious connotation – a mechanism of transcendence, an 'apprehension of the divine through an encounter with that which exceeds the limits of everyday experience and cognition' (Farmer, 2005 p. 170). Through their fandom, followers of divas 'resist and transfigure oppressive banalities' using their stars as a kind of balm, palliatives for healing, and cultural icons to connect with the like-minded. In that way, the diva's body is little more than a voice and a vehicle to organise, in the words of Benedict Anderson (1992), a kind of imagined community.

While she was alive, this fleshiness of Houston's body was necessary as a 'centre' to organise her fans physically. Twitter's role in the death of the star is to become the body's understudy, a new centre around which to culturally unionise. Much like with a concert or a funeral, there is an imperative on 'liveness' that enhances the notion of the Twittersphere as a time and space for collectivity. Tweets can be read later much as a concert can be screened later, but both have a different bodily affect than a live, 'we-were-there' experience found in the process of live-tweeting. That is why in the first hour after Houston's death, two and a half million Twitter users flocked to the site to be the first in their social circles to deliver the news. The surge of tweets about Houston's death in the first hour (one in every four sent) suggested that users wanted to demonstrate their cultural awareness (or cultural capital) to their social circles by using tweets to insert their voices into the new live and global space as quickly as possible.

Affect theorists have grappled with understanding the ways in which we spread our affective states to others (for example, when we walk into a room and 'feel the atmosphere'); I would extend this concern to the ways in which we spread them online. For Teresa Brennan (2004 p. 5), while feelings 'are sensations that have found the right match in words', affects are emotional states beyond language which usually require a physical presence to be felt. Twitter users often enact online a series of affective shortcuts to do what their physical bodies cannot: articulate a bodily affect of grief in an emotionally-neutral space. Using words about feelings, or what I call a 'mechanics of feelings', is a tactic shared among Twitter users to perform their emotional upheaval, often by describing how language fails them. The tactic is now so conventional that the writer's conveyed frustration evokes an affect in the reader who then 'feels' the emotions of the writer somewhat vicariously by drawing lines to a similar experience in her or his own life.

For example, after word broke that Houston had died, fellow pop star Rihanna tweeted 'No words! Just tears #DearWhitney',[2] while Missy Elliott wrote 'This is such a sad moment! I'm speechless I have no words for what I'm feeling right now. Rest in Peace Whitney Houston I love u'.[3] Such sentimental messages depend on articulating the failure of language to stand in for the physical sensation of sorrow. Online spaces are inherently evacuated of this emotional presence, and so users grieving socially must articulate it even if only by claiming they cannot.

A surge of re-tweets quickly followed the initial news break; most users chose to re-tweet grieving stars to intensify their affective space as opposed to re-tweeting emotionally-devoid news organisations. Lil Wayne and Justin Bieber both received more re-tweets – 29,000 and 15,000 respectively – than syndicate news outlet the Associated Press did at just 10,000 (Flemings, 2012). Several celebrities thought to be close to Houston tweeted their 'official' and carefully-crafted messages which further legitimated Twitter as the pre-eminent grieving space, drawing together their own followers to mourn. Their tweets made the news more credible and underscored discourses of cultural anguish. Most celebrity responses, like Mintz's initial tweet, delivered the punching blow of the news in a package of sweet remembrance: 'Jesus Christ, not Whitney Houston. Greatest of all time' wrote Nicki Minaj,[4] while Mariah Carey tweeted 'Heartbroken and in tears over the shocking death of my friend, the incomparable Ms. Whitney Houston'.[5] Christina Aguilera added: 'We have lost another legend. Love and prayers to Whitney's family. She will be missed'.[6]

---

[2]   (rihanna). 11 Feb. 2012, 5:51 p.m. PST.
[3]   (missyelliott). 11 Feb. 2012, 5:16 p.m. PST.
[4]   (NICKIMINAJ). 11 Feb. 2012, 5:30 p.m. PST.
[5]   (mariahcarey). 11 Feb. 2012, 5:26 p.m. PST.
[6]   (TheRealXtina). 11 Feb. 2012, 5:34 p.m. PST.

Remembering the Diva in the Social Sorrow Sphere

Star studies scholars highlight the fetishisation of the 'private' life (the mythological 'authentic' celebrity life) as central to the popularity of the public star persona. According to Marshall (2002 p. 232), after the institutionalisation of the Hollywood press corps and the growth of information about stars' personal lives, 'film celebrities became a blend of the everyday and the exceptional. The combination of familiarity and extraordinariness gives the celebrity its ideological power'. Fans, in turn, created a culture of obsession with the lives behind the unchanging images they saw of their favourite celebrities. As Ewen (1988 p. 101) writes:

> ... it is this objectification of the person that, most probably, explains much of the turmoil and grief, the identity crisis that often accompanies stardom. Perhaps celebrities, too, become uncomfortable in their own skins as they, in the eyes of others, become frozen images ... always the personage, never the person. It is difficult to be a disembodied image.

It was likely just as difficult for Houston to be a disembodied voice, unable to hit the notes she once could effortlessly. According to Coghlan (2012), Houston's early training in the church left her with bad vocal habits, meaning that 'every note she sang damaged [her voice] just a little more. So when we listen to Houston's records, even those from her peak, we are hearing a voice destroying itself'.

Coghlan suggests that this 'destructive urge made Houston great' but that same instinct 'may, ultimately, have killed her'. In being labelled 'The Voice', she was stripped of her personhood and blamed for squandering a kind of protected public resource through years of abuse. The *L.A. Times* wrote that 'the pain, and frankly, disgust that so many pop fans felt during Houston's decline was caused not so much by her personal distress as her seemingly careless treatment of the national treasure that happened to reside within her' (Powers, 2009). After her death, fascination with Houston's private life intensified; as news of her possible overdose and drowning spread, #CrackKills became a trending topic. 'The whole world doesn't revolve around Whitney Houston #crackkills', wrote one Twitter user,[7] while another posted, 'Whitney Houston was a crack head that bitch deserved to Die'.[8] These less reverential tweets electrified a defensive mourning public as Houston's fans corralled ever more tightly in her defence. As so much of Houston's appeal stemmed from her fight against public strife (like many divas before her), an insult to her character meant an offence to her family and, by extension, her fans. '#CrackKills is a very disrespectful trending topic. Show some respect to her memory, her family & friends. R.I.P. Whitney Houston', wrote one user.[9]

---

[7]   (BobbyPropes). 12 Feb. 2012, 12:19 a.m. PST (later removed).
[8]   (Fly_Guy_Rashad). 12 Feb. 2012 (later removed, no timestamp).
[9]   (trendeh). 11 Feb. 2012, 8:33 p.m. PST.

'Have some fucking respect for her god damn. She lost her life. It doesn't matter if it was her own damn fault or not. Grow the fuck up', wrote another.[10]

It was publicly announced that a 'private' funeral would take place on Saturday, 18 February 2012, a week after her death, at her childhood church in Newark, New Jersey. Gossip magazines and entertainment tabloids reported on the personal lives of Houston's family members, including her daughter Bobbi Kristina, to give their viewers and readers a sense of personal access to the family's bereavement. TMZ.com leaked images of the funeral programme under the title 'Whitney Houston Funeral – Programs! Getcha Programs Here!' The *National Enquirer* ran a now-infamous photo of Houston in her casket to her family's reported horror. Although it was invitation only, the funeral was far from an intimate family affair as it was broadcast live on many channels and streamed online. Discourses suggest its privacy made viewers watching at home feel even more connected to her 'private' life through their virtual ticket to the memorial, especially because of the immediacy of the event as a live and global broadcast. The star-studded service was scheduled to last only for two hours but lasted four, as several of Houston's famous guests paid her tribute through song. Worldwide, audiences turned on their television sets and computers to watch the public funeral in what Dayan and Katz (1992) refer to as a 'ceremonial media event'. Thousands more viewers logged in to their Twitter accounts to pay their own tributes to Houston, engaging what Jenkins (2001) calls 'social convergence' to suture their private viewing of her funeral with a mourning, tweeting public.

Many of these tweets carried the tag #WhitneyTributes. 'Precious Whitney, the Lord is your bodyguard now. #whitneytributes' read one,[11] while another user tweeted '#WHITNEYTRIBUTES All Asians & Filipinos will never forget your voice and your music that touched our hearts. You will be truly missed. #WhitneyTributes'.[12] Many users felt it necessary to live-tweet the performances inside the church in order to perform their participation in the proceedings. One Twitter user praised gospel-jazz singer Kim Burrell's performance of 'A Change is Gonna Come': 'Sing it Rev. Kim Burrell!! A change had to come for our hurting angel! ... #WhitneyTributes'.[13] Another user commented on Houston's former movie co-star Kevin Costner's eulogy, remarking, 'Kevin Coster's eloquent words and memories of Whitney touch my soul<3 simply beautiful #whitneytributes'.[14]

Other users demonstrated their intimacy with the story and with Houston's star text by commenting on personal details of the funeral: 'I wish E! [Network] would change it from Whitney Houston The Funeral to her Home Coming. That's what her mother wants. #WhitneyTributes'.[15] Such tweets worked to establish the author

---

[10] (itssadieee). 11. Feb. 2012, 6:29 p.m. PST.
[11] (MaddieHill). 18 Feb. 2012, 10:33 p.m. PST.
[12] (RicoHizon). 18 Feb. 2012 (later removed, no timestamp).
[13] (AishaDavismusic). 18 Feb. 2012, 10:14 p.m. PST.
[14] (blueinoctober2). 18 Feb. 2012, 10:34 p.m. PST.
[15] (nicolepbrooks). 18 Feb. 2012, 09:35 a.m. PST.

as intimately credible and thus closer to the family so as to give the experience of becoming ever-closer to Houston's personal life. Twitter, here, is a public tool one can use to access the private, and through the practice of live-tweeting, that access seems more 'real' than ever. Because the funeral was broadcast live, it was an event to be experienced in the moment and collectively. Users took to Twitter not only as a tool to leave a memory or write a few words of personal remembrance, but to claim their seats in the virtual pews as congregants mourning together in the conforming performance of social sorrow. Through Twitter, they enacted their collective grieving and affect through a mechanics of feelings much like her family gathered in New Jersey, while massifying reverential posts in order to cloak a surge of negative tweets to preserve Twitter as a space for mourning rather than condemnation.

Gleeful Grief: Producing the Act of Social Sorrow

Since our private lives are often modelled on public personas, the loss of a celebrity can mean a partial loss of self. With the resulting destabilisation of identities, fans turn to spaces like Twitter to find others like them who can shore up their fragile subjectivities. According to Turkle (2008 p. 128), the 'others' that fans experience in these spaces are there for validation and mirroring, enabling them 'to postpone independently managing their emotions' and increasing their identificatory options with their followers or those they follow. In so doing, they create what Gergen and Rheingold call the 'saturated self', a 'pastiche of personalities' in which communication technologies have caused us to 'colonise each other's brains … we live in each other's brains, as voices, images, words on screens … We are multiple personalities and we include each other' (quoted in Turkle, 1995 p. 257).

Three days after Houston's funeral, the American TV network FOX aired a Valentine's Day episode of its hit musical comedy *Glee*, called 'Heart'. This episode featured, among a variety of other sob-songs, Houston's famous 'I Will Always Love You', sung by the cast's only African-American actor, Amber Riley. The episode had been shot before Houston's death (Riley, in fact, met and thanked Houston in her Beverly Hilton Hotel room just days before her death), but the producers used the coincidence to drive ratings for the show by publicly dedicating it to her memory and encouraging others to watch and tweet along. Increasingly popular, tweet-along episodes create interactivity between programmes and their viewers who in turn connect with other fans through live tweets. The tweet-along episode became a kind of dress rehearsal (both for the producers and the fans) for the properly-produced memorial episode that aired two months later, 'Dance with Somebody'.

In 'Dance with Somebody', the students of McKinley High's glee club perform their grief of Houston's death by creating shrines in their lockers with candles, flowers and framed photos of the singer. When concerned glee club coach William Schuester asks the school counsellor Emma Pillsbury why they are continuing to grieve two months after Houston's death (a plot manoeuvre to reconcile the delay in the episode's broadcast), she explains that they are outwardly mourning Houston's death but inwardly mourning the loss of their youth as they come close to graduation. Pillsbury, who keeps an assortment of homemade self-help pamphlets, pulls one out she made shortly after Princess Diana's death to use as an analogy to help Schuester understand his students' grieving process:

> I didn't [have a connection to Diana]. I mean every little girl worshipped her. But she was just a physical representation of my pain. I was scared, it was my last year of high school. I was saying goodbye to my teachers and my friends. Diana dying represented the loss of my childhood.

When she finishes her speech, Schuester concludes: 'So, Whitney is their Diana'. This comparison suggests sorrow for the death of a celebrity is similar to or can stand in for other sorrowful experiences. Through the narrative of the episode and vignettes of different kinds of grieving practices, *Glee* teaches its viewers at home how to use the death of a celebrity as a mechanism to process private trauma all the while underscoring the importance of mourning as a public act.

In this way, fans can use stars' deaths as coping strategies to mourn unrelated personal tragedies at a time when others are also openly performing their grief. While Pillsbury crafted a self-help pamphlet to mediate her sorrow, hashtags throughout the episode encouraging viewers to tweet along invited *Glee*'s fans to mediate Houston's death through tweeted memorials. The convergence of the social habits of the TV characters with those of the intended audience illuminates the profit potential of social sorrow, modelling tweeting behaviour to encourage fans to engage in mourning as cultural labour. The more affective the show, the more they struggle to verbalise affect, the more tweets they send, the more likely others in their social circles are to turn on their televisions and join in on the conversation. So while social sorrow may have the capacity to ameliorate great pain and personal strife through collective bereavement, it does so also with a considerable profit margin for the industries that encourage it.

Throughout the course of the episode, *Glee* broadcast the hashtag #GLEEremembersWhitney to drive viewers to the social media site to talk about the episode while they watched. At the very beginning, a graphic also appeared above the tag, reading 'Join New Directions [the name of the glee club] in celebrating the music of Whitney Houston', which characterised Twitter as the pre-eminent social space where the characters of *Glee* were hosting a kind of virtual memorial to which the viewers were invited.[16] Because of the inclusion of the hashtag and its emphasis on liveness, watching the episode as it aired and participating in the discussion online again legitimated the 'reality' of the social

---

[16]   *Glee* is not simulcast across the world or even across the United States, making the experience of liveness also more regional for some viewers, even as this broadcasting practice is not generally well-known.

sorrow sphere as a communal grieving space joined both by the characters and the Twitter users. Among the first tweeting, were those mentally preparing themselves and physically preparing their spaces to watch the episode: 'Gonna watch Glee in a bit ... then write my heart out ... too much pain to hold in ...',[17] and also 'I cant properly mourn someone until I tweet about it and sing along on Glee. Heal me, Lea Michele [an actress in the show]'.[18]

Several users agreed with Pillsbury's suggestion, writing simply 'Whitney was my Diana ... Glee',[19] or 'Whitney was our Princess Diana #glee'.[20] However, some viewers thought the comparison was inappropriate, on both sides of the coin. For example, 'Whitney is more than my diana #glee',[21] versus 'Don't compare Whitney Houston to Princess Diana. One was a crackhead, the other visited crackheads in rehab – smile #Glee'.[22]

Many of the tweets insinuated that watching the episode was a kind of duty they felt they had to endure in order to properly pay tribute to Houston's memory, even if they weren't fans of the show themselves. 'Sigh. I guess for #WhitneyHouston I will watch tonight's #glee #RIPWhitneyHouston' wrote one,[23] while another user commented, 'So im sad 2 say im watching Glee but only cuz they singing all Whitney Houston song!!!'.[24] Some of the viewers who watched the show only out of tribute found themselves moved: 'I only watched Glee cause of the Whitney Houston tribute *wipes tears* back to regular life now',[25] and still others were upset: 'Dear Whitney Houston, On the behalf Glee, they're apologizing for murdering your songs. RIP. Sincerely, Ashten'.[26]

After the tweet-along episode, users reconvened to tweet in familial remembrance: '"Your Love is My Love" thank you #Glee for helping us say goodbye! #gleeremembwhitney' wrote one user,[27] while another responded 'and the tears are streaming down your face ((((((because of glee))))))'.[28] One even claimed the episode would forever help in remembering Houston, a sentiment that was re-tweeted often: '2nights episode of #glee will stay om my DVR 4ever #gleeremembwhitney'.[29] The voice of a diva or the memory of her, carries her fans out of the quotidian, dissolves the self in the service of its repair; she is a cure that enlarges their identities by connecting them together into something bigger.

---

[17] (TheIzze). 24 Apr. 2012, 5:50 p.m. PST.

[18] (cashleelee). 24 Apr. 2012, 4:03 p.m. PST.

[19] (MellieMelATL). 24 Apr. 2012, 6:01 p.m. PST.

[20] (ddriffin). 24 Apr. 2012, 5:05 p.m. PST.

[21] (HearMeRor). 24 Apr. 2012, 5:04 p.m. PST.

[22] (lowereastsmile). 24 Apr. 2012, 5:03 p.m. PST.

[23] (TheHatemonger). 24 Apr. 2012, 6:09 p.m. PST.

[24] (Mskeshia1796). 24 Apr. 2012, 5:43 p.m. PST.

[25] (BrieeHefner___). 24 Apr. 2012, 6:09 p.m. PST.

[26] (AshtennRaee). 24 Apr. 2012, 6:08 p.m. PST.

[27] (ScooterB29). 24 Apr. 2012, 6:06 p.m. PST.

[28] (KittyLeClaire). 24 Apr. 2012, 6:19 p.m. PST.

[29] (DETtoNYC). 24 Apr. 2012, 6:06 p.m. PST.

As one user wrote, 'I've cried, I've laughed, I've been devestated [sic], and I've been repaired, tonight. #GleeremembersWhitney'.[30]

In her study of social media technologies, Turkle (2008 p. 125) writes that people today are not exactly tethered to their devices, but rather 'to the gratifications offered by their online selves. These include the promise of affection, conversation, a sense of new beginnings ... thus more than the sum of their instrumental functions, tethering devices help to constitute new subjectivities'. Spaces provided by services like Twitter are important new sites of mourning that allow us not only to experiment with our own subjectivities, but to expand them outwardly – to colonise and be colonised by the minds of the bodies to whom we are virtually connected, slowly closing the gaps between us in conformity. Working through a mechanics of feelings effaced from most other media, our social sorrow creates a time and space in which our disembodied virtual selves congregate. Twitter, specifically, is an interesting case study as it is an instant, simultaneous and international tool for the expression of emotions (as opposed to national broadsheets, personal letters, discussions and so on). Like the Navy-mother describing the overwhelming feelings she experienced during Houston's performance of the national anthem – as a rainbow connecting her with her deployed son – a social sorrow space is that very rainbow, uniting millions of fragmented selves online in the painful but also pleasurable performance of shared mourning.

As illustrated by a few of the Twitter users' hesitancy to watch the memorial episode of *Glee*, the process of online grieving and paying tribute to a fallen star is one that is ultimately rather normative, and if people step out of that conformed grieving process, they may find themselves outside carefully crafted collective bereavement spaces – and thus, outside social sorrow. After her passing, a Twitter critical mass re-envisioned 'I Will Always Love You' from the power ballad it had become into a tear-stained love song to the singer's memory. Indeed, it was the song that concluded her funeral while anguished fans laboured over their keyboards to describe what they felt.

Bibliography

Albright, Ann Cooper (1997) *Choreographing Difference: The Body and Identity in Contemporary Dance*. Middletown, CT: Wesleyan University Press.

Anderson, Benedict (1992) *Imagined Communities: Reflections on the Origin and Spread of Nationalism*. London: Verso.

Brennan, Teresa (2004) *The Transmission of Affect*. Ithaca, NY: Cornell University Press.

Coghlan, Alexandra (2012) 'Whitney Houston, A Voice that Destroyed Itself', *The New Statesman*, 20 February.

---

[30] (Empress_Laxue). 24 Apr. 2012, 6:06 p.m. PST.

98   *DEATH AND THE ROCK STAR*

Dayan, Daniel and Elihu Katz (1992) *Media Events: The Live Broadcasting of History*. Cambridge, MA: Harvard University Press.

Ewen, Stuart (1988) *All-Consuming Images: Style in Contemporary Culture*. New York: Basic Books.

Farmer, Brett (2005) 'The Fabulous Sublimity of Gay Diva Worship', *Camera Obscura*, 20 (2), pp. 164–95.

Flemings, Hajj (2012) '#WhitneyHouston's Impact on Twitter: Looking at how Trusted News Breaks in the Age of Social Media', *Black Enterprise*, 15 February.

Gergen, Kenneth (2000) *The Saturated Self: Dilemmas of Identity in Contemporary Life*. New York: Basic Books.

Jackson, Shantina (2009), 'Houston, Whitney', *Encyclopedia of African American History, 1896 to the Present. From the Age of Segregation to the Twenty-First Century*, ed. Paul Finkelman. New York: Oxford, p. 460.

Jenkins, Henry (2001), 'Convergence? I Diverge', *MIT Technology Review*, 1 June, p. 93.

Johnson, Samuel (1811) *The History of Rasselas, Prince of Abissinia*. Boston, MA: J. Belcher.

Marshall, P. David (2002) 'The Cinematic Apparatus and the Construction of the Film Celebrity', in Graeme Turner (ed.), *The Film Cultures Readers*. London: Routledge, pp. 228–39.

Powers, Ann (2009) '"I Look to You" by Whitney Houston', *The Los Angeles Times*, 26 August.

Reid, Shaheem (2001) 'Whitney Houston's "Star-Spangled Banner" to Wave Again', *MTV.com*, 17 September.

Turkle, Sherry (1995) *Life on the Screen: Identity in the Age of the Internet*. New York: Simon & Schuster.

——— (2008) 'Always-on/Always-on-you: The Tethered Self', in James E. Katz (ed.), *Handbook of Mobile Communication Studies*. Cambridge, MA: MIT Press, pp. 121–37.

'Whitney Houston Funeral – Programs! Getcha Programs Here!' (2012), *TMZ.com*, 17 February.

Zakreski, Patricia (2006) *Representing Female Artistic Labour, 1848–1890: Refining Work for the Middle-Class Woman*. Burlington, VT: Ashgate.

Other References

'Dance With Somebody'. *Glee* (2012) television programme, FOX, Los Angeles, 24 April.

'Heart'. *Glee* (2012) television programme, FOX, Los Angeles, 14 February.

Oprah's Next Chapter (2012) television programme, OWN, Los Angeles, 1 March.

The Oprah Winfrey Show (2006) television programme, syndicated by Harpo Productions, New York City, 14 September.

The Star Spangled Banner. As Performed at Super Bowl XXV (1991) Whitney Houston video, ABC Sports Inc., distributed by 6 West Home Video (Artista Records, Inc.).

PART III
The Labouring Dead

Chapter 8

Laneways of the Dead: Memorialising Musicians in Melbourne

Catherine Strong

Since 2004, the idea of naming public places, particularly laneways,[1] after dead rock musicians has gained traction with councils in inner-city Melbourne, Australia. In that year, a laneway in Melbourne's central business district (CBD) was renamed 'AC/DC Lane', and although this is not named after a dead musician as such, the figure of the band's deceased singer Bon Scott loomed particularly large in this process. In 2005, a walkway in the Port Phillip suburb of Elwood was named after ex-Crowded House drummer Paul Hester, who committed suicide earlier that same year. In 2013, proposals have been approved for the renaming of laneways in the CBD and St Kilda areas for Divinyls singer Chrissy Amphlett and Birthday Party guitarist Rowland S. Howard respectively.

The establishment of these laneways serves the interests of a number of groups. For the councils, creating a physical association between Melbourne and popular music has the potential to increase the cultural capital of the city, and, as has been the case in other cities such as Manchester and Liverpool in the UK or Aberdeen in the US, may bring benefits such as tourist income and prestige. For the families and other interested parties associated with the dead musicians, there is a lasting, tangible memorial to the departed, which helps preserve their own legacy. Fans gain a physical place that they can visit to remember, pay tribute to and mourn the loss of their idols. Each of these interests, and the ultimate goal of creating a way to remember and honour the deceased, feature prominently in the media and council documentation related to the namings. I will argue that the process of naming Melbourne streets after popular musicians represents an attempt on the part of the Melbourne councils to create, in Pierre Nora's terminology, sites of memory (*lieux de mémoire*), and will consider the conditions necessary for this goal to succeed, and whose interests will be best represented. I will also examine the paradoxical nature of using street names as a way of connecting the memory of extraordinary and creative musicians with physical locations, given the mundane nature of such names.

Nora (1989) has argued that an increase in archives and written history has led to a decrease in lived memory (*milieux de mémoire*), or memory that is shared among people on an everyday basis. This decline produces a need for *lieux de*

---

[1] Laneways are narrower, often cobbled service streets and ex-service streets that connect the main thoroughfares of the city, especially for pedestrian traffic.

mémoire, or sites of memory, places where memory crystallises around certain locations (physical or otherwise) that then help define the identity of a group in the absence of more organic shared memory. Although Nora originally contrasted history with memory and argued that *lieux de mémoire* were necessary only in societies where memory experienced as a part of everyday living had been supplanted by history, the strict distinction he drew between these has generally been rejected in favour of a more dynamic approach to the workings of memory (Rigney, 2008). However, in the cases under consideration here, it may be useful to reconsider Nora's conceptualisation of sites of memory as representations of disconnected memory that is reimposed onto the world in an attempt to stop the past disappearing altogether. Nora (1989 p. 19) argues that because memory and sites of memory act as a type of anchor in an accelerating world where the past and the future bear little relationship to one another, 'the most fundamental purpose of the *lieu de mémoire* is to stop time, to block the work of forgetting, to establish a state of things, *to immortalise death*, to materialise the immaterial' (emphasis added). Importantly, he also notes that a place becomes a *lieu de mémoire* 'only if the [collective] imagination invests it with symbolic importance'. As will be demonstrated below, the places being renamed in Melbourne are not obviously places where the memory of these individuals should or could reside. As such, the processes and decisions to create these memorials present an attempt to 'immortalise death, to materialise the immaterial', by imposing new memories onto existing physical sites. This process is not new; street names are indeed one of the types of *lieux de mémoire* discussed in the *Realms of Memory* series overseen by Nora, and have long been used as an official way of shaping public memory (see Milo, 1997). What is relatively new, however, is the use of the names of dead rock musicians for this purpose.[2]

Music, Place and Memory

While music itself can act as a type of *lieu de mémoire*, in the sense that songs can come to represent certain aspects of the past in a way that helps define a group's identity, it is also often tightly bound to the memories of specific physical locations. This ranges from the association of entire nations or cultures with particular musical forms, through to cities or regions being connected to specific 'scenes' and sounds. On a more local scale, there are examples of streets, venues or addresses that are linked to the memory of a song, band or musician (Connell and Gibson, 2003). These associations have been part of the way popular music resides in and constitutes cultural memory, and have been celebrated (and contested) by fans. Of particular interest to fans have often been the spaces associated with musicians who have died. The traces that fans can discern in the places the

---

[2] This trend has been increasing worldwide since streets were named after the Beatles (for example, Paul McCartney Way and John Lennon Drive) in Liverpool in the 1980s.

deceased once inhabited, the places they died or where they have been laid to rest, are the only physical connection that is now possible. Such places are often sites of spontaneous memorials (for example, flowers and other items left near the tree where Marc Bolan died after his car crashed [McCarron, 1995]) and can be described as *lieux de mémoire* when they eventually become sites of pilgrimages (as the site of Bolan's crash has done), or regular gatherings of fans (for example, at the grave of Jim Morrison in Père Lachaise Cemetery [Margry, 2008]).

However, it is only relatively recently that the connection between place, music and memorialisation has started to be formalised using official processes through the services of governments, councils and city planners. As a case in point, the place in south-west London where Marc Bolan's car crashed now has an official memorial and is 'recognised by the English Tourist Board as a "Site of Rock'n'Roll Importance" in their guide *England Rocks*' (Sanders, 2010). This formalisation has been part of a wider shift in who and what is memorialised in Western societies since the end of the twentieth century. The 'democratisation of the past' has seen groups that were once marginalised or oppressed, including minority ethnic groups, indigenous people and women, given more opportunities to insert their versions of the past into public landscapes (Foote and Azaryahu, 2007; Rose-Redwood, 2008). Public memory, as represented through official strategies around place naming, memorials and debates around what constitutes 'heritage', has become more inclusive and less monolithic, as different versions of the past gain legitimacy and as the nation state loses its hold as an organiser of identity. As a result, while once excluded from official public memory (leaving the creation of memory sites in the hands of fans), popular music has become a celebrated part of heritage in official discourses (Roberts, 2014; Cohen, 2012). This celebration is often happening on a local rather than national level, as with the case studies discussed here.

This move towards regarding popular music as an aspect of heritage is also connected to various commercial, economic and policy considerations, rather than being simply a reflection of a more inclusive attitude to the past. In Australia, it has been calculated that popular music contributes significantly to the economy. Australia is the tenth biggest global market for recorded music (Homan, 2011) and the live sector is worth over $400 million per annum (APRA, 2011). Government policy is increasingly recognising these benefits, along with the social advantages of healthy live music scenes and the other opportunities that encouraging the growth of the 'creative industries' can bring. Constructing a past for a city or nation that incorporates popular music as having been an inherent part of its identity for a long time is one way to shore up support for such activity into the future. It also creates other economic opportunities, as increasingly city councils and national bodies are using popular music as a drawcard to bring tourists in by advertising not only current musical activities, but also connections to music history (Brandellero and Janssen, 2014).

The city of Melbourne, the capital of the Australian state of Victoria, exemplifies these trends. Melbourne has long had a reputation as a place where popular music, particularly live music, flourishes (Homan, 2011), and the Melbourne City Council

106   *DEATH AND THE ROCK STAR*

(MCC) is keen to capitalise on this reputation (Melbourne City Council, 2014). Although the government and music community have not always seen eye-to-eye,[3] since the early 2000s there has been a willingness on the part of councils, in particular Melbourne City Council, to incorporate popular culture into official discourses on the city. This was made apparent in 2004 with the naming of the AC/DC Lane, the first utilisation of rock music in place-naming in Australia.

The naming of public spaces is a highly political act, in that whom spaces are named after and who can do the naming reveals much about which groups hold power within a particular society. Conventions around street names in Australia have tended to see politicians, civic figures, military heroes, pioneers and royalty honoured (Besley, 2005). Comments from officials suggest that the namings discussed in this chapter are part of a broader change in the way naming public space is thought about. For example, in discussing the naming of Paul Hester Walk, Port Phillip mayor Darren Ray stated that

> [t]he majority of the historical markers that we have in the city are still a hangover from the 19th and 20th centuries. But that's changing. In Elwood, and other suburbs in the city, we're starting to recognise the efforts of those who are not just 19th century white engineers or planners. (In Barry, 2005)

However, this broader conceptualisation of who is worthy of recognition in this way is limited to people who have died (Department of Sustainability and Environment Melbourne, 2010 p. 12).

This chapter will now give a brief account of the circumstances under which each of the four case studies considered here originated and the processes that led to their approval, before moving on to a more detailed discussion of the implications of these namings. The cases are divided between two different Melbourne councils (Melbourne City Council, which covers the inner city, and Port Phillip Council, which covers the area around St Kilda), and are also a combination of applications that have been seen through to completion and those that are still ongoing.

AC/DC Lane

AC/DC is one of the most successful Australian rock bands of all time, having sold over 100 million albums worldwide since their formation in 1973. The process through which the laneway in the CBD was renamed in their honour has been documented by Frost (2008), who describes how the notion of AC/DC Lane originated in a newspaper article noting the connections between Melbourne and the band. The journalist's suggestion that one of Melbourne's Corporation Lanes be renamed after them was acted on by Melbourne City Council. The lane was

---

[3]   See Homan (2011) for an account of the 2010 'Save Live Australian Music' rallies protesting the closure of music venues, which drew over 20,000 participants.

opened with much fanfare in October 2004 as 'ACDC Lane' (as the slash was not permitted according to street name conventions), but after repeated incursions by fans to reinstate the slash, the name was changed to 'AC/DC Lane' some years later. Although the laneway is named after the band, and not specifically for Bon Scott (1946–80), the band's singer who died from alcohol poisoning in 1980, it is the Bon Scott-era AC/DC that has been constantly referenced both during the approval process for the laneway (for example, through references to the 'Long Way to the Top' film clip which was shot on Swanston St, a main thoroughfare in the CBD), and visually in the laneway itself. The street art that has at times adorned AC/DC Lane has featured Scott prominently in various ways (see Figure 8.1), while Scott's replacement, Brian Johnson, has been represented far less often (and his predecessor Dave Evans not at all). For this reason, the laneway to a large extent memorialises Scott, although not in the same clear terms as the other spaces discussed below.

Figure 8.1   Artwork of Bon Scott in AC/DC Lane, Melbourne
Photo: Catherine Strong

108   *DEATH AND THE ROCK STAR*

Paul Hester Walk

Paul Hester (1959–2005) was the drummer in internationally successful group Crowded House from 1985 to 1994, after which time he left the group to pursue other interests. On 26 March 2005, he hanged himself from a tree in Elsternwick Park in Melbourne. In the aftermath of his death, it was acknowledged that he had suffered from ongoing problems with depression (Boulton, 2005). In October of the same year, a pathway along Elwood canal in the suburb where Hester lived was named 'Paul Hester Walk' in his honour. It is unclear exactly how the decision to establish a memorial to Hester originated, although a news report four days after his death (Anon., 2005) suggested that 'Melbourne's Bayside Council could erect a memorial to Hester in the park', alongside a quote from a 'council spokesperson' saying that 'if someone approached us we would consider a memorial'. This raises the possibility that the idea of a memorial could have originated in this media report itself. Community consultation led to 207 submissions being made to Council in support of the idea, and seven in opposition, some of which conveyed concerns regarding the manner of his death and the possibility of inadvertently glamourising suicide. The name was made official in October 2005, although there does not appear to have been a public opening or ceremony.

Chrissy Amphlett Lane

Chrissy Amphlett (1959–2013), lead singer of the rock group the Divinyls (1980–2009), passed away in April 2013 from breast cancer, exacerbated by multiple sclerosis. Amphlett is unusual in Australian rock music, in that she is one of a very small number of female performers who have been granted access to the Australian rock canon. Amphlett's death was covered extensively in the Australian media, and prominent Australian public figures, from other well-known musicians to the then-Prime Minister Julia Gillard, made statements lamenting her passing (Anon., 2013).

Only days after her death, the idea of memorialising her via a laneway named in her honour started to circulate. Journalist Jessica Adams initiated an online petition on the site change.org in early May 2013 (with the support of Amphlett's husband), asking Melbourne City Council to 'please dedicate and name a laneway (or other Melbourne city landmark) for Chrissy Amphlett'. This petition was submitted to the Council on 30 July 2013 with over 6,000 signatures (Masanauskas, 2013). In April 2014, this number was still increasing, with close to 7,500 signatories. After an appropriate laneway (Corporation Lane 1639, located near a number of venues where Amphlett had performed) was located, and with no opposition from business or community groups, the Council unanimously approved the renaming on 2 September 2014. However, the Amphlett laneway proposition ran into difficulties created by the Guideline for Geographic Names (Department of Sustainability and Environment Melbourne, 2010 p. 12), which state: 'A commemorative name applied to a locality or road should use only the surname of a person … This approach is to ensure that the emergency and postal services are not delayed through inconsistent application of the name'.[4]

An application for an exemption from this rule in the case of Chrissy Amphlett lane was rejected, and the laneway will be renamed Amphlett Lane. This is likely to have officially happened by the time this volume goes to print.

Rowland S. Howard Lane

Rowland S. Howard (1959–2009) was best known as the guitarist for Melbourne band the Birthday Party (1978–83, originally the Boys Next Door). He spent a large part of his life living in St Kilda, and after he died of liver cancer in 2009, music promoter Nick Haines started a petition to have a specific unnamed laneway, located between Jackson Street and Eildon Road (where Howard once lived), renamed Rowland S. Howard Laneway. The petition, with over 2,000 signatures, was presented to the City of Port Phillip Council, and the proposal was accepted by the Council on 23 April 2013. It has, however, met the same difficulties as the Amphlett application, in that regulations do not allow for more than one name to be used, let alone an initial. An application for an exemption was also rejected in this case. Since a location had already been established, and finding two nearby streets is not viable, Haines has suggested that the Office of Geographic Names' preferred option Howard Lane does not adequately memorialise the singer (and could be mistaken for a tribute to former Prime Minister John Howard, a figure with a public profile that is diametrically opposed to that of Rowland). As of September 2014 the parties behind the naming campaign were still pursuing options that would allow the whole name to be used (personal communication, 3 September 2014), meaning there may still be a long wait before the laneway is established, or that it may not be successful.

Creating Meaning

Having covered the background and the specific circumstances of these naming decisions, I now turn to a discussion of what functions these namings may be called upon to perform and the extent to which they could be considered *lieux de mémoire*. Their possible functions include keeping the memories of these people alive, supporting certain images of Melbourne's identity, and creating links between the individuals and the city. To begin with, the decision to use laneways, particularly CBD laneways, is significant, as they have increasingly been marketed as a unique aspect of Melbourne's urban identity (and indeed could be considered a type of *lieux de mémoire* themselves). A 2007 MCC document notes:

---

[4] This provision was introduced after Paul Hester Walk and AC/DC Lane were named.

110   *DEATH AND THE ROCK STAR*

> The Central City laneway network is a valued and vital part of the city's urban form. They are integral to the city's distinct urban fabric qualities, providing an insight into the city's built form evolution. Lanes provide some of the most important and unique public spaces within the Central City. (Melbourne City Council, 2007 p. 7)

The laneways are used as a marker of difference and a drawcard for the city, distinguishing it from other Australian capitals. For example, Melbourne tourism campaigns in 2010 and 2011 featured these laneways, and they are also prominent in officially sponsored tourist activities such as walking tours (see, for example, the 'Lanes and Arcades Tour' and 'Melbourne Experience Tour' on the official Melbourne tourism website).[5] The use of laneways as memorials is in some ways pragmatic (as it is easier to name an unnamed street than to have a pre-existing name changed), and in other ways exemplifies the changing image of the city as it finds commercial uses for its once-derelict urban spaces that now increasingly denote 'coolness' and authenticity. The use of graffiti, often within the laneways, as a way to promote the city, is another aspect of the same process (Dovey, Wollan and Woodcock, 2012).

Rock music can be used in a similar manner to increase the city's prestige. Using the names of important Australian musicians in these laneways can be seen as an attempt to increase the association between Melbourne and music by embedding it in the urban landscape of the city. That these artists have passed away has the potential to increase the emotional impact of these spaces, and hence increase the benefits that may accrue to the city through their existence. As Connell and Gibson (2003 p. 221) have noted, 'visible "reminders" of the presence of musical scenes and sounds that have since declined or disappeared, or of artists who have died or whose careers are finished, have generated some successful year-round tourism economies' (Liverpool is again an excellent example of this). They go on to note, however, that these 'are difficult to establish, given the relative "invisibility" of music and sound'.

Indeed, a number of difficulties exist in making a meaningful link between a Melbourne laneway and the memory of a deceased musician and their music. One of these is whether there is a pre-existing connection between the place and the person, and if not whether it is possible to create one. As part of the approval process for street naming, evidence is generally provided that the person being memorialised has a connection to the city or area and has made a contribution to it. In some of these case studies, this was more easily done than in others. Some difficulty was encountered particularly with AC/DC, a band whose best-known members were born and raised in Adelaide, and which did not base itself in Melbourne. The application to Council presented the following links:

---

[5]   http://www.visitvictoria.com/Regions/Melbourne/Activities-and-attractions/Tours/Walking-tours.

LANEWAYS OF THE DEAD: MEMORIALISING MUSICIANS IN MELBOURNE 111

> ... the band was formed in Sydney and has performed in Melbourne on several different tours ... the band's drummer Phil Rudd was born in Melbourne as was Mark Evans a former AC/DC bass player. One of the band's most famous videos 'It's a Long Way to the Top' was filmed on a flatbed truck travelling down Swanston Street [a main thoroughfare in the CBD] in 1975. (Melbourne City Council. Planning and Development Committee, 2004 p. 2)

These somewhat tenuous connections raise questions over the extent to which the lane can evoke memories of the band. Despite the fanfare that accompanied the opening of the lane in October 2004, and the subsequent adornment of the street with AC/DC-related street art and posters (particularly at the time of their 2010 tour), by late 2013 these did not appear to have been well-maintained (see Figure 8.1). Indeed, one of the objections raised by local business operators when the laneway renaming was proposed, was that the image of AC/DC was not in keeping with that of the local area, and that 'the type of bars that exist in the area do not reflect AC/DC music styles but range in type from jazz through bar disco to rock and roll, and only one (The Cherry Bar) may play AC/DC music on infrequent occasions' (Melbourne City Council. Planning and Development Committee, 2004 p. 9). Today, the area contains high-end restaurants and sophisticated bars that appear out of keeping with the connotations of hard rock. However, given that AC/DC marketing now extends to the production of a range of wines (Wright, 2013), this may be representative of the changing position of rock as also evidenced by the memorialising discussed in this chapter. Regardless of whether it is an indication of a possible mismatch between concept and surroundings, the laneway's tributes to the band are currently not in good repair.

The Chrissy Amphlett laneway campaign faced similar obstacles, in that Amphlett was born and raised in Geelong, and while she did live in Melbourne for a period of time, most of her life, including her final years, was spent elsewhere (Amphlett, 2009). However, the organisers behind the campaign went to great lengths to ensure the chosen location could be directly connected to Amphlett. This was mainly done through finding a laneway in the immediate vicinity of two venues where Amphlett had performed, but also through emphasising the involvement and approval of members of Amphlett's family, particularly her husband.

The memorials approved by Port Phillip Council for Hester and Howard, on the other hand, were constructed as much more obviously connected to the locale. As noted above, the proposed 'Rowland S. Howard Laneway' is adjacent to the street he lived on, while Paul Hester Walk is also located near the drummer's house in an area he frequented (and a short distance from the park where he died). As such, the applications received by the Council supporting these changes were often about these musicians' contributions to the local community. The Council review on Paul Hester Walk contained submissions that described him as 'lifelong ambassador for Elwood' and 'the best walking advertisement for Elwood you could have asked for' (Port Phillip Council. Strategy and Policy Review Committee, 2005 p. 79). Likewise, when presenting the petition regarding Howard, his sister spoke of how 'as a long time St Kilda resident, Rowland walked down the laneway [to be named after him] most days' (Port Phillip Council, 2013 p. 4). That Howard and Hester not only lived but died or spent their last days in the vicinity of the spaces memorialising them appeared to be a factor in their adoption.

At the same time, however, the Hester and Rowland memorials are very much removed from any musical context, as they are located in highly gentrified or suburban surroundings. Paul Hester Walk has a small sign noting Hester's achievements as a musician, but in neither this spot nor the lane that looks set to become Rowland Lane is there any evidence of memorialisation by fans or any connection to the sights, sounds or ideologies of rock 'n' roll. They are quiet, pleasant, green spaces (see Figure 8.2).

This is perhaps not surprising, though, and may itself be an indicator of the middle-class nature of these types of memorials established through bureaucratic process, and is also further evidence of the increased respectability of rock music. Furthermore, the processes leading up to the creation of all four of these memorials lacked the spontaneous or fan-led elements that have been associated with many of the other places where dead rock stars are remembered (such as the Bolan site mentioned earlier). In all four cases, fans have been involved in the petitioning of the councils, but only as a type of secondary support. The proposals themselves have been put together by family members or industry insiders and primarily backed by supporters with high social capital in this area, including the rock musician Nick Cave and the renowned Australian rock critic Molly Meldrum. However, none of these factors necessarily precludes the effective creation of a *lieu de mémoire*. Nora himself notes that 'monuments to the dead ... owe their meaning to their intrinsic existence' (Nora, 1989 p. 22), and as such do not then require the presence of, or a strong connection to, the dead in any way. In this way, it is the creation of symbolic importance that is vital in the establishment of a site of memory, but it does seem that if a physical site is already associated with the dead person, and/or with whatever it is they are known for, then the naming process is more likely to occur.

This leads to the question of the effectiveness of using street names as a method of memorialisation, especially given the bureaucratic context that surrounds the debates about these names. Street names occupy a strange position in that they crystallise a particular way of thinking about the past that represents specific political interests (Rose-Redwood, 2008), in a way that 'allows them to render a certain version of history not only familiar but also self-evident' (Foote and Azaryahu, 2007 p. 128). At the same time, street names are also an extremely banal feature of the present. As Azaryahu (1996 p. 320) notes, street names are ultimately everyday, ordinary features of the city, and an encounter with them 'usually takes place in the context of mundane activities and does not involve any substantial spiritual experience'. In terms of their possible utilisation as a way of creating *lieux de mémoire*, Hartmuth argues that street names

Figure 8.2   Paul Hester Walk
Photo: Catherine Strong

114　　　　　　　　*DEATH AND THE ROCK STAR*

> certainly help remind people of the existence of these real or potential *lieux*, but most inhabitants might still not know who exactly is behind those names. Thus, it is often merely names without biographies that are inserted into the landscape. They might thereby lack the symbolic element intrinsic to Nora's *lieux de mémoire*. (2010 p. 17; see also Milo, 1997)

A street name alone, then, is of questionable efficacy as a way of keeping the memory of a person alive, and keying a place to that memory.

The bureaucratic obstacles to using full names in Melbourne create more difficulty, as there is a significant difference between 'Chrissy Amphlett Lane' and 'Amphlett Lane', or 'Rowland S. Howard Lane' and 'Rowland Lane'. Although all street names eventually gain other symbolic meanings as they become part of the life of the city, depending on what happens in them, a full name retains the memory of a person more powerfully than part of one. AC/DC is probably the most recognisable of the names discussed here, and there are likely to be few people who would not immediately make the connection between the laneway name and the band. Paul Hester Walk has the benefit of a modest monument that gives an account of the drummer's accomplishments. 'Rowland Lane' and 'Amphlett Lane', on the other hand, might not work as adequate identifiers of the people being memorialised unless significant work is done to give them something more than half a name each.

Conclusion

The attempts described here to create memorials to recently deceased Australian rock stars make the complicated nature of memorialisation clear. As 'monuments of history torn away from the movement of history, then returned; no longer quite life, not yet death, like shells on the shore when the sea of living memory has receded' (Nora, 1989 p. 12), *lieux de mémoire* preserve important symbolic elements of the past. The extent to which laneways can achieve this in Melbourne is unclear, but the final outcome will not be known until all the namings are complete: fans and tourists may indeed flock to Rowland and Amphlett Lanes and through their presence create the symbolic connections that are essential to sites of memory.[6] The failure of this to occur in AC/DC Lane to a great extent, or at all at Paul Hester Walk – locations that are more clearly connected to those they memorialise – suggests a name alone will not bring this about. (By contrast, an Elvis Presley memorial built by fans in Melbourne General Cemetery is regularly visited, with fresh flowers and tributes always adorning the site.) Furthermore, memory and forgetting are always woven together. Rigney (2008 p. 345) suggests that 'while putting down a monument may seem like a way of ensuring

---

[6]　There are signs this may happen in Amphlett Lane – the site chosen was adorned with chalk murals by fans on the night the name change was approved by Council.

long-term memory, it may in fact turn out to mark the beginning of amnesia unless the monument in question is continuously invested with new meaning'.

This leads us back to the problematic nature of *lieux de mémoire*, and their role in preserving the past and maintaining the memory of the dead, as well as maintaining group identity for the living. Certainly, we are now seeing attempts to create new *lieux de mémoire* that relate to rock musicians. Rock is no longer oppositional or rebellious in any more than a symbolic way (if it ever was), as the use of figures from its ranks as street names – a resounding seal of approval from the establishment – attests. This process is also increasingly fragmented; the shared memory of music that came from a population having limited access to it is dissipating in the wake of technological changes. As rock ages, the deaths that thin the ranks of its stars are increasingly less spectacular. Rather than drug overdoses at wild parties, there are deaths from cancer, old age and other unspectacular afflictions. Even Paul Hester's suicide as a divorced middle-aged man suffering the same mental health issues that afflict so many other men of his age group was framed as a very different event to 'tortured soul' Kurt Cobain's shotgun blast. Rock star legends who die young and beautiful create their own memorials; as rock 'n' roll itself ages and former stars are more and more slipping quite gently into that good night, *lieux de mémoire* that reinstate not only their memory but with it the memories of the youth (and perhaps significance) of those able to influence the creation of such memorials may emerge.

The changing nature of popular music, and the changing role that death now plays in it, may have come to a point where it is being recognised that the 'lived memory' of fans is not now enough, leading to attempts to create such sites. The communities that once existed around music scenes such as those that spawned the Birthday Party or the Divinyls have dissipated over time, and as the lived memory (*milieux de mémoire*) associated with these groups disappears, so *lieux de mémoire* and other ways of preserving the artists' memory, including biographies, films and museum exhibitions, become necessary (for a discussion of the memorial preservation of the Manchester music scene of the 1970s and 1980s, see Greig and Strong, 2014). High-profile deaths provide a moment of focus for the crystallisation of these memories through memorialisation. That this can now happen in official ways using public space provides an opportunity to interrogate the intersections between fandom, bureaucracy and commerce. In a way, the identities of these specific individuals may be less important than their association with 'rock music', which could itself be thought of as a broader *lieu de mémoire* that the officials of Melbourne are trying to create an association with more generally, where each official display of alliance with it amounts to an overall connection more important than any of the individual sites. The development of an image of Melbourne as a 'cool' city steeped in live music and with strong connections to the music heritage of the nation can have tangible benefits in terms of tourism dollars and the growth of 'creative industries' that also bring financial benefits.

It should be noted, however, that the remembrance of the artists under consideration here does not hinge on the success or failure of these streets to become *lieux de mémoire*. It is arguable, for instance, that the band AC/DC has already become a site of memory for Australia and rock music fans more generally, regardless of whether or not it is connected to a physical site. The nationwide outpouring of grief over the death of Chrissy Amphlett also points to an enduring legacy that may manifest itself in many different ways. What the examples considered in this chapter point to, nonetheless, is the changing nature of memorialisation of musicians, and complexities in maintaining an after-life support system for dead musicians.

Bibliography

Amphlett, Chrissy (2009) *Pleasure and Pain: My Life*. London: Hachette.

Anonymous (2005) 'Simple Tribute Honours a Star', *Geelong Advertiser*, 30 March, p. 3.

Anonymous (2013) 'Chrissy Amphlett Dead at 53', *The Age*, 22 April, http://www.theage.com.au/entertainment/music/chrissy-amphlett-dead-at-53-20130422-2ia30.html#ixzz2RpO8hvzK, accessed 1 June 2013.

APRA (2011) *Economic Contribution of the Venue-Based Live Music Industry in Australia*. Australasian Performing Rights Association (APRA).

Azaryahu, Maoz (1996) 'The Power of Commemorative Street Names', *Environment and Planning D: Society and Space*, 14, pp. 311–30.

Barry, Evonne (2005) 'Hester Park First Modern Memorial', *MX (Melbourne, Australia)*, 6 July, p. 4.

Besley, Joanna (2005) 'At the Intersection of History and Memory: Monuments in Queensland', *Limina*, 11, pp. 38–46.

Boulton, Martin (2005) 'Hester Walk to Immortalise Musician', *The Age*, 5 October, p. 6.

Brandellero, Amanda and Susanne Janssen (2014) 'Popular Music as Cultural Heritage: Scoping out the Field of Practice', *International Journal of Heritage Studies*, 20 (3), pp. 224–40.

Cohen, Sara (2012) 'Musical Memory, Heritage and Local Identity: Remembering the Popular Music Past in a European Capital of Culture', *International Journal of Cultural Policy*, 19 (5), pp. 576–94.

Connell, John and Chris Gibson (2003) *Sound Tracks: Popular Music, Identity and Place*. London and New York: Routledge.

Department of Sustainability and Environment Melbourne (2010) *Guideline to Geographic Names 2010*, Victorian Government.

Dovey, Kim, Simon Wollan and Ian Woodcock (2012) 'Placing Graffiti: Creating and Contesting Character in Inner-City Melbourne', *Journal of Urban Design*, 17 (1), pp. 21–40.

Foote, Kenneth E. and Maoz Azaryahu (2007) 'Toward a Geography of Memory: Geographical Dimensions of Public Memory and Commemoration', *Journal of Political and Military Sociology*, 35 (1), pp. 125–44.

Frost, Warwick (2008) 'Popular Culture as a Different Type of Heritage: The Making of AC/DC Lane', *Journal of Heritage Tourism*, 3 (3), pp. 176–84.

Greig, Alastair and Catherine Strong (2014) 'Joy Division and New Orders of Nostalgia', *Volume! The French Journal of Popular Music Studies*, 11 (1), pp. 191–206.

Hartmuth, Maximilian (2010) 'History, Identity and Urban Space: Towards an Agenda for Urban Research', in Stephanie Herold, Benjamin Langer and Julia Lechler (eds), *Reading the City: Urban Space and Memory in Skopje*. Berlin: Univerlagtuberlin, pp. 12–22.

Homan, Shane (2011) '"I Tote and I Vote": Australian Live Music and Cultural Policy', *Arts Marketing: An International Journal*, 1 (2), pp. 96–107.

McCarron, Kevin (1995) 'Pilgrims or Tourists? Rock Music and "Shrines" in England', *Critical Survey*, 7 (2), pp. 165–71.

Margry, Peter Jan (2008) 'The Pilgrimage to Jim Morrison's Grave at Père Lachaise Cemetery: The Social Construction of Sacred Space', in Peter Jan Margry (ed.), *Shrines and Pilgrimage in the Modern World: New Itineraries into the Sacred*. Amsterdam: Amsterdam University Press, pp. 143–72.

Masanauskas, John (2013) 'Melbourne City Councillors Support Creation of Amphlett Lane in CBD in Honour of Divinyls Frontwoman', *Herald Sun*, 10 September, p. 7.

Melbourne City Council (2007) *Melbourne Planning Scheme Amendment C105*, MCC minutes, 25 September.

——— (2104) *Melbourne Music Strategy 2014–17*. MCC minutes, 14 June.

Melbourne City Council. Future Melbourne Planning Committee (2013) *Proposed Road Naming to Honour Chrissy Amphlett*. 10 September.

Melbourne City Council. Planning and Development Committee (2004) *Report on Proposed Renaming of Corporation Lane (CL. No 1404) Melbourne as ACDC Lane*, 10 September.

Milo, Daniel (1997) 'Street Names', in Pierre Nora and Lawrence Krietzman (eds), *Realms of Memory: The Construction of the French Past, Part II: Traditions*. New York: Columbia University Press, pp. 363–90.

Nora, Pierre (1989) 'Between Memory and History: Les Lieux de Mémoire', *Representations*, 26 (Spring), pp. 7–24.

Port Phillip Council (2013) *Ordinary Meeting of Council Minutes*, 23 April.

Port Phillip Council. Strategy and Policy Review Committee (2005) *Naming of Reserve after Late Paul Hester*, 3 October.

Rigney, Ann (2008) 'The Dynamics of Remembrance: Texts between Monumentality and Morphing', in Astrid Erll and Ansgar Nunning (eds), *A Companion to Cultural Memory Studies*. Berlin and New York: de Gruyter, pp. 345–56.

Roberts, Les (2014) 'Talkin' bout my Generation: Popular Music and the Culture of Heritage', *International Journal of Heritage Studies*, 20 (3), pp. 262–80.

Rose-Redwood, Reuben S. (2008) 'From Number to Name: Symbolic Capital, Places of Memory and the Politics of Street Renaming in New York City', *Social and Cultural Geography*, 9 (4), pp. 431–52.

Sanders, Jill (2010) 'Roadside Memorials: Highways Authority Policies and Good Practice', *Bereavement Care*, 29 (3), pp. 41–3.

Wright, Shauna (2013) 'AC/DC Introduce Platinum Wine', *Ultimate Classic Rock*, 8 August, http://ultimateclassicrock.com/acdc-platinum-wine/, accessed 20 February 2014.

Chapter 9

Three Faces of Musical Motherhood in Death: Amy Winehouse, Whitney Houston and Donna Summer

Paula Hearsum

Introduction

This chapter considers the representation of female musicianship in recent UK press obituaries, with a focus on the theme of motherhood. The research data set considered was taken over a nine month period, between July 2011 and February 2012. Over this time the popular music industry and fans across the world mourned the deaths of three of its best-selling female artists: Amy Winehouse (1983–2011), Whitney Houston (1963–2012) and Donna Summer (1948–2012). The UK press coverage of their deaths intriguingly indicates that motherhood was used as a journalistic hook to compare them, regardless of whether the artists were actually parents, as in the case of Houston and Summer, or not (Winehouse). This chapter will unpack the meanings of motherhood (Eid, 2002), that most gendered of themes, and its usage, value and cultural politics.

Between July 2011 and May 2012, UK broadsheets included the obituaries of 45 musicians, only four of whom were women (representing 8.3 per cent); of these, three were in the same, albeit broad, musical category of 'rock and pop', justifying their selection for analysis here (the other was the blues and jazz singer Etta James). The data set is small and is intended as a litmus test for an analysis that draws from popular music studies, feminist studies, death studies, media studies and celebrity studies, to probe the ways in which motherhood, as a 'social type' (Negra and Holmes, 2008), was journalistically packaged and presented.

Previously published work utilising obituaries has been drawn from a variety of academic disciplines such as journalism studies (Starck, 2006) and sociology (Fowler, 2007), and has used a variety of methodologies such as a discourse (Moore, 2002) and gendered analysis (Kastenbaum, Peyton and Kastenbaum, 1977), which this research acknowledges and draws upon. What this chapter intends to do is to investigate the unexplored intersection between popular musicians, obituaries and gender, and to suggest that the theme of motherhood plays a part in gendering the specific journalistic texts that obituaries are (Eid, 2002). This broad feminist media studies approach uses discourse analysis. The case studies serve to articulate the extreme positions of motherhood within which women popular musicians are typically cast. The rhetoric of motherhood encapsulated within an obituary, examined through discourse analysis, can expose the socio-historically-specific moralities of life choices. While the key focus here is on an analysis of obituaries, wider overlapping journalistic outputs are also discussed as divisions between obituaries, news and features blur in both production and consumption. Awareness of a continually convergent media landscape is pertinent for this subject, since it was TMZ, the celebrity news website, that broke the news of Michael Jackson's death in June 2009 rather than traditional newspapers. The media evolution encourages us more than ever to not read in isolation, as hypertext enhances our natural patterns of acquiring knowledge. It is appropriate to cast a wider net in data capture to set the context in which obituaries are written and read. While obituaries in the UK only appear in the broadsheets, references within them often draw on broader media outputs which will also be considered.

Obituary Journalism

Journalism operates as a site within which public memory is negotiated (Zelizer, 2004; Kitch, 2008). The coverage of the deaths of our public figures is perhaps most controversially played out in news and feature stories, but also less obviously within obituaries, which offer a formulaic and condensed version of a life story. Those who have examined obituaries historically (Starck, 2006) and their role in formulating a 'collective memory' (Fowler, 2007) concur that what their analysis can offer is socially insightful: '… obituaries can provide a valuable resource. An obituary distils the essence of a citizen's life, and because it is a commemoration as well as a life chronicle, it reflects what society values and wants to remember' (Kitch and Hume, 2008 p. 64).

Obituaries have a very particular structure when it comes to covering parent-child relationships. According to the linguist John Swales (2004 p. 86), a person's life is 'shrunk to an annotated node on the family genealogical tree' with a hierarchy to that detail that begins with the name of the deceased's partner, particularly if married (not always if unmarried), and is followed by the names of their children and grandchildren (Moses and Marelli, 2004 p. 125). Moses and Marelli (2004) demonstrate that an obituary reflects social norms and beliefs about not only death, but also concerning the principles by which lives are lived. What is of pertinence here is their consideration of how the parent-child relationship is mediated. They examine this using Brown and Yule's 'topic framework' (1983 p. 73) through a linguistic analysis of *New York Times* obituaries. These revealed that when children are mentioned, 'the intimacy of these relationships is usually adjectively modified', citing the example of a 'devoted mother' (Moses and Marelli, 2004 p. 127). Using the more generic work on obituaries as a starting point, we can draw on other disciplines to see the extent to which this differs when the subject is a musician. Elsewhere (Hearsum, 2012; 2013a; 2013b) I have demonstrated that musicians are treated differently to other professional groups,

THREE FACES OF MUSICAL MOTHERHOOD IN DEATH 121

and arguably unethically, when it comes to portraying their lives in an unbiased way. As an example of how extreme this biased reporting on musicians' deaths can be, I will examine briefly coverage of the death of Michael Jackson before considering female musicians.

Michael Jackson

The Guardian's obituary of Michael Jackson (Sullivan, 2009), following his death from an overdose of prescription drugs on 25 July 2009, uses adjectives around family relationships to create its own 'psychological autopsy' (Hearsum and Duffett, 2015). Accolades are, often in the same sentence, followed by a negative point. Jackson is crowned the 'King of Pop' but this was 'overshadowed by his private life'. He is described as 'music royalty – one of its biggest stars', but whose 'bizarre life-style and personal notoriety eclipsed his talent and his numerous achievements' (Sullivan, 2009).

Sullivan attributes Jackson's psychological profile to his family upbringing, describing how '[a] combination of dysfunctional family and invasive fame ate away at the essentially private singer' (Sullivan, 2009). His relationship with Debbie Rowe is framed as a conduit for producing children: '[h]is second marriage, to his dermatologist's nurse, Debbie Rowe, in 1996, was equally perplexing to everyone but the couple themselves. They seemed to spend little time together, but Rowe produced his first two children ... They divorced in 1999' (Sullivan, 2009). Sullivan goes on to discuss Jackson's third child and questions his genetic linkage to all three children:

> A third child, Prince Michael II, was born with the aid of a surrogate mother. Despite Jackson's great affinity with children, his behaviour with his own was eccentric. He forced them to wear masks or veils whenever they appeared in public ... A few photos exist of the children without their cover-ups, and their lack of a physical resemblance to Jackson is marked. (Sullivan, 2009)

A visual cue on how to remember an artist is generally provided through the choice of a large image that accompanies the obituary. In the online version of Jackson's obituary, a photo of the singer with his chimpanzee Bubbles has been chosen rather than the typical portrait of the person alone, suggesting the most important relationship in Jackson's life was with his pet.

These selective features demonstrate clearly that including children within journalistic texts is a symbolic device whereby children become 'the ultimate rhetorical gesture' (Kitch and Hume, 2008 p. 168). In the case of Jackson, they are used to emphasise his *difference* and strangeness that had already become the focus of coverage of him, even before his death.[1] Furthermore, references to

---

[1] See Fast's chapter in this volume.

122   *DEATH AND THE ROCK STAR*

children in obituaries signal abandonment by parents in life, and even more so when the parents' death may have been avoided. When a star is seen as having had their life cut short because of their choice to live a 'rock 'n' roll lifestyle', their deviations from the expected role of respectable parent can become even more sensational news.

Whitney Houston

Whitney Houston was a pop and soul diva from the USA who had a long-lasting, successful career until vocal problems and substance abuse led to a decline in her ability to perform and record. She accidentally drowned in a hotel bath tub, and was found to have a number of legal and illegal drugs in her system that contributed to her death.[2]

Houston's obituaries contextualise her as a mother within a 'tempestuous' relationship with Bobby Brown in at least three examples. Firstly, *The Times* (Anon., 2012b) framed her daughter's birth in relation to her own increasing addiction, which was attributed to Brown's proximity. Secondly, *The Telegraph* (Anon., 2012a) described her addiction as a 'demon' and discussed the dissolution of her marriage. Thirdly, *The Independent* (Sturges, 2012) picks up on the violence of the relationship, including during her pregnancy. All three are the antithesis of the way motherhood is currently configured in mainstream media as being about achieving happiness in work and being responsible for and to a child – 'having it all'. What might be considered aspirational has varied but this, as Kawash (2011) suggests, makes it all the more pertinent that 'feminist studies ought to be placing [understanding motherhood] front and center' (Kawash, 2011 p. 970). The construction of parenthood in these examples is contextualised within Houston's drug use, and reproduced elsewhere as Céline Dion's reaction to Houston's death typifies:

> When you think about Elvis Presley and Marilyn Monroe and Michael Jackson and Amy Winehouse, to get into drugs like that … Is it because of the stress and bad influence? What happens when you have everything? What happens when you have love, support, the family, motherhood? You have responsibilities of a mother and then something happens and it destroys everything. (In Wardrop and O'Hare, 2012)

In celebrity culture, the media spotlight turns on the children after their parents' deaths. Indeed, Oprah Winfrey has interviewed both Jackson and Houston's children since their parents' deaths (the former within 18 months, and Houston's daughter a month after her mother died). The metaphorical (and actual) unveiling of Jackson's children both at the media spectacle of his funeral and since (Michaels, 2010),

---

[2]   See Taylor Cole Miller's chapter in this volume.

or even the ways in which the children of the Beatles have stirred media interest in recreating another 'Fab Four' a generation on (Michaels, 2012), are examples of meeting an audience's ongoing desire for connection and continuation of a musical narrative, albeit genetic, with a musical star, after death. Certainly, it is an emotionally charged imperative that Bobbi Kristina Brown, Houston's daughter, voiced in a televised interview with Winfrey: 'I have to carry on the legacy', she said. This comment was much re-quoted in the press coverage of the show through the Press Association syndication (Anon., 2012d), and forms part of the integrated and complex media tapestry that multi-media audiences navigate as they build non-linear understandings of details around a musician's death.

However, few obituaries picked up on Houston's relationship with Nick Gordon, who had lived with her since he was 12, and whom she had acted as a mother towards although never officially adopted (suggesting a hierarchy of parenting). The story did not become common knowledge in the press until Gordon and Houston's biological daughter became romantically involved.

Amy Winehouse

Amy Winehouse was an acclaimed UK rock and soul singer who courted controversy (and gained much publicity) during her life due to her substance abuse, her problematic relationship with her husband and her involvement in a string of violent incidents. She died of alcohol poisoning on 23 July 2011. The theme of adoption and parenting also clearly emerged during the coverage of Winehouse's death in negative and unethical ways lacking any empathy. On 31 July 2011, eight days after her death, *The Mirror* printed the story that Amy Winehouse was planning to adopt a 10-year-old girl, Dannika Augustine, from St Lucia (Anon., 2011a). This story was then picked up in *The Independent* (Anon., 2011b) and *The Metro* (Shah, 2011) in the UK, and spread overseas. In these, the adjective 'troubled' was regularly employed to describe and simplify the behaviour of the singer. Simultaneously, the possibility of motherhood also implied that a transformation was underway, as Winehouse 'had started the process of becoming a mum' (Anon., 2011a). The adoption story, mainly circulated online, was dismissed as untrue within five hours of going live, for instance on the *OK!* website (Hearsum, 2012 p. 187), suggesting it was a fabrication to drive traffic by drawing on a celebrity adoption Zeitgeist (Selman, 2007 p. 32).

Readers potentially take with them wider prior knowledge when consuming the obituary text – a longer narrative arc on which they understand a musician's death. With Winehouse, this may include recollections of her publically articulated wish for a family. In 2008, in a story that covered the news that her husband, Blake Fielder-Civil, had just been sentenced for assault, and which noted that the singer was 'troubled' as well as 'battling a well-publicised addiction to crack cocaine', Winehouse was quoted as saying 'Blake and I can't wait to have kids. I want at least five kids' (Singh, 2008). This was greeted with derision by the press both at the time and in the coverage of her death. Immediately after that interview, in a manner verging on tabloid, *The Times* mocked: 'Not to give you nightmares, but Amy Winehouse has told *OK!* that she and her jail-bird husband cannot wait to have children' (Sherwin, 2008 p. 14). Similarly, an interview from a year later was reused in her obituary in *The Telegraph*, in a section that is traditionally judgement-free but here takes a starkly condemnatory tone:

> Pathetically, Amy Winehouse's hopes for her life with Blake Fielder-Civil seemed touchingly conventional and domestic. 'I've always been a little homemaker', she told an interviewer. 'I know I'm talented, but I wasn't put here to sing. I was put here to be a wife and a mum and to look after my family'. (Anon., 2011c)

In Winehouse's obituaries, *The Independent* encased her desire for children within the context of her marrying Fielder-Civil, which framed marriage as a stable ideal in which to 'settle down'. While obituaries would normally state marital and parental status, it is unusual for a 27-year-old subject. However, for musicians, as part of celebrity culture, noting the status of children (whether they have them or not) is structural fodder, particularly for women, and heightened in the light of the recent vogue of celebrity adoption. Male musicians who have died at the same age but have not had children have not received the same treatment.

Donna Summer

Donna Summer was best known as the vocalist on a number of disco hits in the 1970s (for example, 'I Feel Love', 1977). She died of lung cancer – which she believed was caused by inhaling fumes from the 9/11 attacks – on 17 May 2012 (Hughes and Hough, 2012). Summer was the female singer most positively cast in the sampled obituaries. Her illness was used to demonstrate her close-knit family life, as typified by quotes like this: 'she was diagnosed with cancer 10 months ago and only told her husband and three children' (Daily Mail Reporter, 2012). The restrictive adverb 'only' implies her closeness to her family, and rejects the possibility that she was 'troubled', unlike Houston and Winehouse. What did appear popular to report was the paternal lineage of her three daughters. *The Guardian* and the BBC Online were typical in mentioning that of her three daughters, two were from her current marriage and the eldest, Mimi, from her previous marriage. *The Guardian* noted Summer's divorce date (Sweeting, 2012) and the BBC Online (2012) the brevity of her first marriage. However, the cause of her death (lung cancer) rather than death through misadventure from alcohol poisoning (Winehouse), or accidental drowning with atherosclerotic heart disease and cocaine use as factors (Houston), allowed Summer to be portrayed as putting her role as mother and grandmother first: 'Bringing up her children lowered Donna Summer's professional profile, because she was determined to spend time

THREE FACES OF MUSICAL MOTHERHOOD IN DEATH   125

at home; and in 1994 the family moved from Los Angeles to Nashville, where Donna built up a subsidiary reputation as an artist whose work was shown at exhibitions throughout the world' (Anon., 2012c).

Summer's past negative media coverage (relating, for example, to previous substance abuse or homophobic comments allegedly made by her) disappeared from the visible ether as if a media absolution had been granted. Summer's death saw the press – tabloid, mid-market and quality alike – crown her the 'Queen of Disco' (Cramb, 2012; Daily Mail Reporter, 2012; Samson and White, 2012).

Discourses of Motherhood

What emerges from the coverage of these three musicians, and the way motherhood is made central to discussions of their death, is that obituaries and the coverage of death are places where ideas about what constitutes 'good' and 'bad' motherhood are reinforced. These ideas are closely connected to the manner of death and the perceived 'selfishness' or 'selflessness' of the deceased. Houston's manner of dying, for example, is framed as a selfish action – the linguistic converse of the 'selfless' mother. 'Accidental drowning' might be seen as a tragedy but when it was the result of cocaine use, readers are positioned to see it as a choice made by Houston. This binary opposition between 'selfish' and 'selfless' is a discourse which, Johnston and Swanson (2003) argue, forces women into a 'double bind' to define themselves in terms of their roles as mothers (Johnston and Swanson, 2003 p. 243). Johnston and Swanson's content analysis of the representation of mothers in magazines echoes Moses and Marelli's point (2004, p. 253) that mothers are 'relationally defined through servicing others' (see also Cobb, 2008). When Houston's daughter was hospitalised the day following her mother's death, in a much understandable state of grief, obituaries implied that Houston was to blame for her reckless behaviour resulting in her death (Cockerton, 2012).

Similarly, it appears that the theme of 'self-destruct[ion]' (Boshoff, 2012) evidenced with Winehouse (Palmer, 2011) is played out noticeably more strongly with women than men in the music industry, especially in cases where individuals had either taken their own lives or died through reckless behaviour. Moreover, in her examination of the gendering of suicide representations, carried out by comparing the obituaries of Michael Hutchence and Paula Yates, Jaworski (2008) concluded that 'being a parent ... appear[ed] to matter more in the case of Paula Yates' (Jaworski, 2008 p. 782). Yates fell from grace, from being the first 'celebrity yummy mummy' (Hardyment, 1983 p. 302) to carrying out the worst offence of motherhood – willingly abandoning her children. In the case of Winehouse, this condemnation extends even to potential future children (in combination with relief at the avoidance of such a fate for these hypothetical offspring).

This needs to be considered in a context where the ideological pressure to present oneself as a 'yummy mummy' 'through language of self-perfectibility'

(McRobbie, 2006) has been increasing for female celebrities. In discussing the American actress Sarah Jessica Parker, Deborah Jermyn (2006 p. 77) suggests that stability in a female celebrity's life is equated with 'domesticity, femininity and motherhood', as opposed to a party lifestyle often equated with the music industry cliché of 'sex and drugs and rock 'n' roll'. For those female musicians who embraced the 'rock 'n' roll' life of excess, including Winehouse and Houston, their demise was visually documented in a formulaic succession of 'before and after' pictures both during their lifetimes and as re-runs in the press afterwards. For instance, within the same issue of *The Telegraph*, images of Whitney Houston accompanying her obituary were two non-contentious portraits, one colour image of her singing and the other a black and white head shot of a scene from *The Bodyguard* (Anon., 2012a p. 35). A news feature in the same issue included a more sensational image taken of the singer leaving the Tru nightclub in Hollywood a little worse for wear, two days before her death (McCormick, 2012 pp. 16–17). The contrasting images visually signal the musician's moral failings and signal an inevitable ending.

A spectrum of acceptability in motherhood becomes more apparent when the coverage of those who have died through reckless behaviour is contrasted with the treatment of famous mothers whose deaths are seen as 'not being their fault', and that are framed more in line with the 'good', selfless mother stereotype. This includes Donna Summer, or others who have died as a result of an accident (for example, Kirsty MacColl or Princess Diana [Kitch, 2000 p. 180]). These labels of 'good' and 'bad' mother are, however, not static. Indeed, Nunn and Biressi (2010) have shown that in the coverage of controversial UK celebrity Jade Goody, the reality series that followed her dying and eventual death from cancer carefully showcased her role as a 'working mum'. This, they argued, amounted to a 'media rehabilitation' in which '… she was now sanctioned on behalf of her children's future to be lavishly reimbursed for her final media work with her domestic role as mother and her public role as celebrity finally and neatly fused' (Nunn and Biressi, 2010 p. 51).

With this, the furore of her 2008 racially controversial comments about Indian actress Shilpa Shetty diminished in the coverage of her death and dying. Being a mother was accented as 'primary' in Goody's life (Holmes, 2009 p. 12), and she was cast as a 'devoted mother' in her dying and death (Kavka and West, 2010 p. 217). Walter (2011) argued that when children are part of the picture in the coverage of the death of a famous person, the mediation of their loss is inextricably bound up with religious symbols. For instance, his analysis of online mourning for Goody reveals that the children become 'angels' (Walter, 2011 p. 38). This is juxtaposed with the stereotypes available for women to fall into, which Goc (2007) suggests can either be monsters or Madonnas. This is a paradigmatic set of representations 'from the idealised to the demonised' (Goc, 2007 p. 160), as old as the mythology of Medea and revitalised by the mediated rise in celebrity motherhood.

Conclusion and Future Research

This chapter has shown that the dominant discourse in UK obituaries of female musicians overtly values women's gendered role to procreate, thus upholding a particular parenting style. The case studies offer three faces of motherhood: the good mother (Summer as the role model), the bad mother (Houston as the type to avoid) and the ugly mother (Winehouse – where even the thought of her being a mother seems abhorrent).

In her cross-cultural content analysis of gender in obituaries, Eid (2002) argues that this form of journalism represents the values of the social context in which it is written (Eid, 2002 p. 14). In addition to the mothering tropes discussed above, analysing the articles also exposed lapses in standard broadsheet protocol. For instance, *The Telegraph* used first names as opposed to surnames only or full names, particularly for Amy Winehouse. This slight variation, more typically used by tabloids or the music press which tended to draw on first names more positively to claim Winehouse as part of their community, is used by the broadsheets with a belittling and gendered tendency, which was absent, for instance, in the press treatment of Michael Jackson.

The challenge for journalistic practice is two-fold: to recognise where there has been problematic reporting and to seek ways to circumvent it in the future. Indeed, recognition of poor practice on what went so 'very badly wrong' with the coverage of Winehouse's death led to *The Guardian* offering, with some sarcasm aimed primarily at tabloid and mid-market journalism, seven tips as a 'handy guide' for 'what not to do when a celebrity you've been tormenting for years dies' (Freedman, 2011). In considering the coverage of Michael Jackson's death, Niles (2009) calls for production processes to be tightened up whereby 'Twitterstorms' might be acknowledged as rumour until confirmation is clear. This goes some way towards implementing measures to limit dissemination of inaccurate information. It was interesting to note a correction added to *The Guardian*'s obituary of Amy Winehouse, four days after publication, which changed the term 'fellow junkie' to 'addict' when discussing Pete Doherty in relationship to the singer in its online format (Sullivan, 2011). A year after Winehouse's death, in collaboration with the Society of Editors, the UK Drug Policy Commission published guidance for journalists in order to avoid the term 'junkie' altogether (Society of Editors and UKDPC, 2012). The guidance acknowledges the positive role the media can play in increasing public awareness and support for drug users. It argues that the term 'junkie' discourages rehabilitation because it reinforces the stigma of addiction and does not separate the person from the condition; instead, they suggest the phrase 'dependent drug user' (2012 p. 38).

However, we need to be mindful of the changing media landscape, having ascertained that we acquire our knowledge of a famous person's death through intertextual mediated information before reading an obituary. Increasingly, the functions of obituaries, news and features blur both in production and consumption. This shift means that approaches such as Eid's, which looks at the amount of coverage of women's deaths in mainstream media, may be less relevant. Online users set preferences and can personalise news delivery in a way that earlier obituary studies have yet to consider.

These changes are important because celebrity deaths are the focus of much discussion in social media. For example, Cashmoore (2009) noted that the phrase 'Michael Jackson' led 22 per cent of worldwide Twitter traffic on the day he died, with another 8 per cent having variations. The weekend that Winehouse's death was announced, 10 per cent of all Twitter users (20 million users worldwide) were discussing her death (Verrico, 2011 p. 2). These statistics buck the trend in Death Studies, which, for at least 50 years, have noted a decline in public grieving with concerns that this was impeding the psychological healing process of mourning. In his classic text, *Death, Grief, and Mourning in Contemporary Britain*, Geoffrey Gorer (1965) argued that we should grieve for our own social good, and yet death has been sequestered according to Anthony Giddens (1991 p.161) as it is '… routinely hidden from view … removed into the hands of the medical profession'. More recently, Margaret Gibson (2007) has noted the irony that despite this, death has become very visible in the media in so far as it has become a 'narrative force' (Gibson, 2007 p. 416). This has had an impact on how death is experienced, and how it is reported. In the media, professional contemporary journalists are now expected to give an aggregation of the tweets of the public as well as the famous (just as they used to take public and celebrity reactions in traditional media). The contemporary social media requires performative practice of other celebrities to disseminate their condolences, opinions and reactions to the death of another celebrity through outlets such as Twitter. Page (2012) demonstrates that one's reaction on Twitter allows the tweeter to become as visible as the person they comment on, amounting to the cultural commodification of the 'reaction'.

In addition, it would enrich this research area to consider some missing layers of analysis particularly around social media and user interactivity, a process I have elsewhere termed 'socialcasting' (Hearsum, 2013b). The old 'broadcast' and even 'narrowcasting' models of journalism are both now shaped by, and reflect, the interactive nature and impact of social media. For Winehouse, the re-circulation of the adoption story was propelled with speed via social media rather than traditional media forms. The possibility to re-tweet and post on Facebook, offered by *OK!*'s website, led to the story being picked up by news agencies. The printed press which used those syndicated stories was unable to retract once it had been printed and distributed, unlike the online media outlets. Content that 'triggers emotions' is more likely to be shared (Stieglitz and Dang-Xuan, 2013 p. 219), so when this happens through a magazine and accompanying website whose core demographic is women, then women themselves play an active role in re-circulating these stereotypes of motherhood and perpetuate accompanying discourses.

While academics of new media have considered how technologies have impacted journalism in terms of accelerated speed, there has been little academic examination of significant differences between *what* is being said and *how* it is being said. For Winehouse, rather than the story, the conversations about her and what

THREE FACES OF MUSICAL MOTHERHOOD IN DEATH

her potential motherhood evoked in the public were represented with a desiccation of social compassion through the displaying of mere impressions of grief. It is time to build on the grounding work of linguists such as Page (2012) whose combing of Twitter hashtags and folksonomies (a classification of online content) examines social and economic hierarchies, and is undertaken with a feminist narratological approach. Indeed, probing the ever-expanding media requires, as this analysis of three women singers demonstrates, a variety of interdisciplinary tools in order to truly offer an insight into the cultural construction of journalistic texts.

Bibliography

Anonymous (2011a) 'Amy Winehouse was Adopting Girl of 10', *The Mirror*, 31 July, www.mirror.co.uk/3am/celebrity-news/amy-winehouse-was-adopting-girl-of-10-184082, accessed 2 August 2014.

Anonymous (2011b) 'Amy Winehouse Planned to Adopt', *The Independent*, 1 August, www.independent.co.uk/news/people/news/amy-winehouse-planned-to-adopt-2329891.html, accessed 2 August 2014.

Anonymous (2011c) 'Amy Winehouse Obituary', *The Telegraph*, 23 July, www.telegraph.co.uk/news/obituaries/culture-obituaries/tv-radio-obituaries/8657048/Amy-Winehouse.html, accessed 2 August 2014.

Anonymous (2012a) 'Whitney Houston', *The Telegraph*, 12 February, www.telegraph.co.uk/news/obituaries/culture-obituaries/music-obituaries/9077348/Whitney-Houston.html, accessed 2 August 2014.

Anonymous (2012b) 'Whitney Houston', *The Times*, 13 February, p. 50.

Anonymous (2012c) 'Donna Summer', *The Telegraph*, 17 May, www.telegraph.co.uk/news/obituaries/culture-obituaries/music-obituaries/9273393/Donna-Summer.html, accessed 2 August 2014.

Anonymous (2012d) 'Bobbi Kristina Brown Tells Oprah Winfrey: Whitney Houston was "My Everything"', *The Independent*, 12 March, www.independent.co.uk/news/people/news/bobbi-kristina-brown-tells-oprah-winfrey-whitney-houston-was-my-everything-7562581.html, accessed 2 August 2014.

BBC Online (2012) 'Obituary: Donna Summer', 17 May, www.bbc.co.uk/news/entertainment-arts-18108052, accessed 2 August 2014.

Boshoff, Alison (2012) 'Doomed to Self-destruct: No One Could Save Whitney Houston as She Blew £100 million and Sought Oblivion in Crack Cocaine', *The Daily Mail*, 13 February, www.dailymail.co.uk/femail/article-2100280/Whitney-Houstons-cause-death-Singer-sought-oblivion-crack-cocaine.html, accessed 2 August 2014.

Brown, Gillian and George Yule (1983) *Discourse Analysis*. Cambridge: Cambridge University Press.

Cashmoore, Pete (2009) 'Michael Jackson Dies: Twitter Tributes Now 30% of Tweets', *Mashable*, mashable.com/2009/06/25/michael-jackson-twitter/, accessed 2 August 2014.

Cobb, Shelley (2008) 'Mother of the Year: Kathy Hilton, Lynne Spears, Dina Lohan and Bad Celebrity Motherhood', *Genders*, 48, www.genders.org/g48/g48_cobb.html, accessed 2 August 2014.

Cockerton, Paul (2012) 'Whitney Houston's Daughter Rushed to Hospital from Same Hotel Where her Mum Died', *The Mirror*, 12 February, www.mirror.co.uk/3am/celebrity-news/whitney-houstons-daughter-bobbi-kristina-682500, accessed 2 August 2014.

Cramb, Gordon (2012) 'Disco Queen Donna Summer Dies, 63', *Financial Times*, 17 May, www.ft.com/cms/s/0/b8f579b4-a040-11e1-88e6-00144feabdc0.html#axzz1xaKAvnd5, accessed 2 August 2014.

Daily Mail Reporter (2012) 'Donna Summer, Queen of Disco, Dead at 63 after Secret Cancer Battle', *Daily Mail*, 17 May, www.dailymail.co.uk/tvshowbiz/article-2145891/Donna-Summer-dead-Queen-Disco-dies-63-cancer-battle.html, accessed 2 August 2014.

Eid, Mushira (2002) *The World of Obituaries: Gender across Cultures and over Time*. Detroit, MI: Wayne State University Press.

Fowler, Bridget (2007) *The Obituary as Collective Memory*. New York and Oxon: Routledge.

Freedman, Hadley (2011) 'Amy Winehouse's Death was Badly Reported', *The Guardian*, 26 July, www.guardian.co.uk/commentisfree/2011/jul/26/amy-winehouse-death-badly-reported, accessed 2 August 2014.

Gibson, Margaret (2007) 'Death and Mourning in Technologically Mediated Culture', *Health Sociology Review*, 16 (5), pp. 415–24.

Giddens, Anthony (1991) *Modernity and Self-Identity: Self and Society in the Late Modern Age*. Stanford, CA: Stanford University Press.

Goc, Nicola (2007) 'Monstrous Mothers and the Media', in Nial Scott (ed.), *Monsters and the Monstrous*. Oxford: Media Inter-Disciplinary Press, pp. 149–65.

Gorer, Geoffrey (1965) *Death, Grief, and Mourning in Contemporary Britain*. London: Cresset Press.

Hardyment, Christina (1983) *Dream Babies: Childcare Advice from John Locke to Gina Ford*. London: Jonathan Cape.

Hearsum, Paula (2012) 'A Musical Matter of Life and Death: The Morality of Mortality and the Coverage of Amy Winehouse's Death in the UK Press', *Mortality*, 17 (2), pp. 181–99.

——— (2013a) 'Zappa and Mortality: The Mediation of Zappa's Death', in Paul Carr (ed.), *Zappa and the And: A Contextual Analysis of his Legacy*. Aldershot: Ashgate, pp. 201–16.

——— (2013b) 'Sex and Drugs and Rock and Roll Deaths: How Media Coverage of Musical Celebrities' Deaths Reflects Social Values', 2 May, Child Bereavement Network Conference: Cultures of Grief: Bereavement in Young People's Worlds. http://cbn2013.eventbrite.co.uk/, accessed 4 May 2015.

Hearsum, Paula and Mark Duffett (2015) 'Re-imagining Richey: Celebrity Disappearance, Manic Street Preacher Fandom and Ben Myer's Richard', *Volume! The French Journal of Popular Music Studies* (forthcoming).

THREE FACES OF MUSICAL MOTHERHOOD IN DEATH 131

Holmes, Su (2009) '"Jade's Back, and this Time She's Famous": Narratives of Celebrity in the Celebrity Big Brother "Race" Row', *Entertainment and Sports Law Journal*, 7 (1), http://go.warwick.ac.uk/eslj/issues/volume7/number1/holmes/, accessed 2 August 2014.

Hughes, Mark and Andrew Hough (2012) '"Queen of Disco" Donna Summer "Thought She Became Ill after Inhaling 9/11 Particles"', *The Telegraph*, 17 May, http://www.telegraph.co.uk/news/celebritynews/9273396/Queen-of-Disco-Donna-Summer-thought-she-became-ill-after-inhaling-911-particles.html, accessed 2 August 2014.

Jaworski, Katrina (2008) 'Elegantly Wasted: The Celebrity Deaths of Michael Hutchence and Paula Yates', *Continuum: Journal of Media and Cultural Studies*, 22 (6), pp. 777–91.

Jermyn, Deborah (2006) 'Bringing Out the ★ in You: SJP, Carrie Bradshaw and the Evolution of Television Stardom', in Su Holmes and Sean Redmond (eds), *Framing Celebrity: New Directions in Celebrity Culture*. London: Routledge, pp. 96–117.

Johnston, Deirdre and Debra Swanson (2003) 'Undermining Mothers: A Content Analysis of the Representation of Mothers in Magazines', *Mass Communication and Society*, 6 (3), pp. 243–65.

Kastenbaum, Robert, Sara Peyton and Beatrice Kastenbaum (1977) 'Sex Discrimination after Death', *Omega: The Journal of Death and Dying*, 7 (4), pp. 351–59.

Kawash, Samira (2011) 'New Directions in Motherhood Studies', *Signs*, 26 (4), pp. 969–1003.

Kavka, Musga and Amy West (2010) 'Jade the Obscure: Celebrity Death and the Mediatised Maiden', *Celebrity Studies*, 1 (2), pp. 216–30.

Kitch, Carolyn (2000) 'A News of Feeling as Well as Fact: Mourning and Memorial in American News Magazines', *Journalism*, 1 (2), pp. 171–95.

——— (2008) 'Placing Journalism Inside Memory – and Memory Studies', *Memory Studies*, 1 (3), pp. 311–20.

Kitch, Carolyn and Janice Hume (2008) *Journalism in a Culture of Grief*. New York and Abingdon: Routledge.

McCormick, Neil (2012) 'The Soul Sweetheart Destroyed by Drugs', *The Telegraph*, 13 February, pp. 16–17.

McRobbie, Angela (2006) 'Yummy Mummies Leave a Bad Taste for Young Women', *The Guardian*, 2 March, www.guardian.co.uk/world/2006/mar/02/gender.comment, accessed 2 August 2014.

Michaels, Sean (2010) 'Michael Jackson's Family Open up on Oprah', *The Guardian*, 9 November, www.guardian.co.uk/music/2010/nov/09/michael-jackson-family-oprah?INTCMP=SRCH, accessed 2 August 2014.

——— (2012) 'Beatles – the Next Generation a Genuine Possibility, says McCartney', *The Guardian*, 4 April, www.guardian.co.uk/music/2012/apr/04/beatles-next-generation-possibility-mccartney, accessed 2 August 2014.

Moore, Stephen (2002) 'Disinterring Ideology from a Corpus of Obituaries: A Critical Post Mortem', *Discourse and Society*, 13 (4), pp. 495–536.

Moses, Rae and Giana Marelli (2004) 'Obituaries and the Discursive Construction of Dying and Living', *Texas Linguistic Forum*, 47, pp. 123–30.

Negra, Diane and Su Holmes (2008) 'Introduction', *Genders*, 48, www.genders.org/g48/g48_negraholmes.html, accessed 2 August 2014.

Niles, Robert (2009) 'Michael Jackson's Death and its Lessons for Online Journalists Covering Breaking News', *The Online Journalism Review*, 25 June, www.ojr.org/michael-jacksons-death-and-its-lessons-for-online-journalists-covering-breaking-news/, accessed 2 August 2014.

Nunn, Heather and Anita Biressi (2010) 'A Trust Betrayed: Celebrity and the Work of Emotion', *Celebrity Studies*, 1 (1), pp. 49–64.

Page, Ruth (2012) 'The Linguistics of Self-branding and Micro-celebrity in Twitter: The Role of Hashtags', *Discourse and Communication*, 6 (2), pp. 181–201.

Palmer, Alun (2011) 'Amy Winehouse – A Talent Dogged by Self Destruction', *The Mirror*, 25 July, www.mirror.co.uk/3am/celebrity-news/amy-winehouse---a-talent-dogged-143812, accessed 2 August 2014.

Samson, Pete and Richard White (2012) '9/11 Dust Kills Donna Summer: Disco Queen Blamed Lung Cancer on Twin Towers Poison Cloud', *The Sun*, 18 May, www.thesun.co.uk/sol/homepage/news/4323815/911-dust-kills-disco-queen-Donna-Summer.html, accessed 2 August 2014.

Selman, Peter (2007) 'The Diaper Diaspora', *Foreign Policy*, 158, pp. 32–3.

Shah, Kavi (2011) 'Was Amy Winehouse Planning to Adopt a 10-year-old Girl?' *The Metro*, 31 July, www.metro.co.uk/showbiz/870917-was-amy-winehouse-planning-to-adopt-a-10-year-old-girl, accessed 2 August 2014.

Sherwin, Adam (2008) 'Amy Winehouse: Postscript', *The Times*, 23 July, p. 14.

Singh, Anita (2008) 'Amy Winehouse: I Want Five Kids and to Appear on Countdown', *The Telegraph*, 28 July, www.telegraph.co.uk/news/celebritynews/2446305/Amy-Winehouse-I-want-five-kids-and-to-appear-on-Countdown.html, accessed 2 August 2014.

Society of Editors and UKDPC (2012) 'Dealing with the Stigma of Drugs: A Guide for Journalists', www.ukdpc.org.uk/wp-content/uploads/dealing-with-the-stigma-of-drugs.pdf, accessed 2 August 2014.

Starck, Nigel (2006) *Life after Death: The Art of the Obituary*. Melbourne: Melbourne University Press.

Stieglitz, Stefan and Linh Dang-Xuan (2013) 'Emotions and Information Diffusion in Social Media-Sentiment of Microblogs and Sharing Behavior', *Journal of Management Information Systems*, 29 (4), pp. 217–48.

Sturges, Fiona (2012) 'Whitney Houston: Singer and Actress whose Talent was Overshadowed by Addiction', *The Independent*, 13 February, www.independent.co.uk/news/obituaries/whitney-houston-singer-and-actress-whose-talent-was-overshadowed-by-addiction-6804670.html, accessed 2 August 2014.

Sullivan, Caroline (2009) 'Michael Jackson', *The Guardian*, 26 June, http://www.theguardian.com/music/2009/jun/26/michael-jackson-obituary, accessed 5 May 2015.

——— (2011) 'Amy Winehouse Obituary', *The Guardian*, 23 July, www.guardian. co.uk/music/2011/jul/23/amy-winehouse-obituary, accessed 2 August 2014.

Swales, John (2004) *Research Genres: Explorations and Applications*. New York: Cambridge University Press.

Sweeting, Adam (2012) 'Donna Summer Obituary', *The Guardian*, 17 May, www. guardian.co.uk/music/2012/may/17/donna-summer, accessed 2 August 2014.

Verrico, Lisa (2011) 'One Demon too Many', *Sunday Times: News Review*, 31 July, pp. 1–2.

Walter, Tony (2011) 'Angels not Souls: Popular Religion in the Online Mourning for British Celebrity Jade Goody', *Religion*, 41 (1), pp. 29–51.

Wardrop, Murray and Sean O'Hare (2012) 'Whitney Houston: Latest Reaction', *The Telegraph*, 13 February, www.telegraph.co.uk/culture/music/music-news/9077464/Whitney-Houston-latest-reaction-live.html, accessed 2 August 2014.

Zelizer, Barbie (2004) *Taking Journalism Seriously: News and the Academy*. Thousand Oaks, CA and London: Sage.

Chapter 10
En'shrine'd: Ushering Fela Kuti into the Western 'Rock' Canon

Abigail Gardner

Fela Anikulapo-Kuti was a fearless maverick for whom music was a righteous and invincible weapon. His self-given second name, Anikulapo – which translates as 'the one who carries death in his pouch' – spoke of indestructibility and resistance. It was an apt choice for the creator of an amazingly timeless body of work that for decades has transcended barriers of class and nationality, gathering ever more strength and devotees with the passing decades. Fela was indeed a man who seems always to have been destined for the almost mythical status he has now claimed among music fans around the world.

Busby, quoted in Moore (2010 p. 9)

In the above quote, Margaret Busby, a writer, broadcaster and the UK's first black female publisher, neatly encapsulates the key themes with which this chapter engages: Fela Kuti's threat, his defiance of death itself and his legacy. Kuti's iconographical status and political impact have largely been silenced in the processes of canonisation through exhibition, representation and memorialisation, and are overshadowed by representations of excess and sexuality that are commensurate with worn yet still dominant stereotypes of African men (Hall, 1997; Gilroy, 2004; Leonard, 2007), and mythologies of the rock star (Reynolds and Press, 1995; Rojek, 2001).

Kuti (1939–1997) was a Nigerian musician and the lead exponent of Afrobeat, a term he coined to refer to a style of music that mixed Yoruba call-and-response style vocals, jazz and funk. From 1969 to 1997, he produced nearly 50 albums and toured Europe and the United States, where his first album (*The '69 Los Angeles Sessions*) was recorded. He used his music to critique the Nigerian authorities, for whom he was a formidable and outspoken opponent. He recorded and performed much of this music in a club called The Shrine, which was part of a self-declared 'Republic' that he set up in Lagos in defiance of the Nigerian military regime of the late 1970s. He died in 1997 aged 58, precipitating many obituaries that dwelled on his political rebellion and musical legacy. In these accounts and in what I consider to be his memorialisation through exhibitions and musicals, there is an attempt to configure him as African icon and/or Western rock star. By keeping close to the concept of the 'shrine', a place of collective religious communion, I draw out the

136   *DEATH AND THE ROCK STAR*

ways in which Kuti's posthumous legacy is predicated on two closely entwined discursive processes which I term containment and enshrinement.

This chapter is motivated by a desire to trace out such discursive strategies in order to address how they represent the posthumous Kuti. It engages with the erasing of threatening qualities in death through canonisation processes that simplify complexities, and in this respect benefits from recent work on museology and popular music that are questioning the relationships between institutions and lived musical experience (Leonard, 2007; 2010; 2013). The following personal reflections indicate why such work might be needed. Kuti played at the Brixton Academy in 1988 when mounted police herded the audience (of which I was a member) into the venue and police dogs rounded them up afterwards. The following year he confused my peers at Glastonbury, who, though wanting to dance, were vehement that his sexual politics prevented them from doing so. From these two instances, it appears that in addition to being a direct political threat to the Nigerian Government he was, in the late 1980s, a threat to both white British authority and the white middle-class Left for whom 'World Music' was an emerging scene. I last saw him in 2004 as part of the Barbican's exhibition *Black President: The Art and Legacy of Fela Kuti*, where his legacy was encased and ensured. It is this journey from threat to accolade within Western Anglo-American discourse that I want to travel, seeing in it a number of attempts to incorporate an unwieldy and problematic musical figure into conventional discursive parameters. In doing this, I sketch out two means by which Kuti's death has been discussed and what kinds of *presence* he has had since. To this end, the chapter is divided into two parts. The first considers Kuti's life in order to provide a context for understanding his politics and music. The second focuses on his posthumous presence by dealing with commemoration. It examines first obituaries in UK and US broadsheet papers and the rock press, all 'containing' Kuti within discourses that are reliant on the myth of the rock rebel. It then addresses three types of commemorative events across three continents: the UK exhibition *The Art and Legacy of Fela Kuti* at London's Barbican Centre (2004), the US musical *Fela!* (2008) and the Nigerian *Felabration* festival (1998 onwards). Through these examples, this chapter demonstrates that Kuti has been contained and enshrined in ways that make him accessible, and reduceable, to a Western rock canon.

Containment and Enshrinement

Containment is a commodifying technique that represents Kuti within discursive parameters particular to musical genre and race, generated within a Western regime of representation that has configured African male musicianship in specific ways (Grass, 1986; Olaniyan, 2001; Stanovsky, 1998). Kuti has been commodified, trafficked and depoliticised (Gilroy, 1993) to become representative of an African masculinity, which, allied to a hyper-sexuality, accords with conventions of the Western rock star and with colonial discourses of the black masculine

(Guilbault, 2006; Feld, 1996). These are traced out across rock press and broadsheet obituaries that prioritise Kuti's sexuality and excess as different or Other (Hall, 1997).

Enshrinement venerates by drawing on quasi-religious rhetoric. It refers to what I argue is the memorialising process of curating Kuti, both through exhibition and revival. It is sometimes an extension of containment or imbricated within it, since both are symptomatic of Western techniques of representation. Shrines are places of veneration, communion and devotion, of pilgrimage and sanctuary, lying outside the body politic. The Shrine in Lagos was such a place, a signifier of separateness (from the Nigerian State) and of devotion to, and communion with, Kuti. Understanding enshrinement also involves a discussion of how Kuti's music and his persona might be configured through the interplay between the human and the divine within Yoruba music and culture.

Yoruba culture is, like many other African cultures, one in which music has a primacy within both the spiritual and secular worlds, where 'music can be a bridge to the animating forces of nature or to the spirit world of the ancestors and the unborn, as well as to deities who influence the material world' (Grass, 1986 p. 131). Grass argues that Kuti's music was an extension of the African idea of music being related to 'both ordinary and extraordinary human activity'. Veal's ethnomusicological work notes this too, describing one of Kuti's night-long performances at The Shrine as follows:

> On stage Fela combines the autocratic band leading style of James Brown, the mystical inclinations of Sun Ra, the polemicism of Malcolm X and the harsh, insightful satire of Richard Prior. [He glides] gracefully around the stage in white face paint, which he says facilitates communication with the spirit world. (Veal, 2000 p. 4)

The interplay between these two realms allows us to envisage how Kuti lends himself to being enshrined, but also illustrates how perceptions of threat and elation in his live performance find themselves transformed in death.

Containment and enshrinement operate as curtailing and erasing processes. In the first, Kuti is somehow restricted in order to fit into prescribed containers that are conversant with Western readings of the rock rebel and the African icon. In the second, which is an extension of the first, his extraordinariness, excess and legendary status eclipse his voice. When an artist as musically influential as Kuti is circumscribed within these available models of mediation, this process suggests an ongoing paucity in the possibilities available for representation, as the following sections demonstrate.

Fela Kuti during his Lifetime

Kuti was born in 1939 into an elite Yoruba Nigerian family, the son of a Church of England minister, the Reverend Israel Ransome-Kuti, who was the first president of the Nigerian Union of Teachers, and of a mother, Funmilayo Ransome-Kuti, who was a leading women's rights and anti-colonial activist. He was sent to England to study medicine but went instead to the Trinity School of Music where he specialised in piano and trumpet. He formed his first band in 1961 (Koola Lobitos), which fused jazz with Ghanaian highlife (a musical genre from Ghana popular across West Africa), and worked on a music that became known as Afrobeat. This was characterised by a large brass section, steady bass lines, sax and Fender Rhodes solos over the top, call-and-response lyrics in 'pidgin' English. It was a fusion of musics that had travelled to and fro across the Atlantic and was distinctly 'his'. It is audible in the album *The '69 Los Angeles Sessions* with his band, now called Nigeria 70, where jazz idioms and funk baselines are shot through with the concerns that Kuti voiced about colonialism, African esteem and identity (Stanovsky, 1998).

Kuti was in the United States in the late 1960s when the Black Panther movement was at the height of its influence. In San Francisco, he met and worked with Sandra Smith, who was active in the Black Panther party and introduced him to James Brown and the music of Nina Simone and Miles Davis (Stanovsky, 1998; Lipsitz, 1994). It was his relationship with Smith that exposed Kuti to 'ideas about Pan-Africanism that had been censored in Nigeria' (Lipsitz, 1994 p. 39), arguably radicalising his politics and informing his musical direction. On his return to Lagos, he and his mother changed their middle name from 'Ransome' to the Yoruba 'Anikulapo' (which translates alternately as 'he who carries death in a bag/his pouch'). All accounts suggest that this move from the Anglicised 'Ransome' indicated a rejection of imposed slavery and colonialism and a shift to a Yoruba-identified Afrocentrism. The choice of 'Anikulapo' could be read as a statement of intent towards the overthrow of colonial legacy, and an indication of Kuti's politicisation and potential threat. He also established the 'Kalakuta Republic', a large compound in the outer suburbs of Lagos, which included The Shrine club. Kuti declared the Republic's independence from the rest of Nigeria in 1970. Around this time, his music started to reflect his growing dissatisfaction with the Nigerian political regime, setting the pattern for the remainder of his life; he was constantly in battle with the Nigerian authorities whom he saw as corrupt and elitist. Singing in 'pidgin', a mix of English and creole, enabled his work to travel out of Nigeria across Africa and beyond, widening his potential impact. In 1977, after the residents had been subject to many arrests and beatings from the Nigerian authorities, the Kalakuta Republic was burned down in a violent attack that saw his elderly mother being thrown out of a window, dying later of her injuries. Kuti took her coffin to General Olesugun Obasanjo's barracks, an event he described in the song 'Coffin for Head of State' (1980). He later wrote 'Unknown Soldier' (1981) in reference to the official enquiry that blamed an unknown soldier for the destruction of the compound.

Throughout his life, Kuti performed and was perceived as a sexual and political rebel. His personal life was political and his politics infused his music; in 1978, to mark the Kalakuta anniversary, he married 27 women at once, which Stanovsky (1998) claims was an affirmation of 'tribal culture'. He also released *Zombie*, an album that critiqued the Nigerian military rulers. While performing this album in Accra, Ghana, a riot broke out which resulted in him being banned from entering the country for life. In the same year he established his own political party called 'Movement for the People', and in 1979 put himself forward as a presidential candidate only to have his candidature rejected. Five years later, in 1984, he was jailed for 20 months on trumped up charges of currency smuggling, an incident that saw Amnesty International designating him a 'prisoner of conscience'. Despite international musical collaborations (with Ginger Baker, Gilberto Gil and Paul McCartney among others) he remained, for the Nigerian authorities, an outsider. After dying of an HIV-related illness at the age of 58 in 1997, 1 million people were estimated to have attended his funeral, in defiance of the Nigerian regime for whom he was, even in his coffin, a threat.

His role as rebel is marked, too, in the handful of YouTube clips of him, most poorly recorded (only one is professional, of the Berlin Jazz festival in 1978). He is dressed (in earlier performances from the 1970s) either in an all-in-one trouser suit, 'match-down' style, where the outfit is carefully co-ordinated, patterned or white; or (in later performances) in underpants, chains and white face paint. We might read him in the first as a *Shaft*-like, Blaxploitation figure that draws on 'standard currenc[ies] of black popular culture' (Hesmondhalgh, 2013 p. 82; Railton and Watson, 2011). This is similar to how some rap stars became cemented within Anglo-American popular culture, as inheritors of highly complex legacies linked to the street, crime and sex: the figures of the pimp, the hustler, the 'badman' (Quinn, 2005, cited in Hesmondhalgh, 2013 p. 82). In the second, where Kuti performs bare-chested and in slave chains, he is part of an ongoing discursive regime that fetishises race (Railton and Watson, 2011 p. 128).[1] Here, in a mimetic move, he appropriates the 'super masculine menial' (Cleaver, 1992 pp. 172–3), sending back the fetishising of the 'colonial fantasy' (Mercer, 1994 in Railton and Watson, 2011 p. 127) into an Anglo-American popular culture whose negotiations over colonialism, post-colonialism and diversity are ongoing (Gilroy, 2011). Kuti himself essentialised his blackness vocally, for instance by claiming on stage (Berlin Festival 1978) to be 'an African' presenting 'African music' to stupid Europeans. How he in turn has been presented after his death raises issues of representational strategies that are complex and, at times, conflicting.

Fela Kuti and World Music

This section discusses posthumous representations of Kuti. It begins with obituaries, which are inevitably the first to map out a posthumous identity and serve to benchmark subsequent representations. Stanovsky (1998) in particular notes

---

[1] See also Gina Arnold's discussion of Tupac Shakur's hologram at the Coachella festival, this volume.

140   *DEATH AND THE ROCK STAR*

that his sexual behaviour, perceived misogyny and polygamy have preoccupied mainstream US and UK newspaper obituaries.

Obituaries appeared in specialist US rock magazines (*Rolling Stone*) and UK and US broadsheet newspapers (*The Independent, The Telegraph, The New York Times*) addressed to a knowledgeable and niche audience. They prioritised, as do many online entries on Kuti, his excess and anarchy, both politically and personally: 'Fela (pronounced FAY-la) was a showy, insolent, marijuana-smoking icon, who often made appearances wearing only bikini underwear. In more than 30 years as a dissident songwriter and saxophonist, he was arrested and imprisoned at least a dozen times, most recently in 1993' (Herszenhorn, 1997). 'Fela, 58, Dissident Nigerian Musician, Dies ... the earliest and wildest of Africa's handful of world-famous popular singers' (Sweeney, 1997).

Sweeney's obituary from *The Independent* stays within a narrative that underlines Kuti's distinction, his ability to 'transfix', but also mentions Kuti's audience, whose diversity cut across race and genre, made up as it was of black British and Nigerian fans, not just white 'World Music enthusiasts'.

'World Music' is a shifting category, into which some writers and broadcasters corral Kuti and others do not. The term was established in Britain in 1987 by a group of music promoters and DJs who saw its potential as a genre offering a flight from 'manufactured' 1980s pop for those who sought 'authenticity' (Taylor, 1997). The *New Musical Express* (*NME*) offered a free *The World at One* tape in its October 1987 edition and this, along with the first World of Music, Arts and Dance (WOMAD) festival, organised by Peter Gabriel at Shepton Mallet in 1984, led to music from Africa and Asia beginning to have a small but noted presence. World Music was a convenient marketing term (Pacini, 1993) for anything outside the conventional Western pop or rock format, including musicians who had been recording for years prior to its launch (such as Ravi Shankar). But in the 1980s, Kuti didn't quite fit the 'World Music' slot: his use of jazz and funk was complex and indicated that his 'musicking' (Small, 1998) illustrated the hybridity of the Black Atlantic (Gilroy, 1993; Stanovsky, 1998; Grass, 1986) which was at odds with the fetishisation of 'authenticity' that prevailed within the World Music scene at the time. A 2013 BBC programme, *How to be a World Music Star*, part of a series dedicated to World Music, discussed the careers of the Bhundu Boys, Baaba Maal and Salif Keita, and how Anglo-American labels formatted and marketed them to a Western audience. Kuti did not figure in this history and his inclusion in some broadcasters' and critics' reading of 'World Music', but not in others, illustrates both the slipperiness of the taxonomy and Kuti's own complexity.

Kuti as a *Rolling Stone* Rebel

Kuti has, however, been accepted into a predominantly white male rock canon, and this is exemplified by his inclusion in the *Rolling Stone*'s list '15 Rock and Roll Rebels' (Anon., 2013). *Rolling Stone* was established in 1967, a vehicle for the 'gonzo' journalism of Hunter S. Thompson, and although its lineage is counter-cultural, it is now arguably part of the (predominantly) white US rock establishment. The magazine's short biography on Kuti prioritises his politics both as a Black Panther and as an opponent of the Nigerian state, interweaving this with comments on Afrobeat and the story behind 'Coffin for Head of State' (1980). In this selection of 15 'rebels', Kuti appears alongside Johnny Cash, Public Enemy and Marilyn Manson as the rebellious outsider. *Rolling Stone*'s collection elides the differences and contexts of the individuals, relying instead on the generic description of rock 'n' roll rebel, a stereotype within Western popular culture whose 'extrasonic or extramusical reputation dominated and still dominates' (Olaniyan, 2001 p. 1). Online, the catalogue of rebels exists as a series of image tabs that you can browse through. If you click to the right of Kuti, there is Elvis Costello (an 'angry young man') and to the left, Plastic People of The Universe, a Czech band who were arrested as dissidents before the Velvet Revolution in 1989. *Rolling Stone* refers to the chosen 15 as outsiders and revolutionaries. Three out of these are black: Kuti, Peter Tosh (chosen over Bob Marley as the 'real rebel') and Public Enemy. Including Kuti in this group corrals his music into a recognisable format where the common denominator is one of revolutionary marginality. Kuti's claim to outsider status is, like Tosh's and Public Enemy's, behavioural and raced, while Kuti is the only African, which compounds his Otherness and adds to his allure. Gilroy has eloquently illustrated the links between commodification and blackness (1993; 2004; 2011) and notes how the use of blackness within popular culture works to 'bleed risk, pleasure and excitement into each other as part of selling things and accumulating capital' (Gilroy, 2004 p. 61). This is arguably what Kuti adds to the roster of rebels in *Rolling Stone*. Notwithstanding Gilroy's work on the history of blackness as a commodity in and of itself, his argument foregrounds the historical complexities and contemporary shifts in how blackness is deployed and represented, some of which are visible in how Kuti was 'exhibited' in London in 2004.

Black President: The Art and Legacy of Fela Kuti

The Barbican is an exhibition space established in 1982 in London. Positioned between the City of London and its East End, it has a reputation for staging cutting-edge exhibitions and shows. Its own mission statement introduces itself in the following way:

> A world-class arts and learning organisation, the Barbican pushes the boundaries of all major art forms including dance, film, music, theatre and visual arts. The Barbican exists to serve its wide and diverse audiences – engaging with arts lovers through our unique and inspiring artistic events at the Centre and using our Creative learning programme and free events to introduce new audiences to great arts experiences. (Barbican official website, 2013)

In 2004, it staged the multimedia exhibition *Black President: The Art and Legacy of Fela Kuti*, which consisted of artworks by 34 artists inspired by Kuti, album covers, photographs, and of screenings of the Kuti documentary *Music is the Weapon* (dir. Flori and Tchalgadjief, 1982). The exhibition was synced to BBC Radio 3, with DJs from London's Cargo club where 'Shrine nights' had been hosted during the 1990s. It was indeed commensurate with the Barbican's aim to 'push the boundaries' in its multimedia approach to the exhibition, despite some reviews calling it a 'festival' or a 'celebration' (Longley, 2004). The exhibition was then transferred to New York's New Museum of Contemporary Art. It would be banal to suggest that the curation of Kuti, by incorporating him as museum exhibit, emasculates him and his politics, but the move from performance to exhibit requires some conceptualising since Kuti's appearance as the focus of this exhibition involved a subtle shift of position, from subject to object and from authorial politicised voice to represented figurative type. Recent publications on how music is curated in museums suggest that canonisation is afforded through rendering music and musicians as artefacts in line with the museums' 'institutional logic', which can replicate 'dominant hegemonic versions of history' (Leonard, 2007 p. 147). Such debates are apparent in contemporary reviews of the exhibition.

Despite the re-use of Kuti's album title *Black President*, which carries a very real and symbolic strength marking Kuti as a figure of black authority, reviews of the exhibition suggest that his radical legacy and iconographic status were downplayed to concentrate on his sartorial style and sexuality, thereby rendering him as a sexual radical more in keeping with an established Western concept of the rebellious rock star (Reynolds and Press, 1995). The reviewers noted Kuti's political activism and his charisma, and claimed him as 'Africa's most influential composer', with Longley (2004) in the UK broadsheet, *The Independent*, declaring how he, 'alongside Ravi Shankar, brought "world music" to the rock-fed masses across Europe and the US'. Kuti's music was slotted into the convenient and unwieldy 'World Music' pigeonhole and, with this, lost all sense of distinct musical hybridity and original creativity. Writing in *The Socialist Review*, Johnson (2004) notes that while Kuti's influence and iconographic status were a given in the exhibition, the 34 artists' work featured concentrated on his sexuality. Photographs of Kuti with his 'Queens' (as his wives were called) backstage and in hotel rooms (by Bernard Matussière) foregrounded his sexual prowess. Johnson (2004) acknowledges that this was 'because he had 28 wives and many mistresses, a tantalizing thought in many heads but, in the context of his torture by the government because of his uncompromising rally to the masses to revolt … misses the point', suggesting that this 'emphasis on sex by some of the artists at the exhibition seems like thinly veiled jealous racism'.

At the Barbican, Kuti was an exhibit, canonised and displayed in line with dominant hegemonic constructs (Hall, 1997; Leonard, 2007) and the elation and communion that Veal and Busby refer to are muffled. In contrast, reviews for a successful US musical foreground not only his life but the effect of hearing him and his music.

Fela! and Felabration

Fela! (dir. Lewis and Jones, 2008) is a stage musical based on Kuti's life. It showed off-Broadway in 2008 before successfully transferring to Broadway and London in 2010, before touring across the United States in 2013. It was nominated for 11 Tony awards, winning three for best choreography, best costume design and best sound design. Reviews described Kuti as an 'icon', 'extraordinary', a 'national hero' and 'legendary'. Publicity for the show refers to Kuti as a 'firebrand, iconoclast, rabble-rouser and composer of genius', and his music as 'sensual' (felaonbroadway.com). Its staging aimed to reproduce the décor of The Shrine in Lagos and audience members reflected on how 'this was music that entered your bloodstream' (Ozekhome, 2010). Ozekhome indicates that the experience of *Fela!* was somehow representative of the 'mysticism' and 'voodoo' of Kuti's music and so provided a musical bridge back to the Yoruba aspects of Afrobeat.

With Jay-Z, Will Smith and Jada Pinkett-Smith now executive producers, this musical might be configured as a positive representational process, led as it is by African-American music and media stars and committed to reviving the experience of being at The ('legendary') Shrine, where Kuti was supposed to have often played all night (due to curfews). The emphasis of the musical was also on Kuti 'presented not in the usual militant stereotype, but as a compromised, flawed, even unbalanced soul' (Spencer, 2010). Spencer's review for *The Observer*, a liberal UK broadsheet, offers a counterpoint to the musical's own publicity, indicating perhaps the complexity of reviving such a figure. Thirteen years after Kuti's death, this review is more nuanced than the obituaries of 1997 in similar liberal broadsheets, both UK and US, a position perhaps enabled by the reflection and critical appreciation that has garnered pace since his death.

Fela! returned Kuti to the United States, where he had recorded his first album in Los Angeles in 1969. He did not have any success there during his lifetime, but this show opened up the Stateside market, and Wrasse records synchronised the release of re-issues to coincide with the musical. Such a synergistic response illustrates the ongoing commodification processes that Kuti is prey to, travelling after death across the Black Atlantic (Gilroy, 1993; 2011). This more recent commodification rests on his reputation as a transcendental musical presence, whose stage shows at The Shrine (replicated on Broadway) offered elation and communion and whose legacy is ensured through celebrations like the annual *Felabration* festival, held in Nigeria.

Staged over a week in October (Kuti's birthday), *Felabration* was started in 1998 by Kuti's daughter and includes performances and debates on all things 'Fela'. The event is subtitled 'Forever Lives Afrobeat' and offers a space where successive generations encounter Kuti's music and discuss his ideas. The potential for such occasions to offer affective communal experiences is also borne out by reactions to fundraising concerts. In the summer of 2013, there were *Red Hot and Fela* Live AIDS Charity performances at New York's Lincoln Centre in the United States where audiences could experience 'The defiant spirit and groove heavy music of

144 DEATH AND THE ROCK STAR

Nigerian firebrand Fela Anikulapo Kuti' (www.lcouofdoors.org), and raise money for the fight against AIDS in the process. However, this also exemplifies how Kuti is allied to an illness with latent connotations of sexual excess and promiscuity that feed into racist and rockist stereotypes, whose simplistic veneers mask complex undercurrents, as exemplified by the following comment.

Conclusion

'I'm not dancing to him. He's sexist'. So said one of the people I had gone to Glastonbury Festival with in 1989 when Kuti was playing the main stage. As my friend, a white World Music fan like myself, walked away in disgust, Kuti, resplendent in a white trouser suit, sang, orchestrated his band, played a Fender Rhodes and sang about corruption in Nigeria. What seemed to have upset my friend was that his band consisted of six or seven of Kuti's wives, all painted, many in bra tops and short skirts, dancing languorously and sensually. Kuti's perceived chauvinism seemed to eclipse all else for this friend who walked away. This machismo, I would argue, along with his radical resistance to the Nigerian government, has enabled Kuti to be posthumously corralled into the Western rock canon. As the BBC review of a recent compilation album of his argues, 'his vivid life story ... fodder for the massively successful stage musical – often threatens to overshadow his music' (Chick, 2013). It is easy to see why.

This chapter has argued that the posthumous Fela Kuti is located within discursive parameters that both contain and enshrine him through commodification and memorialisation. Kuti was a complex, paradoxical character. He reframed and added to his own musical heritage, carving out a new sound in Afrobeat, which he used to articulate his dissident political views. This sound was a fusion of Black Atlantic sounds and its message was Pan-Africanist. He was a counter-cultural figure within the context of Nigeria in the 1970s and 1980s, refusing to be imprisoned within colonial matrices whose legacy he sought to subvert, while at the same time essentialising his blackness and announcing his sexual prowess. It seems fair to say that the political intentions of his music might be less apparent to a Western audience and this point might be borne out with a final personal reflection. When Kuti played the Brixton Academy in 1988, a large proportion of the audience were Nigerian and they sang along; every lyric, every satirical jibe at the Nigerian authorities was joyfully vocalised. All I could do was listen and watch. And dance. His music affected me viscerally and the memory of being rounded up by mounted police afterwards has remained with me ever since, pointing to the element that is missing from the *Art and Legacy of Fela Kuti, Fela!* and *Rolling Stone*. Kuti was dangerous. His music's message was politically and sexually radical, shot through with complexities. These have, to a large extent, been overwritten with comprehensible stories of personal excess. They have ensured that Kuti is tamed and fits in after his death where he never did while alive; canonised and taxonomised as rock star rebel and icon.

Bibliography

Anonymous (2013) '15 Rock and Roll Rebels', *Rolling Stone*, 3 June, http://www.rollingstone.com/music/lists/15-rock-roll-rebels-20130603, accessed 6 February 2014.

Barbican official website (2013), http://www.barbican.org.uk/about-barbican, accessed 9 February 2014.

Chick, Stevie (2013) 'CD review – *Fela Kuti: The Best of the Black President*', BBC, http://www.bbc.co.uk/music/reviews/26b6, accessed 29 November 2013.

Cleaver, Eldridge (1992 [1968]) *Soul on Ice*. New York: Random House.

Feld, Steven (1996) 'Pygmy Pop: A Genealogy of Schizophonic Mimesis', *Yearbook for Traditional Music*, 28, pp. 1–35.

Gilroy, Paul (1993) *The Black Atlantic: Modernity and Double Consciousness*. Cambridge, MA: Harvard University Press.

——— (2004) *After Empire: Melancholia or Convivial Culture?* Oxford: Routledge.

——— (2011) *Darker than Blue: On the Moral Economies of Black Atlantic Culture*. Cambridge, MA: Harvard University Press.

Grass, Randall F. (1986) 'Fela Anikulapo-Kuti: The Art of an Afrobeat Rebel', *The Drama Review*, 30 (1), pp. 131–48.

Guilbault, Jocelyne (2006) 'On Redefining the "Local" through World Music', in Jennifer C. Post (ed.), *Ethnomusicology: A Contemporary Reader*. New York: Routledge, pp. 137–46.

Hall, Stuart (2003 [1997]) *Representation: Cultural Representation and Signifying Practices*, London: Sage.

Herszenhorn, David M. (1997) 'Fela, 58, Dissident Nigerian Musician, Dies', *The New York Times*, 4 August, www.nytimes.com/1997/08/04/arts/fela-58-dissident-nigerian-musician-dies.html, accessed 29 November 2013.

Hesmondhalgh, David (2013) *Why Music Matters*. Chichester and Oxford: Wiley Blackwell.

Johnson, Adeola (2004) 'Review of "Black President: The Art and Legacy of Fela Anikulapo-Kuti", Barbican Centre London', *Socialist Review*, October, www.socialistreview.org.uk/article.php?articlenumber=9070, accessed 29 November 2013.

Leonard, Marion (2007) 'Constructing Histories through Material Culture: Popular Music, Museums and Collecting', *Popular Music History*, 2 (2), pp. 147–67.

——— (2010) 'Exhibiting Popular Music: Museum Audiences, Inclusion and Social History', *Journal of New Music Research*, 39 (2), pp. 171–81.

——— (2013) 'Staging the Beatles: Ephemerality, Materiality and the Production of Authenticity in the Museum', *International Journal of Heritage Studies*, 20 (4), pp. 357–75.

Lipsitz, George (1994) *Dangerous Crossroads: Popular Music, Postmodernism and the Poetics of Place*. London and New York: Verso.

146   DEATH AND THE ROCK STAR

Longley, Martin (2004) '*The Black President*', *The Independent*, 3 September, www.independent.co.uk/arts-entertainment/music/features/the-black-president-6162461.html, accessed 6 February 2013.

Mercer, Kobena (1994) *Welcome to the Jungle*. London: Routledge.

Moore, Carlos (2010) *Fela: This Bitch of a Life. The Authorised Biography of Africa's Musical Genius*. Chicago, IL: Lawrence Hill Books.

Olaniyan, Tejumola (2001) 'The Cosmopolitan Nativist: Fela Anikulapo-Kuti and the Antinomies of Postcolonial Modernity in Research', *African Literatures*, 32 (2), pp. 76–89.

Ozekhome, Franklin (2010) 'Fela Kuti and Maxploitation of Afrobeat Music', *Bizcommunity.com*, May 2, www.bizcommunity.com/Article/196/432/47229. html, accessed 3 December 2013.

Pacini, Deborah (1993) 'A View from the South: Spanish Caribbean Perspectives on World Beat', *The World of Music*, 35 (2), pp. 48–69.

Railton, Diane and Paul Watson (2011) *Music Video and the Politics of Representation*. Edinburgh: Edinburgh University Press.

Reynolds, Simon and Joy Press (1995) *The Sex Revolts: Gender, Rebellion and Rock 'n' Roll*. London and New York: Serpents Tail.

Rojek, Chris (2001) *Celebrity*. London: Reaktion.

Small, Christopher (1998) *Musicking: The Meanings of Performing and Listening*. Hanover, NH: Wesleyan University Press of New England.

Spencer, Neil (2010) 'Fela Kuti Remembered: "He was a Tornado of a Man, but He Loved Humanity"', *The Observer*, 31 October, www.theguardian.com/music/2010/oct/31/fela-kuti-musical-neil-spencer, accessed 24 April 2014.

Stanovsky, Derek (1998) 'Fela and His Wives: The Import of a Postcolonial Masculinity', *Jouvert: A Journal of Postcolonial Studies*, 2 (1), July [Republished in *Montreal Serai*, 14 (1), Winter 2001] no page numbers.

Sweeney, Philip (1997) 'Obituary: Fela Kuti', *The Independent*, 2 August, www.independent.co.uk/news/people/obituary-fela-kuti-1243789.html, accessed 7 February 2014.

Taylor, Timothy Dean (1997) *Global Pop: World Music, World Markets*. New York and London: Routledge.

Veal, Michael (2000) *Fela: Life and Times of an African*. Philadelphia, PA: Temple University Press.

Discography

Fela Ransome Kuti and Nigeria 70, *The '69 Los Angeles Sessions*, Sterns, 1 CD, 1994.

Fela Anikulapo Kuti and the Africa 70, *Zombie*, Coconut Records, vinyl LP, 1976.
——, *Sorrow Tears and Blood*, Kalakuta, vinyl LP, 1977.

Fela Anikulapo Kuti, *Coffin for Head of State*, Wrasse Records, vinyl LP, 1980.
——, *Black President*, Arista, vinyl LP, 1981.

—————, *Unknown Soldier*, Uno Melodic Records, vinyl LP, 1981.
Paul Heck and John Carlin et al., *Red Hot and Fela: The Music and Spirit of Fela Kuti*, MCA, compilation album, 2002.

Filmography

Music is the Weapon, dir. Jean-Jacques Flori and Stephane Tchalgadjief, Universal Import, 1982.
How to be a World Music Star, dir. Ellen Hobson, BBC Four, 2013.

Chapter 11
Post-mortem Elvis:
From Cultural Icon to Transproperty

June M. Madeley and Daniel Downes

In his 1986 work *Stars*, Richard Dyer asserts that celebrities embody contradictory social values. Elvis Presley (1935–77) is a slippery signifier who has represented many conflicting elements of American culture. Indeed, 'the post mortem Elvis incorporates what the larger society presents only as binary oppositions and alternative choices – he is both tough and gentle, both spiritual and sexual, both racist and democratic' (Spigel, 1990 p. 182). He was both adored and vilified as a symbol of teen rebellion in the mid-1950s. He represents a simmering masculinity, but in a highly androgynous form. His southern roots implicate Elvis in American race relations, both positively and negatively. It is well-known that his promoters hailed him as a white boy with a black sound. He was a good southern boy who loved his mama, but he was also excessive in his consumption of drugs and food. For some he is a religious icon, for others he is the embodiment of the American Dream – a man of humble origins possessing a unique talent and a driving ambition that resulted in material success. His image remains ambiguous and contradictory, and may be read in various ways by fans who make it their own. As one commentator puts it, Elvis's ability to perform many of the contradictions at the centre of American culture sets him apart from other dead celebrities (Carlson, 1999 p. 75).

In this chapter, we propose to explore the posthumous and continued use of Presley's image, rather than his music. Elvis resonates because of a range of cultural myths that encircle him, 'and the *multiple and contradictory ways* in which he is articulated to those myths' (Rodman, 1996 p. 40, emphasis added). However, the commercial use of Elvis's image by his estate, in the form of Elvis Presley Enterprises (EPE), and their concentrated efforts to control the meanings of those images, transforms Elvis into a transpropertied commodity form exploiting new uses of the right of publicity. Here, we argue that the image of Elvis propagated and policed by EPE has been highly sanitised and made one-dimensional (see Doss, 1999 p. 227; O'Neal, 1996 pp. 89–90; Wall, 1996 p. 120). In addition, we examine the practices of Elvis Tribute Artists (ETAs) to show the tensions between the social and cultural appropriation of his image and his status as a corporately-controlled, transpropertied cultural commodity.

Elvis: Image and Icon

Elvis Presley was part of the first wave of rock 'n' roll, a period that spanned the years 1954–9 (Wald, 2009 p. 201). Along with artists like Billy Lee Riley, Jerry Lee Lewis and Carl Perkins, Presley played an up-tempo blend of country and rhythm and blues that was labelled rockabilly by critics. Presley became so associated with the sound of rockabilly that subsequent descriptions of the genre include a singer who 'sounds like Elvis' (Morrison, 1996 p. 1). He was 19 at the time of his first recording, which made him part of a new breed of performers who represented the same age group as the emerging teen audience buying their music. His success was supported, in part, by his appearances on television, making him one of the first musical celebrities whose career was linked to the new medium, so much so that many people refer not to hearing Elvis for the first time on the radio but to seeing him on television (Wald, 2009 p. 202).

Indeed, as a symbol of rebellious 1950s teen culture in the USA, Elvis is forever associated with his television appearances. 'Elvis's early television appearances [are viewed] as ground-breaking, culture-shattering events' (Rodman, 1996 p. 153), particularly his appearance on *The Milton Berle Show* on 5 June 1956. Rodman argues that this 'performance is the pivotal moment after which neither Elvis, nor rock 'n' roll, nor US culture would ever be quite the same again' (p. 151). It is singled out because this was the first broadcast of Elvis performing without his guitar, his only prop being the microphone. It was not his singing, but how he moved that provoked such strong responses in the audience of the broadcast (both positive and negative) (Rodman, 1996 pp. 148–50).

It can be argued that Presley's musical influence waned by 1958. Indeed, when he returned to America in 1960 after a two-year stint in the Army, he headed for Hollywood where he made 27 films (of the 31 he starred in) between 1960 and 1969 (Elvis Presley Enterprises, 2013b). The final phase of his career began in 1968 and continued to his death. During this period, Elvis was primarily a Las Vegas performer, although his televised *1968 Comeback Special* suggested that he might have ended his career differently. The special was a curious blend of television variety show with comedy skits and staged musical numbers. However, the second half of the show featured Presley and a stripped-down band, playing his old hits in close proximity to a studio audience. Had Elvis returned to his roots as an innovator rather than as a performer he might have found a way to reinvigorate his musical career. Instead, he used the publicity of the special to return to Las Vegas.

Since his death in 1977, Elvis has been of both popular and academic interest less for his musical accomplishments than as an icon of American culture. In her study of Elvis fans, Doss (1999 p. 10) argues that 'after seeing him, his music became secondary'. Rodman (1996 p. 39) agrees that 'no matter how compelling much of his music actually was (and still is), his impact on US culture was never exclusively musical'. In fact, we would argue that his image contributes more significantly than his music to Presley's status in American popular culture.

Cultural icons are created by the active appropriation and use of cultural material that involves both the originator and the recipient of cultural or symbolic information. Cordero (1997–8 p. 602) argues that, 'in our society, icons are created through a partnership of purveyor and populace, whereby the purveyor of a commodity supplies the product, and the consumer – through an active creative practice – appropriates it by investing the product with new meaning'. Further, as Madow (1993 p. 139) claims, attempts to police symbolic use or to promote preferred readings of intellectual property are often frustrated by the persistent participation of audiences in meaning creation because, 'consumers neither uniformly receive nor uncritically accept the "preferred meanings" that are generated and circulated by the purveyors'. As audiences are co-creators of symbolic meaning in their relationship with performers, they also compete with corporate rights holders for control of the meanings they assign to celebrities.

In previous work about authenticity, rock music and culture, specifically rockumentaries featuring the Rolling Stones in their early years, we have argued that cultural goods and musical performers engender relationships between audiences, texts, celebrities and the cultural industries. In the course of developing and managing these relationships, there is often conflict with fans over what can be described as 'the last word' (see Downes and Madeley, 2013 p. 88). Who gets to decide what 'Elvis' will mean at any given time in his career or in his celebrity afterlife? What meanings, images or references to the man will emerge over time and which meanings will dominate? Madow (1993 p. 134) argues that by 'centralizing this meaning-making power in the celebrity herself or her assignees, the right of publicity facilitates top-down management of popular culture and constricts the space available for alternative and oppositional cultural practice'. This process creates a tension between those who view Elvis as a cultural icon (fans and ETAs) and those who seek to use his various incarnations and to control them as sources of revenue (EPE and their corporate partners).

Elvis's image has generated significant income. According to *Forbes Magazine*, which has been compiling an annual list of the top-earning dead celebrities since 2001, Elvis has been the top earner seven times, never falling lower than position four (he came fourth just once – in 2009 when Michael Jackson joined the list). He was the second top-earning dead celebrity on the 2013 list, and 'his estate is still earning steadily thanks to his eternally popular image and his famous home, Graceland' (Pomerantz, 2013). Elvis's posthumous career has included many appearances in contemporary film (Carlson, 1999 p. 74). Carlson has noted that in the mid-1990s there was a shift in how Elvis was portrayed in movies from depictions as himself to depictions as a doppelgänger character or as an Elvis impersonator – from a whole Elvis, to 'a fragmented, dismembered Elvis, a metonymised Elvis, an Elvis of bits and pieces' (Carlson, 1999 p. 74). While Carlson considers a number of possible explanations for this fragmenting of the King in popular culture – his feminisation, familiarity or multiplicity of meanings – he never considers fear of intellectual property lawyers among the possibilities. To understand these fragmentations, we must look to a

152   *DEATH AND THE ROCK STAR*

transformation in intellectual property law since the 1970s that grants enormous power to the estates of dead celebrities.

The Transpropertied Commodity Form

Elvis provides an example of a new form of intellectual property called transproperty based on emerging rights associated with copyright, trademark and celebrity (Downes, 2014). In contrast to the significance that visual representations of Elvis have for fans, critics and academics, is the status his image holds as *intellectual property* owned and managed since 1977 by his former manager, his family and others. The creation of transproperty has been the result of almost a century of interaction between mass media and the law in which fictional characters, authors and celebrities are protected in the marketplace by overlapping forms of intellectual property law. Celebrity rights allow celebrities, their heirs and their representatives to capitalise on the celebrity's likeness long after death. Trademark laws allow for the protection of fictional characters as well as images that are used as markers of corporate identity, and copyright is extended and expanded to protect much more than the expression of original ideas in tangible form. Taken together, these separate forms of intellectual property protection combine to create transproperty. Transproperty claims structure and shape the creative, personal and social uses of iconic characters, whether they are fictional, living or dead.

Thus, while Elvis has become a slippery signifier, it is clear that in one facet of his posthumous life, that in which Elvis is a transpropertied commodity form controlled by EPE, there is definitely a preferred reading. Perhaps more importantly, EPE has been increasingly successful at inserting itself as the entity who authorises more and more uses of Elvis. The commodification of Elvis's image began during his lifetime when Colonel Parker set up Boxcar Enterprises in 1974 to license and merchandise Elvis products. Immediately after Presley's death, Parker signed a deal with Factors Etc. which guaranteed Parker 50 per cent of all merchandise profits (O'Neal, 1996 pp. 30–33; see also Frow, 1995 p. 156). Parker had already sold the masters of Elvis's catalogue of recordings to RCA in 1972 which left the singer's estate to devise new ways to collect revenues from his celebrity after his death. Between 1977 and 1982, his estate and Parker used EPE (another enterprise set up by Parker years earlier to sell Elvis merchandise) to manage their affairs.

After falling out with Parker and through litigation in 1982, Priscilla Presley, as a director of EPE, managed Graceland as a tourist attraction and looked for ways to capitalise on Elvis in order to bolster the estate in trust for their daughter, Lisa Marie. Since the estate disentangled itself from Parker in 1982, Elvis's merchandising has been aggressively policed (Devin, 2009). When Lisa Marie reached the age of 25, she took control of EPE, but Priscilla remained a director. In a 2005 deal that earns Lisa Marie 15 per cent on all uses of Presley's image, control of the company moved outside the family for the first time since 1982 (Serwer, 2005).

POST-MORTEM ELVIS: FROM CULTURAL ICON TO TRANSPROPERTY   153

Of the various forms of intellectual property protection that can be invoked to commercialise creative works and celebrity likenesses, the most important for the afterlife of Elvis is the right of publicity, which has its roots in the right of privacy (Warren and Brandeis, 1890 p. 193). Where the right of privacy was intended to protect private individuals from intrusion into their lives by the press, over time a new right of publicity emerged to protect celebrities from the wrongful or unauthorised use of a celebrity's likeness or name (Prosser, 1960 p. 389). The focus of the right of publicity is to protect the celebrity's identity from economic exploitation.

Over time, a number of American states enacted right of publicity legislation. In some, led by Indiana and Tennessee, and a case initiated by the estate of Elvis Presley, a celebrity's publicity rights extend after their death and are 'descendible'; that is, they can be exploited by heirs or, as in the case of Presley, companies who purchase those rights (Bartholemew, 2011 pp. 315–17). Indeed, the rights to exploit Elvis merchandise have changed hands three times since 2005 (Yan, 2013). Further, trademark and publicity rights cases involving Vanna White, Bette Midler and Tom Waits have made it possible for celebrities or their agents to sue over not only the appropriation or use of a celebrity image, but also for use of their voice and mannerisms (Braatz, 1994).

The model of setting up a corporation to manage the publicity rights of dead artists and authors has become increasingly common since EPE began (see Downes, 2014). By trademarking their business identities, such firms continue to make intellectual property claims, even for works that have gone into the public domain (Schuessler, 2013). In the case of Elvis, EPE manages the dead singer's image using the same strategies of commodification and intellectual property law.

In addition to policing Elvis merchandise, the estate has policed and sanitised Presley's image. Rodman (1996 p. 120) describes how Graceland tour guides were instructed to avoid mention of drugs or the bathroom in their telling of the story of Elvis's death. Eliding such facts 'help[s] to mythologise the man as an almost flawless saint figure, rather than a real and imperfect human being' (Rodman, 1996 p. 121). Doss (1999 p. 221) further demonstrates the estate's control over the King's life story in their replacement of live tour guides with recordings that offer consistency with no fear of off-script slip-ups. The estate has also actively tried to eliminate parodic representations of Elvis by outlawing velvet Elvis paintings,[1] souvenir items such as vials of his sweat, or challenging the sale of paintings of Elvis by serial-killer John Wayne Gacy (Doss, 1999 pp. 214–26). Finally, even though Elvis's last TV special, *Elvis in Concert*, aired in October 1977, and earned the estate $750,000, 'today the decidedly more image-conscious estate refuses to allow this program to be aired or sold' (O'Neal, 1996 p. 41). The estate has

---

[1]   An archetypal example of kitsch, these paintings used bright colours on black velvet and were usually sold by street vendors or at informal markets. Elvis was one popular subject of such paintings which also included nudes, sad clowns and matadors. They were at the height of their popularity in North America in the 1970s.

explained their continued opposition to releasing this special: '[T]here just simply is no way to get it only to the real fans (and we've exhausted all kinds of ideas) without also having Elvis served up to the general public and press for ridicule' (Elvis Presley Enterprises, 2013a). EPE's attempts to sanitise the memory of Elvis, by holding back certain images and performances, contradict the desires and expectations of fans. Clearly, when there is a conflict between fan desires and EPE's vision, EPE increasingly wins.

To summarise, a number of legal cases involving the Presley estate have 'allowed the estate to define the nature of the Elvis property and establish legal control over it. They have also provided the estate's lawyers with the tools by which the property could be subsequently policed and controlled' (Wall, 1996 p. 124). Indeed, the work of policing Elvis's property and publicity rights has made both legal precedent and legal careers (Devin, 2009; Monson, 2012). In the end, the process of making and defending transproperty claims defines a celebrity as primarily a vehicle for commerce. The official Elvis website lists dozens of licensed uses of the King for selling products (see Elvis Presley Enterprises, 2013c). It also provides demographic data suggesting which images of Elvis are recognised by different markets grouped by age, gender and geography.

Branding Elvis as a collection of images works against his status as a cultural icon wherein a performer, alive or dead, adds 'additional grist (mediated or otherwise) ... to the potential pool of symbolic material' (Jones, 2005 p. 5), from which performers and audiences co-construct celebrity and, as stated earlier, negotiate new meanings (also see Cordero, 1997–8 p. 602). The tension between these uses of Elvis becomes particularly obvious in the case of Elvis Tribute Artists.

Elvis Tribute Artists: Contested Mediation

Elvis impersonators and tribute artists arose long before the King of rock 'n' roll died, and contests for the best Elvis impersonation have been going on well prior to EPE beginning its own tribute artist contest in 2007. The fan practice of impersonating or paying tribute to Elvis is a grassroots phenomenon that arose to celebrate Elvis as a cultural icon. '[F]ans' individual and collective appropriation of the fan text' (Sandvoss, 2005 p. 135), in this case Elvis, is in constant tension with the intentions and interests of creators and rights holders.

In 1981, EPE sued Rod Russen, the promoter of a tribute called *The Big El Show*, which featured impersonator Larry Seth. Russen claimed to have an agreement established with Colonel Parker in 1975, but the suit claimed that the show infringed on trademark and right of publicity and that it constituted unfair competition. In the decision the court found that the show was not unfair competition: 'although the promoter had the right to stage his show, he could not utilise the unique Presley indicia which would tend to lead customers to believe that the show was authorised by the estate, a false designation of origin' (Biederman, 2007 p. 279). The merchandise sold was found to be in violation of the right of publicity held by EPE, but the court found that 'there was no likelihood that Larry Seth would be confused with Elvis Presley. The judge disagreed with EPE's argument that *The Big El Show* diminished its ability to license Elvis. In the judge's opinion, an Elvis impersonator did not need a license from EPE to perform' (O'Neal, 1996 p. 147).

Johnny 'Elvis' Spence is reported to be the first Elvis impersonator who toured the US, in 1970 (Williams, 2011). He was also targeted by EPE for legal action during the 1980s, based on perceived infringement of their trademarks (O'Neal, 1996 p. 146). Spence had applied for a license from EPE for his planned concert to commemorate the tenth anniversary of Elvis's death, but had been turned down. Unlike his shows in the 1970s which were performed in fairly small venues, including bars in the Chicago area, the 1987 *Elvis the Way it Was* concert was to be held in a 12,500 seat hall (O'Neal, 1996 p. 146). EPE lawyer C. Barry Ward asserted the company's right of publicity in the cease-and-desist letter: 'We own exclusive right to the name, likeness and image (of Elvis) ... You are not authorized to use the name Elvis or to perform any Elvis impersonation or act, and you are advised to immediately cease and desist' (Ward quoted in Zorn, 1987; parentheses in the original). Despite the mixed judicial decision in the Russen case, in the case of the *Elvis the Way it Was* show, EPE prevailed in an out-of-court settlement with Spence. EPE specifically targeted successful tribute ventures in an effort to gain both economic benefit and legal precedence to establish its rights over all Elvis impersonators (O'Neal, 1996 pp. 146–8). While these actions had some chilling effects on impersonators of the time, EPE was unsuccessful in its legal efforts to fully assert their right of publicity over these performances.

In June 1990, the first EP International Impersonators Convention (EPIIA) was held in Chicago, bringing together Elvis impersonators from all over the world. At the time, the convention did not use Elvis Presley's name because the Presley estate did not license imitations (Spigel, 1990 p. 200). The audience at tribute shows

> ... engage in a very specific and very repetitive ritual with the performers. The performances at the EPIIA made this quite clear since all forty impersonators who sang on stage basically did the same act. Singing mostly the bombastic ballads of the Vegas years, the impersonators walked to the edge of the stage, where, just like Elvis, they gave satiny scarves to women who mingled around the stage waiting for a kiss and the token. (Spigel, 1990 p. 181)

The EPIIA dissolved in 1999 and a new entity called the Elvis Entertainers Network (EEN) was launched soon after. The EEN has switched to the now preferred term of 'tribute artist' to refer to professional performers of Elvis. Tribute artists now embrace this term, but there is no clear universal distinction within Elvis culture between these terms for Elvis performers. The EEN produce events that are sanctioned by EPE, but they also participate in events that are not authorised by EPE. The majority of tribute artists perform without sanction or authorisation by the estate, but their acts usually conform to the conventions observed by Spigel at the first meeting of the EPIIA.

The estate may have given up on suing tribute artists, but they have found new ways to try to control these activities by hosting their own 'Ultimate' contest. In 2007, EPE launched the Ultimate Elvis Tribute Artist Contest which has been running annually, during Elvis week in Memphis, every August since. When promoting their inaugural event, EPE stated that they were looking for the 'best representation of the legacy of Elvis Presley' (Elvis Presley Enterprises, 2013d). The contest rules stipulate that ETAs must refrain from vulgarity and from the use of controlled substances. Most importantly, they must not portray Elvis in a derogatory manner. The contest rules General (Sections 6–10) stipulate the expected conduct of participants as well as the full and exclusive rights of EPE to publicise their performance without compensation to the ETA. As with other depictions of Elvis, EPE champions a fairly narrow range of performance and behaviour for tribute artists who want to participate in their licensed contests. Contestants designate the songs they would like to showcase (in order of preference) and are assigned their song and a band with which to perform. The Preliminary contests, which are authorised but independently produced run-offs to select ETAs to compete in Memphis, have to abide by similar rules and have any of their own unique rules approved by EPE if they are sanctioned as an Ultimate Preliminary. Since the Ultimate contests are authorised, sanctioned and publicised by EPE through Elvis.com and other advertising, the winners tend to be accepted as the Ultimate Elvis Tribute by fans.

Fans embrace these tribute styles because ETAs adhere so closely to the few filmed concerts that exist of Elvis. Their tribute shows, including the tribute concert that the writers attended as part of the research for this chapter, tend to be re-enactments of those filmed concerts. The authors attended a concert by tribute artist Thane Dunn in January 2013. Decades after the first meeting of associated tribute artists, the shows continue to model concert footage of Elvis in the early 1970s. We witnessed the ritual distribution of scarves and also of teddy bears during the show. Thane Dunn's Elvis tribute included martial arts dance moves and on-stage banter that are all reminiscent of the filmed and televised concerts. A fan who saw Elvis in Las Vegas 26 times between 1972 and 1976 indicated that his shows were structured in much the same way as the filmed concerts and very much like ETAs perform him today. She said:

> Elvis did not deter much from his show at all. He always started with the same number, 'CC Rider', and he always ended with 'Wise Men'. Now in between if he'd made a new recording he'd put that in, but he really liked to have his numbers structured. In between numbers he did a lot of chatting with the band. (Francis, 2014)

In this fan's experience, Elvis performed songs in much the same order and in the same way, but the shows varied in the impromptu stories and interactions with the audience. Sadly, there are only a few filmed shows that provide access to these off-the-cuff aspects of Elvis's live performances.

POST-MORTEM ELVIS: FROM CULTURAL ICON TO TRANSPROPERTY   157

There are tens of thousands of performers who pay tribute to Elvis, whether in small venues, large venues or contests to evaluate the best performance of Elvis (see Doss 1999; Spigel 1990). While an accurate count is hard to determine:

> ... what is clear is that in a supposed nation of individualistic do-it-ourselfers, all sorts of Americans look at Elvis and say they want to be just like him. And the Elvis they most want to be – and the one most fans want them to be the most too – is the jumpsuited icon of the 1970s. (Doss, 1999 p. 158)

As we mentioned above, the visual image of Elvis has had a greater impact than his music or, indeed, the man as a musician. Although some ETAs perform young 1950s Elvis, Vegas Elvis is arguably the most mediated televisual image of Elvis. Most of the available concert films on which ETAs base their performances feature Vegas Elvis. *Elvis That's the Way It Is* contains footage of Elvis during his third season in Vegas and was released to theatres in November of 1970, but was also broadcast on NBC in 1975 (released on VHS in 1987 and DVD in 2010). *Elvis on Tour* is a Golden Globe-winning concert documentary that was released in theatres in 1972 (and later on VHS in 1991 and on DVD in 2010). The 1973 *Aloha from Hawaii* concert was the first ever to be broadcast live via satellite across the globe to audiences in 40 countries (released on VHS in 1991 and DVD in 2003 and 2006). Once again, we see the importance of Elvis as a televisual image, especially for tribute artists. Thane Dunn, based in Canada, models his shows and costumes primarily on the 1972 *Elvis on Tour* special (see www.thanedunn.ca). In addition to the official EPE sanctioning of specific tribute performances through their authorised Ultimate contests, the lack of any new music, mannerisms or general behaviour of Elvis to copy, leaves ETAs with limited source material.

Other forms of tribute that less closely adhere to the small cache of images of Elvis in concert, such as the campy performances and recordings of the Latino musician El Vez, are criticised by fans 'largely because they think his hysterically campy act, replete with Chicano Power parodies of Elvis songs like "You Ain't Nothin' but a Chihuahua" ... borders on blasphemy' (Doss, 1999 p. 206). In the example of El Vez, there is an alignment between the reading of Elvis fans and the image of Elvis prioritised by EPE. ETAs from diverse cultural backgrounds (including other Latinos) are accepted within Elvis culture, such as African-American ETAs and Japan's Mori Yasumasa who won the *Images of Elvis* impersonator contest in Memphis in 1992 (Doss, 1999 p. 206). According to Hills,

> Elvis impersonation is a project, it represents recourse to an archive (the precisely catalogued set of jumpsuits and outfits worn on-stage by Elvis; images of Elvis; set-lists and conventionalised details of his stage show), and recourse to a powerful set of memories; those of the fan's lived experience *as a fan*. (Hills, 2002 p. 165)

An Elvis of colour is accepted if the performance conforms to that archive which is largely controlled by EPE and sets limits on not only the conventionalised

158 *DEATH AND THE ROCK STAR*

performance of ETAs, but also on the experiences and memories of fans. The relative scarcity of recorded Elvis source material and the officially sanctioned contests combine with other pressures to accept EPE's preferred readings of Elvis and result in a narrow set of normalised behaviour adopted by most ETAs. Ultimately, EPE incorporates this fan-led activity as a way to make money from people that they were unable to stop through legal means.

Conclusion

The purpose of this chapter has been to outline a tension between the multiple individual and social uses of the cultural icon Elvis Presley. Strategies used to contain and control the use of Elvis are enabled by the flattening of intellectual property laws and the transformation of various forms of intellectual property into an emerging form of transproperty. The transpropertisation of culture significantly strengthens the power of intellectual property holders, such as EPE, to control the meanings associated with their properties.

One of the reasons that ETAs can continue to perform without licensing or overt control by EPE is that it is much more difficult to propertise live performance. Live performances are a key marker of authenticity in popular music and, for Elvis fans and ETAs, there is still room for audiences and performers to negotiate meaning. That being said, through law suits (and the threat of law suits), by restricting access to unflattering performances by Elvis, and by inserting themselves as the dominant vehicle through which tribute artists gain access to larger audiences, EPE has effectively gained the final say in the commercial use of Elvis Presley.

When it comes to Elvis, EPE asserts their rights to have the last word, and presents a sanitised, uncomplicated image of the singer. This leads to a situation where one of the main impacts of Elvis's afterlife on American popular culture is the transpropertisation of the King through descendible publicity rights, the transformation of celebrity images into trademarked merchandise, licensing of new intellectual property and the emergence of companies whose business is the exploitation of the dead.

Bibliography

Bartholemew, Mark (2011) 'A Right is Born: Celebrity, Property, and Postmodern Lawmaking', *Connecticut Law Revue*, 44 (2), pp. 301–68.
Biederman, Donald (2007) 'Personal Rights: The Lanham Act and Other Federal Legislation', in Donald Biederman, Edward Pierson, Martin Silfen, Janna Glasser, Charles Biederman, Kenneth Abdo and Scott Sanders (eds), *Law and Business of the Entertainment Industries*, 5th edition. Westport, CT: Praeger Publishers, pp. 269–80.

Braatz, John R. (1994) 'White v. Samsung Electronics America: The Ninth Circuit Turns a New Letter in California Right of Publicity Law', *Pace Law Review*, 15, pp. 161–222.

———— (1999) 'Bit Parts: Dismembering Elvis in Recent Hollywood Films', *Film Criticism*, 24 (1), pp. 73–85.

Cordero, Steven (1997–1998) 'Cocaine-Cola, the Velvet Elvis, and Anti-Barbie: Defending the Trademark and Publicity Rights to Cultural Icons', *Fordham Intellectual Property Media and Entertainment Law Journal*, 8, pp. 599–654.

Devin, Jonathan (2009) 'The King's Court: Attorney William Bradley of Glankler Brown Protects Elvis Presley's Intellectual Property Rights', *MBQ: Inside Memphis Business*, 13, October, http://www.mbqmemphis.com/MBQ-Inside-Memphis-Business/September-2012/The-Kings-Court/, accessed 13 November 2013.

Doss, Erika (1999) *Elvis Culture: Fans, Faith and Image*. Lawrence, KS: University Press of Kansas.

Downes, Daniel (2014) 'Branding Culture: Fictional Characters and Undead Celebrities in an Era of "Transpropertied" Media', in Teresa Scassa, Mistrale Goudreau, Courtney Doagoo and Madelaine Saginur (eds), *Intellectual Property Law for the Twenty-First Century: Interdisciplinary Approaches to IP*. Toronto: Irwin, pp. 241–62.

Downes, Daniel and June M. Madeley (2013) 'Sympathy for the Circus: The Rolling Stones, Documentary Film, and the Construction of Authenticity', in Helmut Staubmann (ed.), *The Rolling Stones: Sociological Perspectives*. Lanham, MD: Lexington, pp. 81–106.

Dyer, Richard (1986) *Stars*. London: British Film Institute.

Elvis Presley Enterprises (2013a) 'About the King: FAQ', Elvis.com, http://www.elvis.com/about-the-king/faq.aspx#sthash.syiep2OA.dpuf, accessed 10 December 2013.

———— (2013b) 'About the King: Film and TV', Elvis.com, http://www.elvis.com/about-the-king/film_and_tv.aspx, accessed 8 October 2013.

———— (2013c) 'Elvis Presley Brand Guide', Elvis.com, http://www.elvis.com/!userfiles/editor/docs/Partnerships/2013%20Elvis%20Presley%20Brand%20Presentation_FINAL.pdf, accessed 6 September 2013.

———— (2013d) 'Ultimate Elvis Tribute Artist Contest Official Rules and Guidelines', Elvis.com, http://www.elvis.com/!userfiles/editor/docs/2014Rules GuidelinesETA.pdf, accessed 5 July 2013.

Francis, June (2014) 'Interview' [phone], 3 April 2014.

Frow, John (1995) 'Elvis's Fame: The Commodity Form and the Form of the Person', *Cardozo Studies in Law and Literature*, 7 (2), pp. 131–71.

Hills, Matt (2002) *Fan Cultures*. London: Routledge.

Jones, Steve (2005) 'Better off Dead: Or Making it the Hard Way', in Joli Jensen and Steve Jones (eds), *Afterlife as Afterimage: Understanding Posthumous Fame*. New York: Peter Lang, pp. 3–16.

Madow, Michael (1993) 'Private Ownership of the Public Image: Popular Culture and Publicity Rights', *California Law Review*, 81 (1), pp. 125–240.

Monson, Lynn (2012) 'Patents Pending: Precedent-setting IP Cases are his Trademarks', *Motion Magazine*, 28 February, http://www.legalnews.com/motion/article.php?article_id=195, accessed 1 November 2013.

Morrison, Craig (1996) *Go Cat Go: Rockabilly Music and its Makers*. Urbana and Chicago, IL: University of Illinois Press.

O'Neal, Sean (1996) *Elvis Inc.: The Fall and Rise of the Presley Empire*. Westminster, MD: Prima Lifestyles.

Pomerantz, Dorothy (2013) 'Michael Jackson Leads our List of the Top Earning Dead Celebrities', *Forbes Magazine*, 23 October, http://www.forbes.com/sites/dorothypomerantz/2013/10/23/michael-jackson-leads-our-list-of-the-top-earning-dead-celebrities/, accessed 7 January 2014.

Prosser, William (1960) 'Privacy', *California Law Review*, 48 (3), pp. 383–423.

Rodman, Gilbert (1996) *Elvis after Elvis: The Posthumous Career of a Living Legend*. London: Routledge.

Sandvoss, Cornel (2005) *Fans*. Cambridge: Polity Press.

Schuessler, Jennifer (2013) 'Public Domain, My Dear Watson? Lawsuit Challenges Conan Doyle Copyrights', *New York Times*, 15 February, http://artsbeat.blogs.nytimes.com/2013/02/15/public-domain-my-dear-watson-lawsuit-challenges-conan-doyle-copyrights/?_php=true&_type=blogs&_r=0, accessed 18 February 2013.

Serwer, Andy (2005) 'The Man Who Bought Elvis', *CNN Money*, 12 December, http://www.money.cnn.com/magazines/fortune/fortune_archive/2005/12/12/8363137/, accessed 18 December 2013.

Spigel, Lynn (1990) 'Communicating with the Dead: Elvis as Medium', *Camera Obscura*, 8 (2 23), pp. 176–205.

Wald, Elijah (2009) *How the Beatles Destroyed Rock 'n' Roll: An Alternative History of American Popular Music*. New York: Oxford.

Wall, David (1996) 'Reconstructing the Soul of Elvis: The Social Development and Legal Maintenance of Elvis Presley as Intellectual Property', *International Journal of the Sociology of Law*, 24, pp. 117–43.

Warren, Samuel and Lous Brandeis (1890) 'The Right to Privacy', *Harvard Law Review*, 4 (5), pp. 193–220.

Williams, Matt (2011) 'Rockford Area's Very Own Elvis Dies', *Rockford Register Star*, 14 May, http://www.rrstar.com/x600914900/Rockfords-very-own-Elvis-dies-on-eve-of-planned-comeback, accessed 5 April 2014.

Yan, Sophia (2013) 'Sold! Elvis Presley Inc. Has a New Owner', *CNN Money*, 20 November, http://money.cnn.com/2013/11/20/news/elvis-property/, accessed 25 November 2013.

Zorn, Eric (1987) 'Threat to Stop Elvis Show Puts Rocker in a Hard Place', *Chicago Tribune*, 8 July, http://articles.chicagotribune.com/1987-07-08/news/8702190761_1_elvis-presley-enterprises-elvis-show-impersonator, accessed 5 April 2014.

Filmography

Elvis: '68 Comeback Special (Broadcast) dir. Steve Binder, NBC/USA, 1968 (DVD, BMG Video, 2004).

Elvis: Aloha from Hawaii (Broadcast) dir. Marty Pasetta, NBC/USA, 1973 (VHS, Lightyear Entertainment/USA 1991; DVD, Warner Music Vision, 2003; DVD, Sony BMG, 2006).

Elvis in Concert, dir. Dwight Hemion, CBS/USA, 1977.

Elvis on Tour, dirs Robert Abel, Pierre Adidge, MGM/USA, 1972 (VHS, MGM/UA, 1991; DVD, Warner Home Video, 2010; BROADCAST, NBC, 1976).

Elvis: That's the Way It Is, dir. Denis Sanders, MGM/USA, 1970 (VHS, MGM/UA, 1987; DVD, Warner Home Video, 2010).

PART IV
Resurrections

Chapter 12

Performing Beyond the Grave:
The Posthumous Duet

Shelley D. Brunt

Introduction

'Two of America's most wanted in the same motherfucking place at the same motherfucking time', shouts a long-dead Tupac Shakur (1971–1996) as he gestures to his fellow rapper Snoop Dogg, on stage at the Coachella Valley Music and Arts Festival in April 2012 in front of an estimated 75,000 fans. This lyric from his 1996 duet with Snoop, titled '2 of Amerikaz Most Wanted', suddenly generates new meaning within this new context, well over 15 years since the single was released. The 'same place' and 'same time' highlights the unearthly pairing of one living and one dead rap icon; the latter seen as a return from the dead for a performer plagued by speculation about his untimely murder. Yet here on the festival stage, Tupac seems 'alive', resurrected for the purpose of performing beyond the grave. The 'liveness' of Tupac is documented in an official video on Snoop's YouTube channel which captures their posthumous duet from several different cameras (Westfesttv, 2014). The wide angles create a sense of spaciousness – a full shot of Tupac showcases his entire body as he prowls along the stage alongside Snoop – while close-up and panning shots capture the play of light over the curves of Tupac's naked torso. He is incredibly life-like, from his signature chest tattoos to his characteristic bodily movements. The overt sense of realism fuelled speculations by fans and media outlets about the technology used to create the performance. Digital Domain, the special effects company which designed Tupac's digital image, summarised the breadth and depth of public curiosity: 'YouTube videos of the performance amassed 15 million views. Google search results for "Tupac hologram" exceeded 50 million. 2Pac album sales increased 500% … There were thousands of media stories, assessing "virtual 2Pac's" impact on everything from music to entertainment, ethics, technology and intellectual property' (Digital Domain, 2014).

These points of 'impact', ranging from commercial concerns to ethical dilemmas, lie at the heart of the politics of the posthumous duet – a term that can be defined as the co-performance of one living and one dead singer in a new context. These are not new concerns. Technology has long permitted the splicing of voices of the living with recordings by dead singers. However, the integration of aural and visual elements in performance, as presented here with Tupac and Snoop Dogg, prompts an additional level of reality and believability.

166   *DEATH AND THE ROCK STAR*

This chapter considers the posthumous duet as a performance medium in relation to the *visual* as well as aural. It considers the positive and negative rhetoric of 'resurrection', from a miraculous Christ-like second coming which encompasses a pleasurable nostalgia, to an uncomfortable morbidity associated with the gruesome exhumation of a corpse. This chapter summarises and challenges the positive and negative discourses of performing beyond the grave, with a focus on performances on television – the more common incarnation of the posthumous duet. It begins by theorising the posthumous duet as sonic recontextualisation, explaining the overlapping modes of performance that reach beyond the binary categories of 'live' and 'recorded' (see Auslander, 2008; 2002). It continues with a short history of the posthumous duet before examining three case studies of televised posthumous duets from 2006 and 2007.

Theorising the Posthumous Duet: Sonic Recontextualisation

Many scholars have focused on the study of a star's posthumous career, including Rodman (1996) and Doss (2005) on Elvis Presley, Mäkelä (2005) on John Lennon, Jensen (2005b) on Patsy Cline, and Kamberelis and Dimitriadis (2005) on Tupac Shakur. One notable study that sheds light on the posthumous duet in particular is Stanyek and Piekut's, 'Deadness: Technologies of the Intermundane' (2010). Their article explores posthumous duets as 'intermundane collaborations' in terms of temporality, archives, agency and within the history of sound recording, proposing several terms to conceptualise 'deadness' in music.

The numerous concerns about the posthumous duet stem from pre-existing ambiguities about sonic and/or performance re-contextualisation after the death of the performer. Stars do not have an industry shelf life that ends with physical death. In fact, their existing performances continue to circulate in new contexts, such as 'best of' television specials, YouTube channels, in mash-up videos, and more. The nature of twenty-first century mass media means that 'we live in a world of dead people who continue to speak', and continue to sing (Jensen, 2005a p. xxii). Indeed, 'in the age of recording media', as Bauman (cited in Bode, 2007 p. 37) has long argued, 'things no longer live and then die – instead they appear and disappear, with the possibility of appearing again'. This connects with Feld's (1996 p. 13) discussion of schizophonic mimesis, a concept that highlights the indexical connections between a sound, its creator and its new reinvented form, and draws on other studies of splitting and copying (Attali, 1985), not to mention the authenticity and value of the new creation when compared with the original (Benjamin, 1969). Auslander (1992 p. 30), moreover, notes that the issues surrounding the digital manipulation of existing audio material for new purposes involves an 'important nexus of cultural discourses: performance, technology, and the law'. These three aspects are seen in his example of a drumming track, originally recorded by Led Zeppelin's John Bonham but now edited, reordered and reworked long after Bonham's death for the Frankie Goes to Hollywood song 'Relax'.

The resulting drum track, manipulated by technology and without the consent of the performer, both is and isn't Bonham's performance, thus raising questions of artistic practices, ethical intent and intellectual property rights. While these are also applicable to the posthumous duet, one of the fundamental differences between this audio-only example and the televised posthumous duet is the additional visual component; this is a relatively recent development.

A Recent History of the Posthumous Duet

It is unclear as to when the first posthumous duet was created. Stanyek and Piekut (2010) suggest that the first posthumous collaboration occurred when dead tenor Enrico Caruso's voice from a 1907 recording was dubbed with live musicians for a 1932 release. Vocal collaborations between dead and living singers emerged in the 1950s, perhaps as a result of experiments with analogue editing techniques. Several more were produced in the following decades, however it was not until the late 1980s and early 1990s that the posthumous duet was duly acknowledged as a unique form within popular music.

Many such duets during the 1990s were between family members. For example, the single 'There's a Tear in My Beer' featured a collaboration between father Hank Williams Senior (1923–53) and son Hank Williams Junior for the album *The Best of Hank and Hank* (Curb Records, 1992). By this stage, the audio-only posthumous duet had extended to the music video format to suit the demands of the MTV-influenced industry, and performance footage of both living and dead singers was now expected. The best-known posthumous duet video comes from this era, featuring father Nat 'King' Cole (1919–65) and daughter Natalie Cole. Their song 'Unforgettable' was the lead single for her 1991 album *Unforgettable ... with Love* (Elektra/WEA), and the music video featured new colour footage of Natalie interspersed with pre-existing black and white footage of Cole from a 1957 episode of the *Nat King Cole Show*. In the 2000s, children of deceased stars have continued to produce posthumous duets by way of tribute to the deceased's illustrious career, and to reinvigorate their own repertoire. Lisa Marie Presley, for example, recorded an internet-only release of 'In the Ghetto' (Spinner.com, 2007) with her father in 2007 to commemorate the 30th anniversary of Elvis's death. This historical trend of family duetting has afforded the posthumous duet a romantic and favourable image. In this context, the advances of technology have permitted the manipulation of performances, resulting in the realisation of a magical 'if only ...' performance between deceased parents and their offspring.

Posthumous duets between unrelated singers are a more recent occurrence. In 2007 an album of Dean Martin (1951–87) duets was recorded with performers such as Joss Stone and Robbie Williams for the 10-year anniversary of Martin's death. Titled *Forever Cool* (Capitol, 2007), this collection demonstrated another function of the posthumous duet: to allow a star's charm, appeal and 'coolness' to persist beyond the grave. At the time of the release, Martin's daughter Gail

168　　　DEATH AND THE ROCK STAR

announced to the press that the album would 'reach so many ages and so many different generations' (Méndez, 2007). This indicated that posthumous duets between former and current stars were part of a strategy of reinvigorating cool hits from the past in order to find relevance with today's audience. In addition, she noted that her 'Dad would have adored it': a comment that effectively pre-empted and answered the unspoken question about whether the star would have consented to the use of his music in this new context had he been still alive. Here, the issue of the dead's distinct lack of agency (a point taken up later in this chapter) is avoided, due to a family member's authority to speak on their behalf. However, not all relatives of deceased stars consider posthumous duets to be desirable for a star's brand. When Janie Hendrix, CEO of Experience Hendrix, was asked if she would consider 'partnering up with her dead stepbrother' for a song, her reply was curt and disparaging: 'No. We kind of look at [the posthumous duet] as the karaoke version of playing with Jimi ... We try to keep things as authentically correct and as pure as possible' (cited in Méndez, 2007).

In many ways, retaining the 'authenticity' and 'purity' of a dead musician's image or back catalogue of music is now out of the hands of gatekeepers and copyright holders such as Janie Hendrix. In the digital age of free audio-visual editing software and YouTube uploads, fans are now able to (legally and illegally) cut, paste and display an unending array of composite images and audio material in public forums. The abundance and public acceptance of mash-up performances featuring deceased stars are also sustained by twenty-first-century modes of consuming audio-visual products (such as music videos and live DVDs), which continue to circulate in the marketplace and find rerelease long after a star's death. In particular, the online or televised posthumous duet exemplifies 'digitextuality', in that 'digital fabrications function as real-time experience of a sort to overcome not only time and space, but life and death' (Everett, 2003 p. 32). As such, the posthumous duet can be envisioned as a means to resurrect not only the dead star's image but also that star's career.

The years 2006–7 were a particularly fruitful period for televised posthumous duets in the UK and the USA. This may have been due to an increase in technological developments that enabled the production of posthumous duets, or perhaps it was indicative of a sustained public interest in this musical form. Three examples from this period – produced only months apart – are particularly useful to illustrate some of the concerns raised so far about the posthumous duet. The first is a television advertisement produced for BBC Radio 2 about an 'amazing line-up' (2006) of musicians. Although it does not feature a posthumous duet on camera, per se, it presents a stage scenario which enables a discussion about contrived performance relationships between the dead and living. The second is a television programme for BBC 1 that is dedicated to the posthumous duet, titled *Duet Impossible* (2006), which focuses on technology as a means of fulfilling a performance 'dream' for the living star. Lastly, the third considers the ethics surrounding the 'duty of care' toward a deceased star in one performance from the 'Idol Gives Back' episode of the *American Idol* television series (2007).

BBC Radio 2's *Amazing Line Up* – Manufacturing Dead-Living Relationships

In September 2006, a series of innovative videos screened on UK television to promote BBC Radio 2's new audio playlist. The star of the campaign was a long-dead Elvis Presley (1935–77) alongside two other dead stars: singer Marvin Gaye (1931–84) and drummer Keith Moon (1946–78). The setting was a large music hall, where an in-house audience cheered wildly at what seemed to be the start of a popular music concert. Elvis introduced the members of his all-star band, one by one, including 'the man with the beautiful voice: Marvin Gaye', and the living musicians which included all-female vocal group The Sugababes 'on backing vocals', Led Zeppelin's Jimmy Page 'on lead guitar', ex-Oasis member Noel Gallagher 'on rhythm guitar', soloist Sheryl Crowe 'on bass guitar' and Stevie Wonder 'on piano'.

This unlikely grouping of living and deceased performers from a variety of genres serves to visually and aurally encapsulate Radio 2's new focus on musical diversity – a point that was underscored by the station's new slogan which appeared during the final frames of the advertisement: 'What an amazing line-up, all day every day' (DFGW for British Broadcasting Corporation Radio 2, 2006).[1] The unusual promotional video became a surprise internet hit. It was uploaded to YouTube, sent to email inboxes as a viral video, and later uploaded to view on the BBC website. In an interview with UK newspaper *The Daily Mail* (2006), the BBC's head of marketing, Rochelle Fox, articulated the broadcaster's delight in the video's popularity: 'We've had a fantastic response from all over the world. We've had people emailing and asking [about it] which is quite unusual for a promotional trailer'.

The unprecedented interest in the advertisement, and the technology involved in creating a seamless collage of performers, prompted the BBC to request the commissioned advertising agency DFGW (now Freud) to publicly explain how the concert footage was manufactured. Using DVDs, the BBC's own archive library and even YouTube, pre-existing performance footage from noteworthy concerts over several decades were cut, pasted and carefully edited together. DFGW revealed, for example, that footage of guitarist Noel Gallagher was taken from his 2003 Royal Albert Hall concert with The Who and Friends, that the shots of Marvin Gaye were taken from his Live in Montreux show of 1980, and that the footage of Presley came from his famed 1973 concert, Aloha from Hawaii, where he introduced his band. In addition, DFGW recorded new audio material, most likely voiced by an Elvis impersonator, so as to weave these sections together and such that Presley appeared to introduce the members of his present-day 'amazing line-up'.

---

[1]   See Grainge (2010) for an analysis of the Elvis advertisement within the paradigm of 'brandcasting', as a means of promoting BBC Radio's brand in a complex audio-visual-digital media environment.

The extraction of performers from their original context and their repurposing in the new advertisement could suggest a moment of 'hauntology', a concept devised by Derrida (1994) and revised by the music writer Reynolds (2011), which involves the resurfacing, or haunting, of once-forgotten anachronistic music styles or techniques from the archives. However, it can be argued that none of these well-known popular music performers have left the public's consciousness, nor are they presented in a sepulchral manner. In fact, one of the key features of the video is the creation of interpersonal on-stage relationships between the band members. The footage is edited in a way to suggest friendly exchanges between the on-stage stars, evidenced by carefully edited glances, smiles and gestures. After Elvis introduces Keith Moon, for example, Moon steals the limelight by presenting a playful and virtuosic drum roll which cuts Elvis's introductions short. Suddenly silenced, Elvis looks backward over his shoulder to grin at Moon, before slowly shaking his head as if to say 'not again! that's typical behaviour!', as you would to a close friend. Elvis also points directly at Stevie Wonder when introducing him, with both men in the same frame, and nonchalantly says 'play it Stevie!' as the crowd cheers and Stevie begins riffing on the piano. Elvis also waves his arm toward The Sugababes singers, who stand from their upright stools, and slightly bow, wave, clap or clasp their hands in a 'thank you' prayer position toward Presley and the crowd. The camera cuts away to the front row of the audience, where women grin delightedly, while cheers and applause continue to rise and fall in volume over the entire video. The video shows a band that is on the best of terms, and ready to perform to an appreciative crowd.

Despite the realism, these relationships could never have existed outside an editing suite. The power of the producers of this video is undeniable, as is the lack of agency of the dead, the malleability of the star image, and how it can be manipulated after the star has died. Would Gaye, Moon and Presley – all consummate performers of rock, soul and other genres – have wanted to be in a band with pop singers The Sugababes? What of the questions about tampering with the sacred image of the King (his voice and his body) in order to manufacture new relationships and performance scenarios? These questions are about the producer's intent, but they are also about a perceived positive response from fans. Lisa Bode's studies (2010; 2007) on the reanimation of dead actors for new filmic contexts (by, for example, putting new words in dead actor's mouths) provides an entry point to understanding the issue of manufacturing performance relationships in the context of the posthumous duet. In particular, Bode looks at a case study of Marlon Brando (1924–2004). The star was filmed for the original *Superman* film in 1978 and, using previously unseen footage and existing audio alongside new computer-generated images, was posthumously reanimated for a role reprisal in the 2006 sequel *Superman Returns* (Bode, 2010 p. 64). In considering why this was done, Bode notes that 'the impulse beneath digitally reanimated stars [is] one that aims to eliminate this temporal distance [for fans], to bring the dead and the past back to a semblance of life in the present' (Bode, 2007 p. 37). The reanimation of Elvis for the *Amazing Line-Up* promotion elicited both positive and negative

PERFORMING BEYOND THE GRAVE: THE POSTHUMOUS DUET

feedback from fans. However, the BBC spokesperson Rochelle Fox insisted that the ad was not 'shocking or salacious' but instead 'really heart-warming' (*The Daily Mail*, 2006). Without a doubt, this advertisement's marketing strategy relied on an audience's presumed desire to see an uplifting display of past and present stars of popular music performing together in a concert that, without technological interference, could never be.

Duet Impossible – Fulfilling a Performer's Dream through Technology

Just a few months after the *Amazing Line-Up* aired, and perhaps with a view to capitalise on the public's interest in this ad, the BBC presented the December television programme *Duet Impossible* (British Broadcasting Corporation, 2006). It featured such posthumous pairings as the female vocal group The Sugababes with Dusty Springfield (1939–99) for 'Dancing in the Street', singer-songwriter Katie Melua with Eva Cassidy (1963–96) for 'Somewhere over the Rainbow', and male vocal group Westlife with Roy Orbison (1936–88) for his song 'Pretty Woman'.

The return of a musical icon in a posthumous duet serves to maintain the deceased star's media presence and to nourish what Jenson (2005a p. xxi) calls their 'afterimage', thus helping to keep the star 'alive'. However, this programme was framed from the perspective of the living performer: it was a chance for living musicians to fulfil their 'dreams' by singing with the deceased (a discourse that is also adopted for posthumous duets between family members). Steve Smith, the producer and director of *Duet Impossible*, posted a promotional blurb for the programme on his website, noting that the show would 'make the musically impossible become possible as some of today's biggest pop stars get a chance to sing a duet with one of their all time idols' (Smith, 2008). The Christmas Eve timing of the show continued the rhetoric of 'dreams come true', at the height of nostalgic holiday season programming about Christmas miracles and the birth of Christ. The religious connotations were reinforced by references to heaven, where the deceased now dwelled and continued to make music: 'Stars from yesteryear make a comeback from the big gig in the sky and perform live on stage with stars of today', claimed Smith (2008).

The *Duet Impossible* performances were not only framed by the Christmas miracle, but also the rhetoric of startling audio-visual effects – from holograms to optical illusions – within the 'techno-spectacle' (see Spencer-Hall, 2012; Harris, 2013; also Arnold in this volume). Through the 'magic of modern technology', claimed Smith (2008), we are able to see humans triumph over death. Certainly, the technology was impressive: the BBC used an advanced rotoscoping production technique, where a performer's outline is traced and then cut, allowing the image to be inserted into the new video context. It seems that if viewers were not engulfed in nostalgia upon seeing a deceased star performing once again, then they would be awe-struck by the technology used for the programme. In reality, there was an ambivalent response to the programme. Some writers debated the merits of the

172   *DEATH AND THE ROCK STAR*

performances. For example, music journalist Jim DeRogatis of the *Chicago Sun-Times* noted that

> there's no two ways around the mercenary aspect of live musicians with dubious
> connections to the dead flaunting their stuff ... It's all really "Wizard of Oz",
> except behind the curtain is not a little man, but a corpse ... the technology
> is astounding. We can do anything ... [but] it doesn't mean we should.
> (DeRogatis cited in Méndez, 2007)

In this way, the 'dream fulfilment' for the living has a sinister side. It can be deemed
an exploitative act of self-interest that directly benefits the living performer, who
is capitalising on the deceased's star image. And the dead, of course, have no
agency or decisional power in such matters. The final example further unpacks the
relationship between living producers and dead artists, with reference to the notion
of 'duty of care'.

American Idol – Duty of Care toward the Dead

The final posthumous duet example discussed here is 'If I Can Dream' from the
'Idol Gives Back' episode of *American Idol*, broadcast on Fox on 25 April 2007.
The duet was performed by Céline Dion and Elvis Presley on the 30th anniversary
of his death. Host Ryan Seacrest sets the scene for the duet via aggrandising
language that forewarns television viewers to expect an extraordinary performance:
'Now prepare to be startled. Prepare for magnificence. Prepare for a duet you
thought was impossible!' (Fox Broadcasting Company, 2007). The duet is
'impossible' because Elvis is presumably about to be brought into the present to
sing with a living star, as is the usual premise for a posthumous duet. However,
Seacrest reveals that there is a twist – viewers will instead witness a posthumous
duet that is set in the past when Elvis was still alive. To achieve this, Seacrest
declares that 'Céline Dion is travelling back to the year she was born, 1968, to
sing with the man who is and always will be the world's greatest idol!'[2] The screen
quickly fills with a re-configured digital logo featuring the words 'American Idol'
in a psychedelic, hippy 1960s font, and the year '1968' is written underneath in hot
pink to underscore the time-travel illusion. The song then begins with sweeping
360-degree footage of Dion, who wears a modern black suit and walks onto the
Idol stage in front of the studio audience. The 2007-style *American Idol* production
and lighting remains, and the only indication that this is set in the past is when
Presley appears alongside her in a white, 1960s-style safari suit. This footage of

---

[2]   The theme of 'going back in time' is also adopted for *Duet Impossible*, where the
band McFly supposedly travel back to the 1960s to perform 'Shout' alongside a 15-year-old
Lulu. This is not a posthumous duet, however, because all performers are still living, and in
fact present-day (2006) Lulu joins in at the end of the performance.

PERFORMING BEYOND THE GRAVE: THE POSTHUMOUS DUET   173

Presley, made possible via rotoscope techniques from Presley's 1968 *Comeback Special* (National Broadcasting Company, 1968), is supplemented by an on-stage body double for wide shots, so as to heighten the believability of the duet.

The temporal logic of this performance is undeniably skewed. Dion would have been a baby in 1968, unable to sing Elvis. So what is the purpose of this retro-themed performance? It can be argued that the symbols of 'pastness' in this performance – from Seacrest's explanation, to the old-fashioned on-screen lettering, and Presley's dated clothing – tap into a collective memory of a musical past. Audiences already familiar with the primary footage of Presley's classic performance are invited to experience a nostalgic wistfulness at seeing it again, and him again, on prime-time American television in 2007. Moreover, they are also encouraged to feel excitement about seeing 'the world's greatest idol' perform in a new context outside his known catalogue of performances, and within the contemporary context of *Idol*. In this instance, the posthumous duet is part of the 'spatial imaginary' – a term developed by Roberts (2014 p. 275) in his article concerning popular music and the culture of heritage – where the past is not hidden or buried but existing instead in a state of 'co-presence' with the present.

This very clear combination of past/present and old/new, may help create what Lisa Bode calls 'a contemplative viewing distance' for audiences (2007 p. 38), which makes the dead 'watchable' (2007 p. 38). Certainly, footage of Elvis's living, performing body and voice has long been circulated since his death. But this performance, arguably more so than the other two examples discussed in this chapter, generates questions about agency and will with regard to the King of rock 'n' roll – perhaps the most important popular musician of all time.

A star's posthumous image is constructed and defined by how they are remembered, and 'for the posthumous celebrity, the "real" person can no longer shape his or her story, but this doesn't stop the process of story evolution and transformation' (Jensen, 2005a p. xxii). Indeed, what 'we' – as the creators of these posthumous duets – should or shouldn't do is of pivotal concern to a star's legacy. In this instance, Dion and Presley are edited in a manner so as to stare into each other's eyes, sing in harmony, gesture politely to each other, and perform intimately. Would Elvis have wanted to sing with Dion at all?

This performance initiated new discussions online – some favourable, some scathing – centring around *Idol*'s duty of care toward the dead (see Bode, 2010 p. 61). Such discussion indicates a perception that the posthumous duet is not merely about reshuffling sound bites, data files and pixels. Flying in the face of all common sense, the duet has become, for many viewers, a means of retrieving the voice and flesh and bones of a human being. This is why there is heated speculation over a star's 'agency, will, and capacity for independent action', even in death, because these are aspects that make stars so attractive to begin with (Bode, 2007 p. 39). The human body has died, taking with it this control. Instead control and power have shifted toward the creators of the posthumous duet, encapsulated in the question posed by America's ABC (2007): 'Who should *Idol* resurrect next?'

174   *DEATH AND THE ROCK STAR*

Conclusion

By its very definition, a star is a performer 'whose figure enters into subsidiary forms of circulations, and then feeds back into future performances' (Ellis, 1958 p. 91). In the rise to celebrity, stars – including musicians and singers – become known to the public primarily through their appearances in different media texts (Dyer, 1986 [1979] pp. 68–72). As a result, the star image becomes 'all that is publicly known about the star' (Gledhill, 1991 pp. 214–17). Indeed, the phenomenon of stardom relies on such a strong media presence that stars 'can only exist *as stars* in the ethereal non-spaces of media texts and public imagination' (Rodman, 1996 p. 101; emphasis in original). For fans, a popular music star's image is so valuable that it becomes, even in death, 'more tightly held and more powerful than the real person on which it is based' (Fraser and Brown, 2002 p. 202).

For the deceased star, whose status is always unstable, ambiguous (Dyer, 1991) and dependent on public attention (Alberoni, 1972), the posthumous duet offers possibilities to increase their media presence after death (or in Presley's case, long after he has 'left the building'). Indeed, to rephrase the lyrics of Elvis Presley from 'If I Can Dream', while they can think, while they can talk, while they can stand, while they can walk and even when their bodies can no longer do any of these, the star image will continue to find resonance – even from beyond the grave.

Bibliography

ABC News (2007) 'Elvis on "Idol": How it was Done', 27 April, http://abcnews. go.com/GMA/story?id=3087711, accessed 16 August 2014.

Alberoni, Francesco (1972) 'The Powerless Elite: Theory and Sociological Research on the Phenomenon of Stars', in Denis McQuail (ed.), *Sociology of Mass Communication*. Baltimore, MD: Penguin, pp. 75–98.

Attali, Jacques (1985) *Noise: The Political Economy of Music*. Minneapolis, MN: University of Minnesota Press.

Auslander, Philip (1992) 'Intellectual Property Meets the Cyborg: Performance and the Cultural Politics of Technology', *Performing Arts Journal*, 14 (1), pp. 30–42.

——— (2002) 'Live from Cyberspace: Or, I was Sitting at my Computer this Guy Appeared he Thought I was a Bot', *Performing Arts Journal*, 24 (1), pp. 16–21.

——— (2008) *Liveness: Performance in a Mediatized Culture*, 2nd edition. Abingdon and New York: Routledge.

Benjamin, Walter (1992 [1969]) 'The Work of Art in the Age of Mechanical Reproduction', in *Illuminations*. Translated by Harry Zohn. London: Fontana, pp. 211–44.

Bode, Lisa (2007) '"Grave Robbing" or "Career Comeback"? On the Digital Resurrection of Dead Screen Stars', in Kari Kallioniemi, Kimi Kärki, Janne Mäkelä and Hannu Salmi (eds), *History of Stardom Reconsidered*. Turku: International Institute for Popular Culture, pp. 36–40.

————— (2010) 'No Longer Themselves? Framing Digitally Enabled Posthumous "Performance"', *Cinema Journal*, 49 (4), pp. 46–70.

Derrida, Jacques (1994) *Spectres of Marx: The State of the Debt, the Work of Mourning and the New International*. Translated by Peggy Kamuf. London: Routledge.

Digital Domain (2014) 'Virtual 2Pac' movie, http://digitaldomain.com/projects/2711, accessed 29 May 2015.

Doss, Erika (2005) 'Elvis Forever', in Steve Jones and Joli Jensen (eds), *Afterlife as Afterimage: Understanding Posthumous Fame*. New York: Peter Lang, pp. 61–78.

Dyer, Richard (1986 [1979]) *Stars*. London: British Film Institute.

————— (1991) 'A Star is Born and the Construction of Authenticity', in Christine Gledhill (ed.), *Stardom: Industry of Desire*. London: Routledge, pp. 132–40.

Ellis, John (1985) *Visible Fictions: Cinema, Television, Video*. London: Routledge.

Everett, Anna (2003) 'Digitextuality and Click Theory: Theses on Convergence Media in the Digital Age', in Anna Everett and John T. Caldwell (eds), *New Media: Theories and Practices of Digitextuality*. London: Routledge, pp. 29–45.

Feld, Steven (1996) 'Pygmy Pop: A Genealogy of Schizophonic Mimesis', *Yearbook for Traditional Music*, 28, pp. 1–35.

Fraser, Benson P. and William J. Brown (2002) 'Media, Celebrities, and Social Influence: Identification with Elvis Presley', *Mass Communication and Society*, 5 (2), pp. 183–206.

Gledhill, Christine (1991) 'Signs of Melodrama', in *Stardom: Industry of Desire*. New York: Routledge, pp. 207–29.

Grainge, Paul (2010) 'Elvis Sings for the BBC: Broadcast Branding and Digital Media Design', *Media Culture Society*, 32 (45), pp. 45–61.

Harris, Matthew (2013) 'The Hologram of Tupac at Coachella and Saints: The Value of Relics for Devotees', *Celebrity Studies*, 4 (2), pp. 238–40.

Jensen, Joli (2005a) 'On Fandom, Celebrity, and Mediation: Posthumous Possibilities', in Steve Jones and Joli Jensen (eds), *Afterlife as Afterimage: Understanding Posthumous Fame*. New York: Peter Lang, pp. xv–xxiii.

————— (2005b) 'Posthumous Patsy Clines: Constructions of Identity in Hillbilly Heaven', in Steve Jones and Joli Jensen (eds), *Afterlife as Afterimage: Understanding Posthumous Fame*. New York: Peter Lang, pp. 121–41.

Kamberelis, George and Greg Dimitriadis (2005) 'Collectively Remembering Tupac: The Narrative Mediation of Current Events, Cultural Histories, and Social Identities', in Steve Jones and Joli Jensen (eds), *Afterlife as Afterimage: Understanding Posthumous Fame*. New York: Peter Lang, pp. 144–70.

Mäkelä, Janne (2005) 'Who Owns Him? The Debate on John Lennon', in Steve Jones and Joli Jensen (eds), *Afterlife as Afterimage: Understanding Posthumous Fame*. New York: Peter Lang, pp. 171–90.

Méndez, Teresa (2007) 'The Day the Music Didn't Die', *The Christian Science Monitor*, 12 October, http://www.csmonitor.com/2007/1012/p13s01-almp.html, accessed 23 October 2014.

Reynolds, Simon (2011) *Retromania: Pop Culture's Addiction to its Own Past*. London: Faber and Faber.

176   *DEATH AND THE ROCK STAR*

Roberts, Les (2014) 'Talkin Bout My Generation: Popular Music and the Culture of Heritage', *International Journal of Heritage Studies*, 20 (3), pp. 262–80.

Rodman, Gilbert B. (1996) *Elvis after Elvis: The Posthumous Career of a Living Legend*. London: Routledge.

Smith, Steve (dir.) (2008) 'BBC Duet Impossible', 30 November, http://www.stevesmith.tv/Steve%20Smith/Duet%20Impossible.html, accessed 23 October 2014.

Spencer-Hall, Alicia (2012) 'The Post-mortem Projections: Medieval Resurrection and the Return of Tupac Shakur', *Opticon1826*, 13, pp. 56–71.

Stanyek, Jason and Benjamin Piekut (2010) 'Deadness: Technologies of the Intermundane', *TDR: The Drama Review*, 54 (1), pp. 14–38.

The Daily Mail (2006) 'Elvis Superband Ad "A Surprise Internet Hit"', 13 October, http://www.dailymail.co.uk/tvshowbiz/article-410214/Elvis-superband-ad-surprise-internet-hit.html, accessed 14 July 2014.

Westfesttv (2012) 'Tupac Hologram Snoop Dogg and Dr Dre Perform Coachella Live 2012', 17 April, https://www.youtube.com/watch?v=TGbrFmPBV0Y, accessed 23 October 2014.

Discography

Natalie Cole, *Unforgettable ... with Love*, Elektra/WEA, 1 CD compilation, 1991.

Dean Martin, *Forever Cool*, Capitol, 1 CD compilation, 2007.

Lisa Marie Presley, 'In the Ghetto', Spinner.com, online release, 2007.

Hank Williams Senior and Hank Williams Junior, *The Best of Hank and Hank*, Curb Records, 1 CD compilation, 1992.

Filmography

Duet Impossible (2006) television programme, British Broadcasting Corporation, BBC One, 24 December.

Elvis [1968 Comeback Special] (1968), television programme, National Broadcasting Company, NBC, 3 December.

Elvis (2006) television advertisement, DFGW for British Broadcasting Corporation, BBC Radio 2, September.

'Idol Gives Back: Part Two'. *American Idol* (Season six, Episode 33) (2007), television programme, Fox Broadcasting Company, 25 April.

Chapter 13

There's a Spectre Haunting Hip-hop: Tupac Shakur, Holograms in Concert and the Future of Live Performance

Regina Arnold

> In effect, the dead black body may be an ultimate figure of regulation, unruly desire and its risks fully mastered.
>
> Barrett (1999 p. 306)

Rap stars have been known to be late to their gigs, but no one has ever been later than Tupac Shakur. On 15 April 2012, when he took the stage at the Coachella Festival to sing alongside the rappers Snoop Dogg and Dr Dre in the form of a hologram, he had been dead for 15 years. That night, Shakur appeared on stage around midnight, greeting the crowd with the words, 'You know what this is? What's up Dre? What's up Snoop? What the fuck is up, Coachella?' He then performed his song 'Hail Mary', segueing half-way through into a duet with producer/performer Snoop Dogg on the song '2 of Amerikaz Most Wanted'. During the five-minute-long special effect, Shakur's digitised image strode across the stage, turned around, danced in time with and even conversed with (the live) Snoop. The performance was so well synchronised that both men seemed to be standing on the same white line drawn across the stage, and when it was over, the fact that the long dead Tupac had headlined Coachella immediately became both a conventional media and a social media sensation via Twitter and Facebook, Instagram and YouTube.

Shakur's 'live' performance was not the first of its type, it was just the lengthiest and the most surprising. Will.i.am appeared via hologram talking with Anderson Cooper on CNN on election night 2008. Al Gore appeared as a hologram at Live Earth Tokyo. Céline Dion even sang a duet with a hologram of Elvis Presley on an episode of *American Idol*.[1] Shakur's performance at Coachella, however, was unique in that it didn't merely project a pre-recorded message in a 3D manner to a mediated audience; rather, by presenting itself to a live audience, it passed off what was billed as a *new* performance by a dead man as a *current* one. The difference here is not just academic: Tupac Shakur as a

---

[1]   See the chapter by Shelley Brunt in this volume.

current, creative artist is distinctly different from a dead, inactive artist, and his work can thus be circulated differently. This chapter seeks to interrogate some of the theoretical problems that Shakur's holographic image raises, for example, how the use of his digitised body at Coachella may have reappropriated the meaning of his life and work. I argue that inserting an iconic and politically-charged singer, whose work in the 1990s redefined rap as a site of counter-hegemonic speech, into a benign entertainment context, permanently and inevitably changes the symbolic weight of his oeuvre. Additionally, although the use of a hologram in place of a human complicates, enriches and may even emancipate the experience of rock performance, there are troubling aspects to it too. If, as Walter Benjamin argues, the moving picture 'burst this prison-world asunder' (1968 p. 236), then holograms that purport to reanimate dead people might do the same thing, only with a different set of consequences.

Another more pressing issue relates to ethics and race. One legacy of slavery is that images of black male bodies haunt American culture. Billie Holiday famously sang about 'black bodies swinging in the Southern breeze', in her song 'Strange Fruit' (1939), and that is not the only image of African-Americans caught up in violence in the media. There is, for example, a famous 1955 photograph of murdered Mississippi boy Emmett Till's dead body, which writer Evelyn C. White remembers looking at with her friends in the pages of *Jet* magazine: 'We'd silently gaze at Emmett's photo for what seemed like hours ... in his pummelled and contorted face, I saw a reflection of myself and the blood-chilling violence that would greet me if I ever ventured into the wilderness' (White, 1995 p. 581). White's distinct memory may not linger in the minds of young people today, but the more recent histories and photographs of black murder victims like Oscar Grant, Trayvon Martin, Justin Davis and Mike Brown ensure that similar images and ideas are still in circulation.

The real Tupac Shakur was, like all humans, a complicated being. But Shakur's holographic body, dancing above the crowd at Coachella in its transparent trousers, is a cartoon thug, comely and compelling, hardly confrontational. Appearing as it does in the midst of a nostalgic revisitation of gangsta rap, his hologram can be read as merely a racially fetishised aspect of his humanity as a whole. Stuart Hall (1997 p. 268) claims that fetishism is 'a displaced form of representation', a strategy for 'both representing and not representing the tabooed, dangerous or forbidden object of pleasure and desire'. The hologram of Tupac provides just this sort of alibi, a license for unregulated voyeurism. In other words, audiences who might have felt shame, fear or simply discomfort at a Tupac Shakur (or other gangsta rap) show in 1994 are now allowed access to a manageable, displaced 'part' of Tupac, the part in this case being what is essentially his shadow cast on a (mylar) wall.

Resurrection

In 1996, at the age of 25, Tupac Shakur was shot in a drive-by after attending a boxing match in Las Vegas, and eventually died from his wounds.[2] Since then, his production company has released eight LPs which have sold 25 million copies (Greenberg, 2011). According to writer, historian and hip-hop analyst Michael Eric Dyson (2006), Shakur is widely considered the world's most influential rapper, and one of the most important figures in the genre's brief history (see also Chang, 2005; Dimitriadis, 2009; Kitwana, 2002). Shakur, whose mother Afeni Shakur was a well-known member of the Black Panthers, is widely considered to have merged hip-hop aesthetics with a wider political message, which Dyson argues resonated deeply with the black community – at least, that portion which sees itself as deeply in conversation with hip-hop. In that world, Tupac 'is perhaps the representative figure of his generation' (Dyson, 2001 p. 13).

The popularity of dead rock stars is nothing new: in 1981, *Rolling Stone* magazine famously ran a cover story on the continuing interest in Jim Morrison, headlined '[h]e's hot, he's sexy, and he's dead' (Breslin, Hopkins and Williams, 1981). But as Barrett (1999 p. 306) has noted, the dead body is one thing; the dead black body is another. Hence, the 'resurrection' of Tupac Shakur's body as a performing hologram at Coachella raises some questions that holograms of Elvis Presley, Princess Leia and Céline Dion do not. First, why Tupac, and why now? One simple answer lies in Coachella's most prominent feature: reanimating the careers of dormant twentieth-century rock acts. The process is not disinterested: festivals like Coachella live and die by their blockbuster line-ups and surprise guests, and in order to justify enormous ticket prices, Coachella's organisers have engineered the reunions of long defunct bands like the Pixies, Throbbing Gristle, Pavement, Outkast and Bauhaus, whose lead singer Peter Murphy appeared on stage hanging upside down by his ankles.

But even by Coachella's standards, the presence, so to speak, of Tupac Shakur, was a spectacular coup. Murphy sang 'Bela Lugosi's Dead', but Tupac Shakur actually sang *while* dead. Although referred to as a hologram in most media accounts, the image was in fact a 2D illusion that used CGI animation and a special screen to create the sensation of liveness.[3] It was enormously realistic. Sweat glistened on Tupac's chiselled body, which was clad in almost see-through parachute pants. A medallion, dangling from his neck, seemed to sway in the air in time to the music. Most bizarre was the invocation of his location, Coachella, a place he couldn't possibly have played in his lifetime, and hence a rhetorical gesture that powerfully evoked the man's actual presence. The image,

---

[2] The murder remains unsolved, although a widely credited report in the *LA Times* (Phillips, 2002) claims that a member of a Los Angeles gang was responsible.

[3] In this chapter, I will continue to refer to the effect as a hologram, because it is popularly thought of as such. In the social media world, 'HoloPac' is a common term referring to this event.

which was created by Digital Domain Media Group and projected by AV Images on a piece of mylar stretched across a mirror, was created pixel by pixel, frame by frame, from scratch. According to Ed Ulbrich, a member of the company, the concert sequence was not simply a projection of already-seen material. 'This is not found footage. This is not archival footage. This is an illusion', he told *The Wall Street Journal*. The sequence was said to cost upwards of $300,000 (Smith, 2012).

Shakur was the ideal choice for resurrection at Coachella for many reasons. First, quite a few of his fans believe he faked his death. The reason for this belief is in part rooted in the black community's desire for this to be the case (Kamberlis and Dimitriadis, 2005 p. 260). Additionally, Shakur referred to his own death repeatedly in songs like 'Niggaz Done Changed' (Rich, 1996), and the video for the song 'I Ain't Mad at Cha' depicted him getting shot and dying, suggesting to some that his 'death' was pre-planned and staged. Today, websites devoted to theories about Shakur's 'faked' death abound, as googling the words 'Tupac alive' quickly demonstrates.[4] Even for those who are clear on his status as corpse, his resurrection at Coachella worked artistically because of the way it was foreshadowed by his lyrics, images and videos, and the Tupac's-death-as-hoax, Tupac-as-legend or Tupac-as-ghost narratives. His resurrection as a hologram also resonated handily with his status as the modern-day embodiment of mythic African-American figures like Br'er Rabbit and Stagger Lee (Dimitriadis, 2009; George, 1998; Dyson, 2006). What is more, Tupac's presence at Coachella made sense because over half of his recordings were released posthumously; one of these is actually called *Tupac: Resurrection* and is the soundtrack to a successful documentary from 2003 of the same name. But mostly, his return made sense because he is already haunting hip-hop – that is to say, his cultural legacy is still present in current music's contemporaneous form. His short career and violent death have made him the byword for authenticity in gangsta rap. His work, for instance, is invoked by Eminem's barely fictionalised character in the film *8 Mile* (2001) as the acme of authenticity, when the white rapper accuses his rivals of being 'no Pacs'. The importance of his legacy in rap has led to his work being the subject of several scholarly classes and seminars held at the universities of Washington, Harvard and Berkeley, and there is a Tupac Shakur archive at Atlanta University.

His critical acclaim, mass popularity and tragic, early and contested death certainly make Tupac Shakur's one of the most dramatic figures in the history of twentieth-century popular music, and this legitimising process continues even as his digital resurrection raises important ethical and aesthetic questions about the use of holograms in performance settings. The estate of Tupac Shakur gave permission for the use of his image at Coachella, just as they allow the use of his music in films, samples, books and other texts. In fact, his estate welcomes recombinant uses of his work. For example, the mix-tape *2Pac: Rap Phenomenon II* (2003) features Shakur's lyrics over updated beats from more recent rap hits, with new verses added by well-known acts like 50 Cent and Busta Rhymes.

---

[4] For example, see http://www.donmega.com/20-reasons-why-tupac-is-still-alive.php.

THERE'S A SPECTRE HAUNTING HIP-HOP 181

Nonetheless, performing as a hologram seems different, because it implicates his actual body as much as his intellectual body of work. Perhaps the technological resurrection of a body in order to make it converse with someone on stage should be considered a different kind of violation of copyright, because, as I'd like to suggest here, it is one that is implicitly violent – not just because of the Frankenstein-like elements inherent in the notion of reanimating long-dead flesh, but because forcing the reanimated body in question to sing, dance and say the words of someone else has overtones of puppetry, minstrelsy and voodoo, activities that have artistic and historical links to slavery. Gilroy (2001 p. 255) has questioned what he calls the 'epidermization' of the black body, suggesting it is time we break with images and words that celebrate both 'the scar on tortured flesh' and 'the gleeful reduction of the black body to its biochemically programmed, naturally physical superiority' (p. 258). And while I agree in theory that epidermisation essentialises race, in the singular case of the hologram, the discourses around identity politics, hip-hop and body politics are worth revisiting.

Appropriation

Coachella is an American popular music festival that debuted in 1999, 30 years after Woodstock, but the utopian discourse of Woodstock still percolates in the rhetoric surrounding it. There is nothing remotely countercultural about the festival's aims or its audience, yet Coachella's publicity material includes images that emphasise some of the more iconic symbols already defining Woodstock: teepees, for example, and a vast American-inflected landscape. Ethnic diversity may not be a prerequisite of communal utopia, but at large outdoor festivals set in out-of-the-way rural settings, diversity is mostly present on stage, as a spectacle. By contrast, the audience appears to be socio-economically, or at least educationally, homogeneous. In one self-reported poll on the festival's official website, Coachella-goers reported themselves as being 4 per cent African-American, or one-third of the proportionate demographic in the US on the whole (Ethnic Demographics, 2013); another poll reported that a full 94 per cent were high-school graduates, with the majority of those either in college or graduated (Your Educational Status, 2013). These figures do not correlate to US demographics (where only 33 per cent hold degrees), and the socio-economic status of concert-goers is also skewed towards the upper-middle-class, since the costs involved mean that the typical attendee there spends over $600; in addition, ticket purchase requires a credit card.

As anyone who has attended a large outdoor festival like Coachella or Bonnaroo will recognise, this isn't really a particularly trenchant observation; perhaps it merely concretises an aspect of popular music consumerism and hence complicates some of the more radical discourses that underpin long-standing practices surrounding folk, rock and rap music and their uses in festival settings (for more on these, see Frith, 1981; McKay, 2000; Bennett, 2004; Regis and Walton, 2008; Lebrun, 2009). However the territory becomes slightly more ominous when the ghost of Tupac

182   *DEATH AND THE ROCK STAR*

Shakur steps onto it. Although this is a reductionist category, 'gangsta rap' does qualify Shakur's musical output, and there is strong evidence that Shakur's music has special significance to African-American listeners, or did at the time of its release. Kamberlis and Dimitriadis (2005 p. 148) described Shakur's cultural role in black communities as bearing the legacy of the black power movement, both through his status as the son of Afeni Shakur and through songs like 'Keep Ya Head Up' (1993), 'White Man'z World' (1996), and 'Only God Can Judge Me' (1996). That Shakur's work was understood this way in black communities has been concretised by Dimitriadis' work in an inner-city youth centre, where Shakur was idolised. According to the author, Shakur provided a profound emotional outlet for these young people, appearing to them as 'an invincible outlaw who settled his problems swiftly and violently, providing feelings of physical invulnerability to an often intensely vulnerable population' (2009 p. 152). When Shakur died, Dimitriadis found that many of the young people he worked with were enormously reluctant to believe he was dead.

Since his death, Tupac's recorded musical output has increasingly appealed to listeners of all races. Superficially, then, his ghostly presence at Coachella 2012 merely demonstrates a rise in rap's popularity with mainstream white listeners. However, I would argue that, because the predominantly white and well-off audience at Coachella appears to be delecting in the spectacle of a black male body, it could also have signified a far more complicated transformation. Dr Dre, who was the driving force behind the 'resurrection', may have intended this hologram duet as an homage, rather than an appropriation, but Railton and Watson (2011 p. 128) have shown how black male bodies in music videos perform 'a very specific racial fetish, one built around a pull between envy and fear, attraction and repulsion, admiration and threat'. They observe that the marginalised masculinity of black men in music videos 'deploy(s) the conventions of Western art to sculpt and fetishize the black male body into an erotic object of contemplation [while also] working to transform and dissect that body into an object of scrutiny and curiosity' (p. 126). The use of Tupac's body in this manner falls directly into this paradigm, with its deadness combining with its blackness to reduce his artistic identity to the simplified signifier of black male body. Indeed, the word 'dissect' can correlate both to the corpse itself, and to the way that film gets edited – or in this case, digitised – to create new robotic movements and actions. In addition, like the black male nudes in Robert Mapplethorpe's works of art and the nude photos of Paul Robeson in Richard Dyer's study 'Crossing Over' (1986), Tupac's holographic hard body highlights the romanticisation of the very words that he had tattooed in Gothic script across his torso: 'Thug Life'. In the video of the performance, those words glow across his skin, spelling out one particular significance – that of holy gangsta rapper. All other meanings are elided, and he is now fixed in the Zeitgeist as a digitised ghost.

The reductive use of Tupac as a hologram raises other issues in terms of race. According to Baker and Nelson (2001 p. 232), the bound black body – in literature, music, film, popular culture and elsewhere – is a 'bedrock for the construction of racism in the United States'. They argue that archetypes of the bounded black body recur in the American mediascape at regular intervals – from James Byrd to Emmett Till, Rodney King, Amadou Diallo and Abner Louima – reminding us again and again of the millions of bound black bodies deposited by ships in America. Echoes of this can be seen in entertainment contexts. At the famous all-black music festival Wattstax, held at the Los Angeles stadium in 1972, Isaac Hayes appeared on stage, similarly half-clad, like Tupac, but with his sculpted upper-body draped in golden chains. Tupac's animatronic appearance at Coachella is strongly reminiscent of that image, but only in relief, as its opposite. Wattstax drew an almost entirely black audience, and one that was local to the area. Hayes's chains, whether perceived as satirical or angry, were also worn with a measure of self-parody. The gesture could be read as an in-joke about the legacy of slavery.

By contrast, Coachella is a very different arena in which to display a black body bound, in this case, by the restrictions of technology: the mylar, the pixels, the projector. Because its audience has been drawn from across the country to a field, any gesture made by a rap artist in this arena could be understood in a variety of ways, none of which are likely to spring from a common understanding of the artist. Moreover, the presence, or invocation, of an artist will have a different valence if the artist is dead. Hayes's chains were meant as a mark of both solidarity and triumph, aimed at an audience who, in broad terms, were sharing both his aims and his gains. This is not the case here. Tupac's music was written for and about an audience that had a similarly shared context, but removed to the context of Coachella, his glowing skin and harsh tattoo come across as mere décor, a hipster's fantasy of (to flip the FBI's description of Martin Luther King) a dangerous negro. In fact, Shakur has been rendered harmless by mortality, technology and time.

The cultural appropriation of African-American musical forms is nothing new in popular culture, but a fresh appraisal of it seems in order regarding the ways that technology may be reinscribing older patterns of co-option. In its early days, rap music was an arena where cultural appropriation turned into a hegemonic struggle for legitimacy, as white performers like the Beastie Boys and Eminem rapped their way into the canon. Today, rap has a global presence that makes discussions about the racial make-up of its practitioners and its listeners much more complicated than in the past. Yet its global reach and international audience does not negate the constant spectre of appropriation; indeed, the cultural appropriation inherent in the hologram of Tupac seems to be categorically different from that which involves rap, since it is not his music that has been commodified – that happened long ago – but some kind of afterglow of his body.

Barrett (1999) argued that the rhetoric surrounding Tupac's death – the notion, for example, that he was 'a hip-hop James Dean' – was rooted in the pleasure, and expectation, of white audiences for young black men to fulfil their destinies as mere bodies at work.[5] Tupac and rappers like him, Barrett (1999 p. 311) contends,

---

[5] The same comparison was made by Michael Eric Dyson (2001), and appeared on MTV News (Baker, 2001), *The Guardian* (Ojumu, 2004), *The Washington Post* (Flock, 2011)

184 DEATH AND THE ROCK STAR

exist at a 'cash nexus' somewhere between capitalism and critique. Hence, Tupac's death merely underscores the fact that 'a highly consequential social production from dead black bodies proves to be, all at the same time, a substantial feat of phantasm (and) a profitable social transaction' (Barrett, 1999 p. 312). In short, Barrett theorises that Tupac will be more profitable dead than alive – as he has been.

Conclusion: The Future of Holograms

Photographic stagecraft such as the device that created Tupac (a special effect colloquially known as 'Pepper's Ghost') has been around since the middle of the nineteenth century. Yet it is only recently that it has begun appearing as a metaphor for artistic and economic corruption. In William Gibson's novel *Spook Country* (2007) an artist places holograms of dead celebrities in the spots where they died, giving rise to a ghoulish form of tourism. More recently, David Eggers' *A Hologram for the King* (2012) describes a failed US marketing man hired to make a sales pitch via hologram to a Saudi Arabian king; in the end, the king backs a rival Chinese company that simply offers a cheaper package. Both these books expose how the use of flashy technology can be punctured by simple economics. Perhaps it shouldn't be so surprising, then, that the same deflating apparatus is at work here.

At the time that Tupac's ghost walked at Coachella, plans were supposedly in the works for other dead rock stars to be put to use (that is, put on tour) in a similar fashion, but so far none has come to fruition. To date, there is no holographic Elvis on tour, no Jimi Hendrix, no Jim Morrison, no John Lennon, no Kurt Cobain, although there is a holographic Michael Jackson, who currently performs in Las Vegas alongside Cirque du Soleil and who appeared at the Billboard Music Awards in 2014, and many of the remarks in this article about the haunting nature of dead black bodies would apply to his hologram as well (see Arnold, 2011). As noted earlier, the creation of these illusions is extremely expensive, and clearly their success depends in part on an audience's suspension of disbelief. While many remarks made here about who would or would not make a 'good' hologram are mere speculation, it seems safe to say that the most commercially effective ones will be those that are the most 'haunting', and that their power to haunt will depend not only on the manner of their death (tragic, violent, sudden, premature) but more importantly, on the genre of their music. Beebe (2002 p. 329) has argued that the process of mourning takes different cultural forms – that is, it differs for rock, and for hip-hop. Beebe contrasts the deaths of Cobain and Tupac, locating the future of mourning in part in the perpetual 'presentness' of televisuality that (he argues) now foregrounds the divergent ways that popular music is consumed and presented across media. In the world of mourning, the musical genre seems to matter. After his death, videos of Cobain performing live,

---

and *The Atlantic* (Hamilton, 2012).

in an episode of *MTV Unplugged*, were perpetually in circulation, emphasising his liveness, as befits a rock band. But the Tupac videos most frequently circulated after his death (especially for the song 'Changes') emphasised his mortality – a nuance that echoes the split between the rock economy, wherein stars make their name by touring and performing live, and the rap economy, which relies more on the sales of recorded music made in studios.

In short, while posthumous Cobain videos present him as still alive, Shakur's videos present him as a composite of his media representations, thus reconciling mass mediation and mourning in ways that seem to be specific to the hip-hop community (Beebe, 2002 p. 329). While the full fields of Coachella do not represent 'the' hip-hop community, this reconciliation of images may go some way towards explaining why Shakur's hologram was such a big hit online after the festival audience disbanded. A resurrected Kurt Cobain playing guitar and singing, as he does continually in videotapes of *MTV Unplugged*, may not have had the same effect that Tupac, who seemed to have leapt straight into the future to perform a brand new show, had. In order to achieve that effect, the makers of holograms need to pick their subjects carefully, and the best subjects may be those (like Tupac and Jackson) whose bodies bear the legacy of American slavery on their skin. Lennon and Cobain also died violently, and by guns, but their bodies simply don't resonate in the same way.

Meanwhile, the currency of Shakur's performance-while-dead also points in a different direction, by reminding us that the more audiences, or rather people in general, rely on avatars, CGI and cyber-generated images to provide them with music, art and cultural products, the more valuable the live body becomes. As Benjamin (1968 p. 215) predicted with his discussion of aura, presence is now at a premium; high ticket prices for concerts reflect this. In the age of Vines, Photoshop and Instagram, nothing is more prized in a celebrity appearance than an unscripted remark: it is now the only reliable mark of the real. Hence, Shakur's hologram serves as a reminder of the ascendancy of false signifiers by underscoring his lack of volition as a participant. He is being held hostage in a hologram, so to speak. This is significant because what is at stake here is more than just the worth of an artist's *oeuvre*. It is his credibility as a speaker. Benjamin (1968 p. 222) has said:

> The authenticity of a thing is the essence of all that is transmissible from its beginning, ranging from its substantive duration to its testimony to the history which it has experienced. Since the historical testimony rests on inauthenticity, the former, too, is jeopardized by reproduction when substantive duration ceases to matter. And what is really jeopardized when the historical testimony is affected is the authority of the object.

That the object in this case is human is what gives this instance its double-edged poignancy.

As Benjamin makes clear, then, what is unsettling about the hologram as performer is not that it happened, or even that, having happened, a real person's story has now shifted slightly away from mythic spokesperson for the underclasses towards digitally-altered phenomenon, on par with Hatsune Miku, the (fictional) Japanese Vocaloid hologram currently on tour with Lady Gaga. What is unsettling here is the obvious inference that if Tupac Shakur *were* to rise, this probably isn't what he'd say: he has lost not only agency, but authority and authenticity. Unlike the uncanny, the holographic performance doesn't *reveal* that which is hidden, it removes it entirely, to all intents and purposes silencing the speaker by taking away their authority as a speaker once and for all. Benjamin (1968 p. 226) once compared a cameraman to a surgeon: cutting into, reshaping and penetrating a patient's body through their art. The creators of Tupac Shakur's hologram did more than merely penetrate his corpse. They also forced it to dance to somebody else's music, to speak someone else's words, a process which at the very least has been ill thought-out and at worst represents yet another appearance of a bound black body in America; yet another strange fruit hanging from a different kind of tree.

Bibliography

Arnold, Regina (2011) 'Profit without Honor: Michael Jackson in and out of America, 1983–2009', *Journal of Popular Music Studies*, 23 (1), pp. 75–83.

Baker, Houston A. and Dana D. Nelson (2001) 'Preface: Violence, the Body and "The South"', *American Literature*, 73 (2), pp. 231–44.

Baker, Soren (2001) 'Tupac: The Legacy Grows along with Catalog', MTVnews.com, http://www.mtv.com/news/1442116/talk-about-life-after-death-tupac-legacy-grows-along-with-catalog/, accessed 4 March 2014.

Barrett, Lindon (1999) 'Dead Men Printed: Tupac Shakur, Biggie Smalls, and Hip-hop Eulogy', *Callaloo*, 22 (2), pp. 302–22.

Beebe, Roger (2002) 'Mourning Becomes …? Kurt Cobain, Tupac Shakur and the "Waning of Affect"', in Roger Beebe, Denise Fulbrook and Ben Saunders (eds), *Rock over the Edge: Transformations in Popular Music Culture*. Durham, NC: Duke University Press, pp. 311–34.

Benjamin, Walter (1968) 'The Work of Art in the Age of Mechanical Reproduction', in Hannah Arendt (ed.), *Illuminations*. New York: Harcourt, Brace & World, pp. 217–52.

Bennett, Andy (ed.) (2004) *Remembering Woodstock*. Aldershot and Burlington, VT: Ashgate.

Breslin, Rosemary, Jerry Hopkins and Paul Williams (1981) 'He's Hot, He's Sexy, He's Dead', *Rolling Stone*, 17 September, http://www.rollingstone.com/music/news/hes-hot-hes-sexy-hes-dead-rolling-stones-1981-jim-morrison-cover-story-20110701, accessed 16 May 2014.

Chang, Jeff (2005) *Can't Stop, Won't Stop: A History of the Hip-hop Generation*. New York: St. Martin's Press.

Dimitriadis, Greg (2009) *Performing Identity/Performing Culture: Hip-hop as Text, Pedagogy, and Lived Practice*, 2nd edition. New York: Peter Lang.

Dyer, Richard (1986) *Heavenly Bodies: Film Stars and Society*. London: Macmillan.

Dyson, Michael Eric (2001) *Holler If You Hear Me: Searching for Tupac Shakur*. New York: Basic Civitas.

——— (2006) 'Tupac: Life Goes On'. *The Free Library*, 1 September, http://www.thefreelibrary.com/Tupac: life goes on: why the rapper still appeals to fans and ... -a0153898385, accessed 26 August 2014.

Eggers, Dave (2013) *A Hologram for the King*. London: Hamish Hamilton.

Ethnic Demographics (2013) Coachella Forums, Polls, http://www.coachella.com/forum/showthread.php?63620-Coachella-Ethnic-Demographics-for-2013, accessed 9 September 2013.

Flock, Elizabeth (2011) 'Tupac Shakur Talented Rapper and Society Bad Boy Died Fifteen Years Ago Today', *Washington Post*, 13 September, www.washingtonpost.com/blogs/blogpost/post/tupac-shakur-talented-rapper-and-society-bad-boy-died-15-years-ago-today/2011/09/13/gIQAkChRPK_blog.html, accessed 23 May 2014.

Frith, Simon (1981) '"The Magic that Can Set You Free": The Ideology of Folk and the Myth of the Rock Community', *Popular Music*, 1, pp. 159–68.

George, Nelson (1998) *Hip-hop America*. New York: Viking.

Gibson, William (2007) *Spook Country*. New York: G.P. Putnam's Sons.

Gilroy, Paul (2001) *Against Race: Imagining Political Culture Beyond the Color Line*. Cambridge MA: Harvard University Press.

Greenberg, Zack O'Malley (2011) 'Tupac Earning Like He's Still Alive', Forbes.com, 31 May, https://music.yahoo.com/blogs/chart-watch/chart-watch-50-cent-sales-slide-002425382.html, accessed 26 September 2014.

Hall, Stuart (1997) 'The Spectacle of the Other', in Stuart Hall (ed.), *Representation: Cultural Representations and Signifying Practices*. Milton Keynes: Open University Press, pp. 223–90.

Hamilton, Jack (2012) 'Hologram Tupac Was Inevitable', *The Atlantic*, 17 April, www.theatlantic.com/entertainment/archive/2012/04/hologram-tupac-was-inevitable/255990, accessed 3 December 2013.

Kamberlis, George and Greg Dimitriadis (2005) 'Collectively Remembering Tupac: The Narrative Mediation of Current Events, Cultural Histories, and Social Identities', in Steve Jones and Joli Jensen (eds), *Afterlife as Afterimage: Understanding Posthumous Fame*. New York: Peter Lang, pp. 144–67.

Kitwana, Bakari (2002) *The Hip-hop Generation: Young Blacks and the Crisis in African American Culture*. New York: Basic Civitas.

Lebrun, Barbara (2009) *Protest Music in France: Production, Identity and Audience*. Farnham and Burlington, VT: Ashgate.

McKay, George (2000) *Glastonbury: A Very English Festival*. London: Victor Gollancz.

Ojumu, Akin (2004) 'Hip-hop Hero', *The Guardian*, 27 June, www.theguardian.com/film/2004/jun/27/popandrock.2pac, accessed 12 September 2013.

188 *DEATH AND THE ROCK STAR*

Phillips, Chuck (2002) 'Who Killed Tupac Shakur?' *Los Angeles Times*, 6 September.

Railton, Diane and Paul Watson (2011) *Music Video and the Politics of Representation*. Edinburgh: Edinburgh University Press.

Regis, Helen A. and Shana Walton (2008) 'Producing the Folk at the New Orleans Jazz and Heritage Festival', *Journal of American Folklore*, 121 (482), pp. 400–440.

Smith, Ethan (2012) 'Rapper De-Light: Tupac "Hologram" May Go on Tour', *Wall Street Journal*, 16 April, http://online.wsj.com/news/articles/SB1000142 4052702304818404577348243109842490, accessed 2 August 2013.

White, Evelyn C. (1995) 'Black Women and Wilderness', in Teresa Jordan and James Hepworth (eds), *The Stories that Shape Us: Contemporary Women Write about the West*. New York: Norton, pp. 377–85.

Your Educational Status (2013) Coachella Forums, Polls, http://www.coachella.com/forum/showthread.php?27058-Your-educational-status, accessed 9 September 2013.

Discography

2Pac, '2 of Amerikaz Most Wanted', *All Eyez on Me*, Death Row/Interscope Records, 1 CD compilation, 1996.

———, 'Changes', Interscope Records, 1992/1998.

———, 'I Ain't Mad at Cha', *All Eyez on Me*, Death Row/Interscope Records, 1 CD compilation, 1996.

———, 'Keep Ya Head Up', *Strictly 4 My N.I.G.G.A.Z.*, Interscope Records, 1 CD compilation, 1993.

———, 'Only God Can Judge', *All Eyez on Me*, Death Row/Interscope Records, 1 CD compilation, 1996.

———, *Tupac: Resurrection*, Interscope Records, 1 CD compilation, 2003.

Billie Holliday, 'Strange Fruit', *Strange Fruit: 1937–1939*, Jazzterdays Records, 2000.

Makaveli, 'White Man'z World', *The Don Killuminati: The 7 Day Theory*, Death Row/Interscope Records, 1 CD compilation, 1996.

Busta Rhymes and Eminem. *2Pac; Rap Phenomenon II*. Hosted by DJ Vlad, Dirty Harry and Green Lantern. Various Artists, 2003.

Richie Rich featuring 2Pac, 'Niggaz Done Changed', *Seasoned Veteran*, Def Jam, 1 CD compilation, 1996.

Filmography

2Pac: Resurrection, dir. Lauren Lazin, Amaru Entertainment, 2004.

Wattstax, dir. Mel Stuart, Columbia Pictures, 1973.

Chapter 14
Post-mortem Sampling in Hip-hop Recordings and the Rap Lament

Justin A. Williams

Composers have the advantage of being shrouded in myth: we can propel fantasies of omniscience upon them. Pop stars torment us with their inconvenient humanness – their tax problems, their noisome politics, their pornography collections, their unwanted comebacks. No wonder the greatest legends are the artists who die young.

Ross (2004 p. 204)

It is death, not love, that is on hip-hop's mind.

Cobb (2007 p. 124)

I'm a meet you up at the crossroads.

Bone Thugs-n-Harmony, 'Crossroads' (1995)

'How many brothers fell victim to the streets? … Be a lie if I told ya that I never thought of death'. These lyrics are from the chorus of 'Life Goes On' by Tupac Shakur (who recorded under the name 2Pac) on the album *All Eyez on Me* (1996), the last album released before he was murdered on 13 September 1996 in Las Vegas. This example illustrates the way that rappers, particularly those associated with 'gangsta rap', are often preoccupied with death, both using the threat of death to intimidate others and reflecting on the everyday dangers of drugs and gang cultures in the inner cities.[1] This can become a type of self-fulfilling prophecy, in that some of the behaviour espoused in gangsta rap can indeed come true for the rappers themselves, as was the case with Tupac Shakur. Following the death of a prominent rap star, there will be a process of mourning, and there have been a number of rap laments for the most influential of deceased rappers and DJs.[2]

---

[1] This is not to suggest that all lyrical content of gangsta rap accurately portrays the lifestyle of every rapper associated with the genre, but the influence of gang culture on Compton rappers, for example, does have an effect on their ethos and mindset.

[2] The term 'rap lament' was used in Krims (2000 p. 78) with a few select examples in passing. He also discussed the concept at greater length at a hip-hop conference in

DEATH AND THE ROCK STAR

This chapter discusses instances of US rappers sampling the voice of a deceased rapper, what I call 'post-mortem sampling', that is, the use of a recording (sound or image) of a deceased artist with great cultural heft – for example, figures such as Elvis Presley, Kurt Cobain, Freddie Mercury, John Lennon and Michael Jackson. In post-mortem sampling, authenticity can be claimed through the use of the recorded sound or image, and its framing through recontextualisation. The presence of the Tupac hologram at 2012's Coachella festival, performing with Dr Dre and Snoop Dogg, reveals an intensification of the impulse to 'sample' murdered rappers to multiple ends. I will show how deceased rappers are lamented, through both the lyrical citation of such artists and the sampling of their voices, with particular reference to the hip-hop 'martyrs' The Notorious B.I.G. and Tupac Shakur. Rappers such as Jay-Z (Shawn Carter), Eminem (Marshall Mathers) and Nas (Nasir Jones) sample the voices of Shakur and B.I.G. post-mortem, and both the sampled voice (with its biographical associations) and the sonic organisation of the beat provide new meaning in their updated contexts.

The second part of the chapter will discuss an extended case study of death and mourning in rap from Compton-based[3] rapper The Game, an artist who arguably extends the lineage of gangsta rap culture. Rap laments are by no means reserved for deceased rappers, as subjects include family, friends and members of the neighbourhood (or 'hood') in general, and an analysis of The Game's 'My Life' (2008) reveals a number of facets of West Coast gangsta rap and its social contexts. 'My Life' demonstrates the intersections of The Game's invocations of previous rappers as lineage, the death culture of Compton's gangs and a rap lament that exemplifies the Christian overtones within African-American cultures.

The Rap Lament

The term 'lament', from the Latin *lamentum*, most generally refers to an artistic expression of grief or sorrow, 'a set or conventional form of mourning; a song of grief, an elegy; *esp.* a dirge performed at a death or burial; also, the air to which such a lamentation is sung or played' (Rosand, 2014). Laments are found in ancient Greek texts as well as the Bible, and lamentations over the death of Jesus Christ are one of the most pervasive in Christian art. In Western art music, opera is perhaps the genre that has most fully codified and aestheticised the lament. The 'Lamento' of Italian opera has produced a number of noteworthy laments, including Monteverdi's *Lamento d'Arianna* (1608) and Purcell's aria 'When I am Laid in Earth' (1688) from *Dido and Aeneas* (known as 'Dido's Lament'). Musical features of these laments include a descending, four-chord harmonic progression that begins in minor and ends

---

Wuppertal in March 2009. I am grateful to him, as always, for his support and know his memory will live on through his work and that of all whom he influenced.

[3] Compton is a city in Los Angeles County, south of Downtown Los Angeles, and primarily known for its history of gang activity.

POST-MORTEM SAMPLING IN HIP-HOP RECORDINGS 191

on the V chord (for example, g minor – D7 first inversion – C first inversion – D). In the case of Purcell, the bass line falls from the ĝ down to the d̂ chromatically, and the 'falling' element of the lament is a musical feature found in laments of many genres. Historically, it has often been a woman who sings or recites the lament, whether in poetry or in opera. The female voice may include sobbing, falsetto, sighs and other vocal techniques that have come to signify lamentation. In post-Second World War popular culture, the presence of strings, such as the use of Barber's *Adagio for Strings* (1936) for funerals and in films that contend with death, have become a sonic feature of more contemporary laments (Howard, 2007).

In rap music, the subgenre that most often intersects with themes of death is gangsta rap, also labelled 'reality rap'. It is called the latter as it often consists of rappers discussing the social realities around them, which for many inner city impoverished minorities include not only gang activity, and the loss of family and friends as a result of such cultures, but also topics of drugs, sex, parties and other stereotypical African-American leisure activities (for example, playing dominoes). It is not a coincidence, then, that many of the rap laments that exist are from artists associated with gangsta rap. It is not uncommon in US gangsta rap albums to hear one track which depicts drug and gun crime, even threatening others with such violence, and another track which laments the loss of friends and family through such activity. In such laments, the religious aspects concerned with death are often present, as part of a long history of Christian values manifested in African-American music and cultures more broadly (Quinn, 2005 p. 147). It is often the case, for example, for African-American gangsta rappers to have grown up in Christian households, and to frequently attend church. Singers with gospel music backgrounds, including Nate Dogg, represent a pervasive mix of the sacred and profane in African-American culture, and sing about God as well as drugs, crime and women as 'hos' (Quinn, 2005 p. 152; also Dyson, 1997).

For rappers who have been murdered, it is a case of life imitating art that reports on specific social conditions. As journalist Touré wrote after the death of The Notorious B.I.G.: 'I can see now that the murder and killings are coming from the same hands that make the beats and rhymes; how is living in hip-hop any different from living in the dysfunctional black family writ large?' (Touré, 1997 p. 30).

Quincy Jones wrote after Shakur's death that 'The tragedy of Tupac is that his untimely passing is representative of too many young black men in this country' (quoted in Quinn, 2005 p. 180). In other words, death in US gangsta rap culture is prevalent both in real life and in song lyrics, and becomes the 'representation' aspect of reality rap or gangsta rap, and perhaps adds to its voyeuristic appeal as well (as the 'ghetto' is a point of public fascination and imagination). As the quotes above suggest, however, both the real deaths and their laments are a political commentary on the urban 'underclass' and the social, economic and political conditions which have led to such a death-fuelled habitus of poverty, guns, drugs, crime and gang activity.

Perhaps the earliest example of a 'rap lament' is Pete Rock and C.L. Smooth's track 'T.R.O.Y. (They Reminisce Over You)' from 1992, which laments the death of friend Troy Dixon. The track sonically belongs to an era slightly earlier than the subsequent examples, and would fall under the jazz/bohemian rap genre rather than reality rap, distinctions articulated by Krims in his 1980s–1990s rap genre system (Krims, 2000). Early reality rap examples would include Ice Cube's 'Dead Homiez' from 1990, Geto Boys' 'Six Feet Deep' (1993), Scarface's 'I Seen a Man Die' (1994), Bone Thugs-n-Harmony's 'Crossroads' (1995) and rapper Eazy-E and Master P's 'I Miss my Homies' (1997). One of the most famous rap laments is about The Notorious B.I.G. in Puff Daddy's 'I'll Be Missing You' (1997) which uses The Police's 'Every Breath You Take' (1983). Musically, many of these tracks include figures and gestures that encourage mourning: strings including piano, and descending minor mode harmonic progressions as well as a slower tempo than in other rap tracks. In the rap lament, the male rapper subverts the traditionally female-voiced lament, although it is not a simple replacement, as many of the mid-to-late 1990s laments and beyond (such as 'I'll Be Missing You') include a female voice on the chorus. A number of rap songs have either lamented the loss of family and friends, or have lamented the death of significant rap artists, or a mix of both, and in either case can serve as allegory for figures who represent the current situation of young African-American males more generally.

The death cultures of gangsta rap also created an environment where artists were ruminating on their own death within rap lyrics before they had died. Tupac Shakur, for example, was shot in 1994, but the theme of death already pervaded his lyrics and music videos, including on the songs 'How Long Will They Mourn Me?' (1994), 'Bury Me a G' (1994) and 'Death around the Corner' (1995), in addition to 'Pour out a Little Liquor'[4] (1994), which is dedicated to any friends and family he had lost.[5] The title of The Notorious B.I.G.'s first album was *Ready to Die* (1994), and he stages shooting himself at the end of the album (on the track 'Suicidal Thoughts'). The Notorious B.I.G. wrote 'You're Nobody (Til Somebody Kills You)' (1997) for his next album *Life after Death*, and this song was later used by rapper Rick Ross for 'Nobody' (2014), in which Ross reflects on being the target of a drive-by shooting in 2013. These examples demonstrate how gangsta rap at the turn of the twenty-first century is a contemporary manifestation of the tendency for artists and poets to ruminate on death, in this case death caused largely by the excessive gun crime and gang cultures that exist in the locales where the art form originated.

---

[4] The tradition of offering libations to God or a spirit in memory of lost loved ones goes back to ancient times and is found in gangsta rap culture often as a 40 oz bottle of liquor to 'pour one out' or 'pour one for my homies'.

[5] Shakur's preoccupation with death and the afterlife is made visually apparent in his concept for the 'I Ain't Mad at Cha' (1996) music video, in which he is shot and dies in the ambulance on the way to the hospital. Before the song begins, Shakur is greeted in heaven by Red Foxx and then raps in the company of Nat 'King' Cole, Billie Holiday, Dorothy Dandrige, Sarah Vaughan, Jimi Hendrix, Miles Davis, Louis Armstrong, Sammy Davis Jr, Josephine Baker and Marvin Gaye. The track appears on *All Eyez on Me*, but the single was released only after Shakur was murdered.

Post-mortem Sampling

Digital sampling (known more colloquially as 'sampling') has been a prominent technique in rap music production since at least the mid-1980s, and sampling has also been used in rap and elsewhere to memorialise dead stars. What I have called 'post-mortem sampling' is defined as the digital sampling of the voice or image of an artist after he or she has died (usually at a young age), and the insertion of this segment in a new context (Williams, 2013 p. 122). As many of the previously mentioned rap laments consist of lyrics referring to lost friends, family and important figures in rap history, digital sampling technologies allow other methods by which to memorialise through rap music production.

Importantly, as the Alex Ross quotation at the beginning of this chapter suggests, when the star dies 'before their time', their artistic qualities are usually preserved whereas the more mundane and embarrassing aspects of their life become more understated. Sociologist Lee Marshall's (2007 pp. 141–2) work on stars and death describes this process, as he notes:

> Death ... creates the tendency to both erase the human failings of a particular star (unless they are part of an image of a difficult, tortured artist) and to create a particular star teleology – a rationalization of an entire career that creates its own logic and leads to a logical conclusion.

Many art worlds have canonical figures who have died young, and this early death often adds a symbolic strength to their works. In music, examples cover the worlds of classical music (Pergolesi who died age 26; Mozart at 35), jazz (Charlie Parker at 35) and rock (Jim Morrison, Janis Joplin, Jimi Hendrix and Kurt Cobain who all died at 27). Although many living artists have a celebrity 'aura', the 'dying young' narrative additionally mediates the reception of a celebrity voice. In other words, the recognisable voice as signifier is given new meaning when the artist has passed away, assuming that knowledge is shared among a significant quantity of listeners. Rather than an impersonator, for example, the digital sampling of a deceased artist's voice maintains the artist's 'authenticity' in a way that imitation or emulation would not. The importance of the voice to post-mortem sampling cannot be overstated: the voice and its characteristics can become a signifier for an image, a personality, and the specific narratives associated with that star image. If it is a prominent figure whose death has received significant coverage, then it is safe to conclude that a substantial number of listeners will recognise this element of the narrative in post-mortem sampling.

From the late 1980s onward, because of new samplers commercially available on the market, digital sampling became an easier and swifter process, and this of course has had repercussions for post-mortem sampling and hip-hop music. Sampling and other forms of borrowing are extremely common in hip-hop music and culture (Williams, 2013), thus post-mortem sampling is one manifestation of broader intertextual practices in the genre.

194 *DEATH AND THE ROCK STAR*

In relation to the sampling of dead artists, Stanyek and Piekut (2010) write of the 'intermundane', the relationship between live and dead labour in late capitalist production. They note that we are living in the 'age of the splice': 'If the late-19th-century urge was to embalm (sounds floating, inert, in the formaldehyde of tin, wax, or resin), since World War II, the tendency has been to recombine' (2010 pp. 16–17). Stanyek and Piekut also note that 'the logics of recombination surface in multi-track tape technology and begin to recondition the very nature of global music production' (p. 17). This allows artists to use previous labour to new ends, 'resurrecting' the 'star aura' of past voices in new ways.

There have been a number of notable 'duets with the dead' (Goodman, 2000) in the digital era that combine the intermundane late-capitalist relationship between 'bio- and necroworlds' (Stanyek and Piekut, 2010 p. 14): Natalie Cole's rendition of 'Unforgettable' with her late father in 1991 (and music video) may be one of the most high profile (Stanyek and Piekut, 2010),[6] but other examples include Tony Bennett with Billie Holiday for 'God Bless the Child' (1997), Kenny G. with Louis Armstrong for 'What a Wonderful World' (1999, and discussed by Whyton, 2010), Angela Gheorghiu with legendary soprano Maria Callas in the 'Habanera' from Carmen (2011), and most recently, Susan Boyle with Elvis for 'Oh Come, All Ye Faithful' (2013) (see also Brunt, this volume). These recorded voices do not only serve the purpose of bringing the dead back to life, metaphorically speaking, but allow the living to have a dialogue with the past, in a co-existence of past and present, or dead and living, in conversation. As one might expect, such examples are the subject of intense debate among fans and critics, and in many ways, the prevalence of digital sampling and collaboration in standard practices of hip-hop make such 'duets' arguably less conspicuous. As we will see, however, in many cases it is a combination of the star aura in post-mortem sampling with musical structures which encourage mourning that encode meaning in rap laments.

Post-mortem Sampling of Tupac and The Notorious B.I.G.

While there exists a number of rapper deaths lamented by the rap community (Proof, Big L, Guru, Cowboy of the Furious Five, Scott La Rock, Big Pun, Aliyah, Jam Master J, DJ Screw, the Beastie Boys' Adam Yauch), Tupac Shakur and The Notorious B.I.G. tower above the rest in terms of both the number of songs about them, and the respect they receive as two of the most respected rappers in history. There exist numerous examples, official and unofficial (for example, mixtapes), of the post-mortem sampling of Biggie and Tupac, in particular from the early-to-mid 2000s, that demonstrate their impact on the genre.

---

[6] More recently, Nat 'King' Cole has had an entire album dedicated to 'updating' and creating new versions of his music through sampling his voice, entitled *Re: Generations* (2009).

In 1996 and 1997, Tupac Shakur and The Notorious B.I.G. (real name Christopher Wallace, also referred to as Biggie Smalls or simply Biggie) were murdered within six months of each other and became the first rap artists bestowed symbolic immortality.[7] Their 'feud' was described in the media as a war between West Coast (represented by Tupac) and East Coast (represented by Notorious B.I.G.) rappers, which even led to speculation that Biggie was responsible for Tupac's murder and that those associated with Tupac murdered Biggie for revenge. Their deaths, in many ways, became a place marker event in hip-hop historiography, a point when the media, fans and artists started to question their own roles in the feud, and the geography of rap's mainstream moved to the US South for a number of years, almost evading engagement with the two coasts for a period of time.

Films and books about the murders of Tupac and Biggie have also added to the mystique surrounding their still unsolved murders,[8] in addition to albums and mixtapes by other artists who keep dead rap stars within cultural memory, further bolstering a hero system within rap and hip-hop culture. Both artists have now sold more albums dead than they did when alive, and murals and T-shirts keep the iconography of the artists in popular consciousness. Furthermore, rappers who sample hip-hop 'martyrs' such as Tupac and Biggie add to the creation of new identities, creating tributes that simultaneous bolster the already-existing prestige of the dead artists and become part of narratives or lineage belonging to newer rap artists. Rappers who use the symbolic immortality of Tupac Shakur and The Notorious B.I.G. to their own ends create alliances and associations within rap subgenres, both creating memorial processes and encouraging canon formation.

Two examples I have explained at greater length elsewhere include Jay-Z's 'A Dream' from *The Blueprint 2* (2002), and Nas's version of 'Thugz Mansion' (also 2002) on *God's Son* (Williams, 2013 pp. 103–39). In 'A Dream', Jay-Z recounts a dream he had about the late Notorious B.I.G. The middle verse is a sample of B.I.G.'s first verse on 'Juicy' (1994) from *Ready to Die*. Biggie's widow, Faith Evans, is also featured on the Jay-Z track, her female voice bringing a historical association with lament reinforced musically by the falling f♯m-E-D harmonic progression.

For his album *God's Son* (2002), rapper Nas used the Tupac song 'Thugz Mansion' from the posthumously released album *Better Dayz* (2002). Nas re-names the track 'Thugz Mansion (N.Y.)', uses the same solo acoustic guitar backing track

---

[7] Tupac Shakur was gunned down at an intersection in Las Vegas following his attendance of the Mike Tyson–Bruce Seldon fight on 7 September 1996. The Notorious B.I.G. was shot in similar fashion on 9 March 1997 in Los Angeles. Tupac was 25 years old and B.I.G. was 24 when they were murdered.

[8] There are a number of theories surrounding both murders which have spawned numerous books and documentary films, including Scott (1997), Sullivan (2002) and Broomfield (2002). See Williams (2013 pp. 110–18) for a much longer description of Shakur's posthumous reception.

(an uncommon timbre for hip-hop 'beats') and inserts a verse from Tupac about rapping in heaven ('Dear momma don't cry, your baby boy's doin good/Tell the homies I'm in heaven and they ain't got hoods'). The topic of death had a personal poignancy for Nas as his mother had just died of cancer, a fact reflected in the lyrics to this track and others on the album (both Tupac more generally and Nas on *God's Son* lyrically express tropes of the 'suffering artist'). Both the examples mentioned re-place the deceased artist in between the rappers' verses and, interestingly, echo and reverb is added to the post-mortem sampling of the voices. These features, not found on the originals, give a 'sonic halo' within the current context which further distances the live rappers from the deceased one.

For Jay-Z's tribute, sonic elements associated with hip-hop (scratching, rapping, sampling) are combined with elements associated with the more traditional lament (repeating descending bass line and female singing). He portrays a Notorious B.I.G. whose voice only surfaces in a nostalgic moment of remembrance, while Jay-Z's description of the dream attests to B.I.G.'s nod of approval ('just keep doin' your thing, he said'). Nas's tribute uses Shakur's verbal depiction of a 'Thugz Mansion' found in heaven, with the middle verse as Tupac's commentary from heaven. The use of acoustic guitar on the track suggests unmediated authenticity, and in this context, also encourages mourning. The reference to Tupac by Nas associates the latter with the late rapper, as the third verse by Nas demonstrates ('my love goes to Afeni Shakur/'Cause like Ann Jones, she raised a ghetto king in a war'), Nas compares Tupac's mother with his own in this verse. Ironically, Tupac criticised Nas while he was alive, but being faithful to Shakur's desire not to collaborate with Nas in his lifetime seems to be of little concern to Nas, and to other artists such as Eminem who choose to utilise such voices.

Eminem (Marshall Mathers III) is another rapper and producer to whom Shakur's mother Afeni gave permission to access and use previously unreleased Tupac tapes. The result included three Eminem-produced tracks for the 2003 documentary *Tupac Resurrection*, and the 2004 album *Loyal to the Game* which was released under Tupac's name but produced by Eminem and his production team. The song 'Runnin (Dyin to Live)', on the *Tupac: Resurrection* soundtrack, includes features common to Eminem's production at the time: a slightly sped-up vocal sample as the chorus material (Edgar Winter's 'Dying to Live'), synth strings and a driving one-note bass figure in a minor mode. The track uses dialogue and interviews with Biggie and Tupac as bookends, and the music video shows an empty studio with holographic-effect projections of the rapper (in some ways similar to the Tupac hologram at Coachella in 2012), stock footage of the two rappers, alternating with a string section of all African-American individuals dressed in white. Interestingly, although Eminem's authorial presence as producer is firmly audible on the track (as 'sonic signature'), he is nowhere to be found vocally or in the music video. This is not the case for *Loyal to the Game*, where Eminem does rap, placing Tupac and Eminem digitally as 'collaborators' even though the two come from separate micro-eras or generations in hip-hop history (1991–6 and 1999–present, respectively).

POST-MORTEM SAMPLING IN HIP-HOP RECORDINGS   197

While Eminem's tracks act as tribute (especially for the songs from *Tupac: Resurrection*), using Eminem's production styles on them to interlink an Eminem aesthetic (voice and music) with a Tupac aesthetic (voice) creates a hybrid construction that is not dissimilar to other mixtapes or the use of previous material in sample-based hip-hop more generally. What is different is the prestige that both 'star texts' bring to the tracks, and thus we find an intersection of a hip-hop icon with the aura of dying young, and a highly successful and controversial 'white rapper' who has successfully placed himself within a predominantly black lineage.[9]

The Game and 'My Life' as Rap Lament

Compton-based rapper The Game (Jayceon Terrell Taylor) is an example of someone who strengthens the bonds of lineage between himself and preceding West Coast gangsta rap artists (in particular, Dr Dre, Snoop Doggy Dogg, Ice Cube and Tupac Shakur). His first album, *The Documentary* (2005), was a highly intertextual album, with guest raps and production from a number of artists, and his lyrical references, which frequently mentioned canonical rap stars from the past 20 years, were most overt. For example, the chorus on the title track references a number of important rap debut albums, including Notorious B.I.G.'s *Ready to Die* (1994), Jay-Z's *Reasonable Doubt* (1996), Ice Cube's *Death Certificate* (1991), Dr Dre's *The Chronic* (1992) and Nas's debut *Illmatic* (1994). This is one of many methods he uses to position himself within a lineage of predominantly African-American gangsta rappers. In addition, The Game mentions Tupac, Biggie and other canonical rappers (on 'We Ain't', he proclaims of canonical rapper Eminem, with whom he collaborates on the track, 'Shady one of the greatest like Biggie n' Pac was'). The Game's dogs are named Biggie and 'Pac, as we find out on one of his tracks, and on 'Let Me Put You on The Game', in addition to mentioning 50 Cent, N.W.A., Snoop, Flava Flav and other rappers, he states: 'This ain't another one of those, this the rebirth of Dre/The rebirth of L.A., the rebirth of hip-hop/Another memorial for Makaveli and Big Pop' (referring to Shakur's alter ego 'Makaveli' and B.I.G'.s nickname 'Big Poppa'). This line is also used for the track 'I Never Change' (featuring verses by Tupac, Jadakiss and The Game) on *Tupac Duets* (2006), a mixtape CD created by DJ Mello and DJ Cinema. The track even uses previous Tupac lyrics that say 'the game' to create the illusion of a Tupac-endorsed 'shout-out' to the rapper. These mixtapes are common, and frequently and arguably a much more intensified and varied instance of post-mortem sampling, yet copyright and other legal and commercial factors prevent them from being official releases.

The Game also continues the tradition of the rap lament more generally, not only lamenting the loss of earlier rappers, but of other people in his neighbourhood.

---

[9] Eminem also produced tracks for posthumous releases from Notorious B.I.G., notably the track 'It Has Been Said' for *Duets: The Final Chapter* (2005).

The song 'My Life', from his third studio-released album *L.A.X.* (2008), most convincingly expresses these sentiments in a number of ways. Lyrically, he criticises life in the ghetto and wants to get out, citing a list of ways of dying, from being shot, to overdosing on drugs, to suicide. In addition to name-checking Kurt Cobain, another music star who died young, The Game mentions Biggie, and refers to him as having been 'crucified', suggesting that Biggie's death represents a type of martyrdom as well as drawing on the authenticity of being from the same geographical and socio-economic background. Further to this idea, he raps: 'Ain't no bars, but niggas can't escape the hood/They took so many of my niggas, that I should hate the hood/But it's real niggas like me, that make the hood'. The chorus accurately summarises the 'survivor's guilt' that The Game feels. The chorus features Lil' Wayne in his heavily auto-tuned style of singing (sung through auto-tune software rather than as a post-production tool, creating a quasi-robotic sound): 'Dear Lord, you've took so many of my people ...' and asking why he hadn't taken him instead. Although the chorus sounds mechanical, there are sighs and swoops in the vocal which suggest lamenting patterns.

The form of the song is simple verse-chorus and follows the same five-chord, two bar, harmonic progression throughout: |g♯m – d♯m – |E – B – F♯/A♯ – | which in g♯m follows the roman numeral progression i-v-VI-III-VII$_6$. The roman numeral progression does not particularly suggest in itself a lament, in that it is not a descending set like i-♭VII-♭IV-V, but if one looks at the last two chords in particular, the B-A♯ which then resolve down to g♯m, this does indicate a $\hat{3} - \hat{2} - \hat{1}$ in the bass which would suggest a falling figure (rather than a V-I, for example). Rolling quavers outlining the chords are played on piano keyboard, which emphasises the downbeats (a chordal piano texture also heard on John Lennon's 'Imagine', for example). The song opens with the chorus and piano only and the beat enters for the first verse, staying there throughout the song.

The music video shows The Game (and Lil' Wayne) in Compton, singing and rapping from a cemetery, this initial scene being juxtaposed with scenes of shootings and murder in the same neighbourhood. The Game often goes over to a dead body lying in the street, which echoes the message in the lyrics. As the track fades, synth strings appear and a final white screen shows a Bible verse from Galatians 2:20 – 'I have been crucified with Christ and I no longer live, but Christ lives in me. The life I now live in the body, I live by faith in the Son of God, who loved me and gave himself for me'. The images are not unlike scenes from 1990s 'hood films' like *Boyz n the Hood* (dir. Singleton, 1991), and these rap laments often contain religious connotations, usually Christian values, found in the historically black churches (The Game says in 'My Life', 'And you wonder why Kanye wears Jesus pieces?', referring to the need for support from a higher power when those around you pass on). 'My Life' represents an artistic expression of grief related to the death cultures in Compton, and laments the loss of those who are a product of those cultures. The song and music video include some updated elements of mainstream contemporary rap styles (for example, use of auto-tune), while maintaining themes of death and loss found in rap and in earlier musical laments.

US gangsta rap culture is complex, but ultimately risks ending up in a vicious circle: the music often reports violence, crime and murder, but at times has also glorified it, and the rap lament mourns those from the same death culture that was celebrated on other tracks.

Conclusion

From Dido's 'Remember Me' in *Dido and Aeneas* (1688), to Kendrick Lamar's 'Promise that you will sing about me' in the song 'Sing about Me, I'm Dying of Thirst' (2012), laments serve a dual function: to mourn the loss of someone and to remember and/or memorialise them. Dido and Lamar are ultimately singing of themselves, becoming conscious of their own mortality (in Dido's case, she then kills herself due to the grief of losing Aeneas). In gangsta rap, the artists' preoccupation with death creates more lyrical content that others can sample or reference after the rapper passes away. Laments are arguably more prevalent in rap than in other popular music genres, and the widespread practice of digital sampling in hip-hop provides the opportunity to sample artists post-mortem, creating and strengthening collaborative bonds while mourning the artist.[10]

Although newer artists like Kendrick Lamar are taking a more critical stance against the death culture of gangs than some previous artists have, its presence in rap lyrics demonstrate that it is still a troubling, all-too-pervasive social phenomenon. The post-mortem sampling of the voices of deceased rappers in hip-hop derives from a complex mix of factors: the ubiquity of sampling and other forms of intertextuality in both official and unofficial releases (for example mixtapes), a culture of death which artists mention and invoke, the fan and media reception of artists who die young and the narratives which add to their star texts, and subsequent rappers who want to lament rappers and others, while potentially wanting to add themselves to a canon or lineage of rappers. The age of recording and digital reproduction means that the voice of the rapper, and the voices of others, will continue to be invoked, producing ever-shifting entities which continue to provide meaning throughout hip-hop's stylistic developments and historiography.

---

[10] Though in some ways, the fashion for the post-mortem sampling of rappers has subsided since the mid-2000s (Tupac's sixth and final official posthumous album *Pac's Life* was released in 2006), many rappers still discuss death on a wider level, both in the context of dead rap icons and as part of the larger social contexts which make death prevalent in African-American ghettos rife with gang activity. One example includes Kendrick Lamar's *Good Kid, m.A.A.d City* (2012), which describes the gang culture in Compton and is much more overtly critical of it than his predecessors. Furthermore, Nas's use of the late Amy Winehouse on 'Cherrywine', for his album *Life is Good* (2012), is much less conspicuous in that it sounds like a jazz sample (due to Winehouse's 'retro-formalist' style of singing) rather than a specific lament for Winehouse.

Bibliography

Cobb, William Jelani (2007) *To the Break of Dawn: A Freestyle on the Hip-hop Aesthetic*. New York: New York University Press.

Dyson, Michael Eric (1997) *Between God and Gangsta Rap: Bearing Witness to Black Culture*. Oxford: Oxford University Press.

Goodman, Fred (2000) 'Duets with the Dead: Homage or Exploitation?', *New York Times*, 16 January, http://www.nytimes.com/2000/01/16/arts/music-duets-with-the-dead-homage-or-exploitation.html, accessed 10 February 2014.

Howard, Luke (2007) 'The Popular Reception of Samuel Barber's "Adagio for Strings"', *American Music*, 25 (1), pp. 50–80.

Krims, Adam (2000) *Rap Music and the Poetics of Identity*. Cambridge: Cambridge University Press.

Marshall, Lee (2007) *Bob Dylan: The Never Ending Star*. Cambridge: Polity Press.

Quinn, Eithne (2005) *Nuthin' but a G Thang: The Culture and Commerce of Gangsta Rap*. New York: Columbia University Press.

Rosand, Ellen (2014) 'Lamento', *Oxford Music Online*. Oxford University Press, http://www.oxfordmusiconline.com/subscriber/article/grove/music/15904, accessed 12 April 2014.

Ross, Alex (2004) 'Rock 101', in Mickey Hart (ed.), *Da Capo Best Music Writing 2004*. Cambridge, MA: Da Capo, pp. 230–42.

Scott, Cathy (1997) *The Killing of Tupac Shakur*. London: Plexus Publishing.

Sullivan, Randall (2002) *LAbyrinth: Corruption and Vice in the L.A.P.D.* Edinburgh: Canongate Books.

Stanyek, Jason and Benjamin Piekut (2010) 'Deadness: Technologies of the Intermundane', *TDR: The Drama Review*, 54 (1), pp. 14–38.

Touré (1997) 'Bigger than Life', *The Village Voice*, 19 March.

Whyton, Tony (2010) *Jazz Icons: Heroes, Myths and the Jazz Tradition*. Cambridge: Cambridge University Press.

Williams, Justin (2013) *Rhymin and Stealin: Musical Borrowing in Hip Hop*. Ann Arbor, MI: University of Michigan Press.

Filmography

Biggie and Tupac, dir. Nick Broomfield. Film Four, 2002.

Boyz n the Hood, dir. John Singleton. Columbia Pictures, 1991.

Index

'27 Club', 6, 65, 65n2, 193
2Pac, *see* Shakur, Tupac
50 Cent, 180, 197

ABBA, 68
AC/DC, 66–7, 103, 106–7, 109n4, 110–11, 114, 116
African-American, 12, 47, 49–50, 94, 143, 157, 178, 180–83, 190, 191–2, 196, 197; *see also* black
Afrobeat, 2, 135, 138, 141, 143–4
Aguilera, Christina, 91
Aliyah, 194
Allin, GG, 2, 8, 33–43
American Idol (television series), 168, 172–3, 177
Amphlett, Chrissy, 2, 103, 108–9, 111, 114, 116
Armstrong, Louis, 192n5, 194
Astaire, Fred, 47
Augustine, Dannika, 123
authenticity, 5, 26, 29, 92, 110, 139, 151, 158, 166, 168, 180, 185–6, 190, 193, 196, 198
auto-tune, 198

Baker, Ginger, 139
Baker, Josephine, 192n5
Barber, Samuel, 191
Bauhaus (band), 179
Beastie Boys, 183, 194
Beatles, 67–8, 123; *see also* Bootleg Beatles
Bee Gees, 2
Bennett, Tony, 194
Berry, Chuck, 64
Bhundu Boys, 140
Bieber, Justin, 91
Big Bopper, 5
Big L, 194
Big Poppa, *see* The Notorious B.I.G.

Big Pun, 194
Biggie, *see* The Notorious B.I.G
Biggie Smalls, *see* The Notorious B.I.G.
Birthday Party (band), 103, 109, 115
Björn Again, 68
black, 12, 47, 49–50, 51, 55, 136, 139–40, 142, 149, 178–9, 183, 191, 197–8
blackness, 8, 135–6, 139, 141, 144, 182
bodies, 12, 178–9, 181–6
culture, 139, 149, 180, 183, 198
minstrelsy, 55
see also African-American
Black Panthers, 138, 141, 179
Blaxploitation, 139
blues, 19, 46, 119
the body, 3, 4, 17–18, 21–2, 26, 29, 33–5, 38–9, 42, 46, 51–2, 54, 78, 87, 88–90, 178–9, 181–6, 198
and affect, 40, 88, 90–91
black, 12, 178–9, 181–6
'body politics', 18, 38, 40, 42, 181
erotic, 51
and death, 17, 21–2, 26, 33–4, 38, 166, 179, 184
and society, 26, 35, 38, 88
and subversion, 8, 20, 26, 33–4, 38, 42
and the voice, 4, 46, 88–90, 170, 173
Bolan, Marc, 105, 112
Bone Thugs-n-Harmony, 192
Bonham, John, 166–7
Bonnaroo, 181
Bootleg Beatles, 67–8
Bowie, David, 81–2
Boyle, Susan, 194
Boyz II Men, 80
Brando, Marlon, 170
Brock, Dave, 68–9
Brown, Bobbi Kristina, 93, 123, 125
Brown, Bobby, 122
Brown, James, 46–7, 137, 138

202   *DEATH AND THE ROCK STAR*

Brown, Mike, 178
Bubbles (Michael Jackson's chimp), 48, 121
Burrell, Kim, 93
Byrd, James, 183

JJ Cale, 2
Callas, Maria, 194
capitalism, 7, 9, 42, 184, 194
Carey, Mariah, 91
Carter, Shawn, *see* Jay-Z
Caruso, Enrico, 167
Cash, Johnny, 73n2, 141
Cassidy, Eva, 171
Cave, Nick, 112
Charles, Ray, 73n2
Chauvin, Louis, 65n2
Chopra, Deepak, 49
Chopra, Gotham, 50
Cirque du Soleil, 54, 184
Cline, Patsy, 166
Coachella, 11, 165, 177–85, 190, 196
Cobain, Frances Bean, 76
Cobain, Kurt, 1, 2, 5, 9, 63, 65, 74–8, 79,
    81–2, 115, 184–5, 190, 193, 198
Cole, Nat 'King', 2, 167, 192n5, 194
Cole, Natalie, 167, 194
commemoration, 17, 23–6, 28, 120, 136
Corbijn, Anton, 74, 77, 79–80
Costello, Elvis, 141
Costner, Kevin, 93
Coughlin, David, 77
Counterfeit Stones, 68
country, 150
Cowboy (rapper), 194
Crash, Darby, 75
Crowded House, 103, 108
Crowe, Sheryl, 169
Cruyff, Johan, 22
Ice Cube, 192, 197
The Cure, 67
Curtis, Ian, 2, 5, 9, 74–82

Puff Daddy, 192
Dalida, 1
Dandrige, Dorothy, 192n5
Darrell, Dimebag, 6
Davis, Justin, 178
Davis, Miles, 138, 192n5

Davis Jr, Sammy, 192n5
Dean, James, 61, 183
Diallo, Amadou, 183
Princess Diana, 9n3, 95, 96, 126
Dion, Céline, 122, 172–3, 177, 179
disco, 111, 124
diva, 87, 88–90, 92, 96, 122
Divinyls, 103, 108, 115
Dixon, Troy, 191–2
DJ Cinema, 197
DJ Mello, 197
DJ Screw, 194
Nate Dogg, 191
Snoop Dogg, 11, 165, 177, 190, 197
Doherty, Pete, 127
Doors, 68–9
Dr Dre, 177, 190, 197
Drake, Nick, 67
Dunn, Thane, 156–7
Dylan, Bob, 77

Eazy-E, 192
El Vez, 157
Electric Boogaloos, 47
Elephant Man (Joseph (John) Merrick),
    48
Missy Elliott, 91
Eminem, 180, 183, 190, 196–7
emo (genre), 3
Evans, Dave, 107
Evans, Faith, 195
Experience Hendrix, 168

Facebook, 128, 177
Factors Etc., 152
Factory Records, 77
Faye, Karen, 54
Fela!, 136, 143, 144
Felabration, 136, 143
Fielder-Civil, Blake, 123–4
Fischer, Martijn, 29
Flava Flav, 197
folk, 67, 181
Foucault, Michel, 38–41
Foxx, Red, 192n5
Frankie Goes to Hollywood, 166–7
funeral, 2, 6, 8, 9n3, 11, 21n5, 22, 33–4,
    89–90, 93–4, 97, 122, 139, 191

funk, 46, 135, 140
Furious Five, 194

Kenny G., 194
Gacy, John Wayne, 153
Lady Gaga, 186
Gallagher, Noel, 169
The Game (rapper), 12, 190, 197–8
Gaye, Marvin, 169, 192n5
Geordie (band), 66n4
The Germs, 75
Geto Boys, 192
Gheorghiu, Angela, 194
Gibb, Robin, 2
Gibb, Steve, 21n4
Gil, Gilberto, 139
Glee, 88, 89, 94–7
Goody, Jade, 126
Google, 45, 165
Gordon, Nick, 123
Gore, Al, 177
goth, 3
Graceland, 151, 152, 153
Grammy, 87, 89
Grant, Oscar, 178
Grohl, Dave, 76
grunge, 1, 74, 76
Guru (rapper), 194

Haines, Nick, 109
Harrison, George, 62
Harvey, Leslie, 5
Hayes, Isaac, 183
Haynes, Todd, 77
hashtag, *see* Twitter
Hazes, André, 2, 8, 17–30, 34
    bedankt, 17, 21–2
Hazes, André Jr, 28n9
Hazes, Rachel, 23
Hazes, Roxanne, 28n9
heavy metal, 3
Hendrix, Janie, 168
Hendrix, Jimi, 61–2, 65, 66, 168, 184,
    192n5, 193
Hester, Paul, 2, 103, 106, 108, 109n4,
    111–12, 114, 115
highlife, 138
hip-hop, 12, 179, 184–5, 191, 193, 195–7

Hole (band), 76
Holiday, Billie, 178, 192n5194
Holly, Buddy, 5, 61, 63–4
hologram, 165–6, 171, 177–86, 190, 196
homo economicus, 40–41
Honoré, Annik, 80
Hook, Peter, 77
Houston, Pat, 87
Houston, Whitney, 2, 5, 9, 10, 87–97, 119,
    122–7
Howard, John, 109
Howard, Rowland S., 2, 103, 109, 111–12,
    114
Hutchence, Michael, 125

icon, 18, 22, 30, 61–70, 87, 90, 135, 137,
    140, 143–4, 149–52, 154, 158, 165,
    181, 197
    iconicity, 65, 69
    iconography, 135, 142, 195
Incredible String Band, 67
Instagram, 177, 185
Internet, 45, 50, 62, 167

Jackson, Joe, 48
Jackson, Michael, 2, 8, 45–55, 120, 121,
    122, 127, 128, 151, 184–5, 190
Jackson 5, 46, 48
Jadakiss, 197
Jam Master J., 194
James, Etta, 119
Japan (band), 67
Jay-Z, 143, 190, 195–6, 197
jazz, 111, 119, 135, 138, 140, 192, 193,
    199n10
    gospel-jazz, 93
Johnson, Brian, 66n4, 107
Johnson, Robert, 65
Johnson, Samuel, 87, 88
Jones, Brian, 65, 66
Jones, Nasir, *see* Nas
Jones, Quincy, 46, 191
Joplin, Janis, 65, 66, 81, 193
Joy Division, 5, 74–7, 80, 81

Kalakuta Republic, 138
Keita, Salif, 140
Killer Queen, 68

King, Martin Luther, 183
King, Rodney, 183
'King of Pop', 47, 51, 121;
    see also Jackson, Michael
The King Singers, 78
Klein, Arnold, 49
Kodikian, Raffi, 77
Koola Lobitos, 138
Kuti, Fela, 2, 10, 135–44

La Rock, Scott, 194
Lamar, Kendrick, 199
lament, 12, 108, 189–99
Led Zeppelin, 166, 169
Stagger Lee, 180
Lennon, John, 6, 9, 62, 63, 67–8, 104n2,
    166, 184–5, 190, 198
Lewis, Jerry Lee, 64, 150
levenslied, 18–21, 24, 28–9
levenspop, 19; *see also polder blues*
lieux de mémoire, 103–5, 109, 112–16
Lil' Wayne, 198
Live Aid, 62, 64
Louima, Abner, 183
Love, Courtney, 76
Lulu, 172n2

Maal, Baaba, 140
McCartney, Paul, 104n2, 139
MacColl, Kirsty, 126
McFly, 172n2
Madonna, 47, 48, 51, 53
Makaveli, 197; *see also* Shakur, Tupac
Manson, Marilyn, 141
Mapplethorpe, Robert, 182
Marley, Bob, 141
Martin, Dean, 167
Martin, Trayvon, 178
Martyn, John, 67
masculinity, 8, 50–52, 139, 149, 182
    and race, 136, 139, 178, 182
Mathers, Marshall, *see* Eminem
May, Brian, 69
mediation, 1, 8, 9, 10, 28, 61–4, 66, 89,
    126, 137, 157, 177, 185, 193, 196
Meek, Joe, 75
Meldrum, Molly, 112
Melua, Katie, 171

Melvin Produkties BV, 23, 28n8, 29
memory, 8, 10, 29, 62–5, 69, 77, 92, 94,
    96, 114–15, 144, 154, 173
    cultural memory, 64, 104, 192n4, 195
    generational memory, 61, 65, 70
    sites of memory, 94, 96, 103–5, 110,
        112–115; *see also lieux de mémoire*
    social/public memory, 29, 75, 82, 105,
        115, 120, 173
Mercury, Freddie, 2, 9, 62, 64, 68, 69, 190
Midler, Bette, 153
Hatsune Miku, 186
milieux de mémoire, 103, 115
Minaj, Nicki, 91
Mintz, Aja Dior, 87, 91
mixtape, 180, 194, 195, 197
Monroe, Marilyn, 122
Monteverdi, 190
Moon, Keith, 169–70
Morphine (band), 5
Morris, Stephen, 76
Morrison, Jim, 5, 65, 66, 69, 75, 81, 105,
    179, 184, 193
motherhood, 10, 119–20, 122–9
Motown, 47, 48
mourning, 2, 22, 34, 61–3, 88–9, 91–7, 103,
    119, 128, 185, 189–90, 192, 196, 199
    collective, 89, 93–5
    and grief, 61–2, 88, 91, 190
    methods, 6, 62, 88–9, 91
    online mourning, 63, 88, 94
    spaces of mourning, 88–9, 91, 97
Mozart, 193
Murphy, Peter, 179

Nas, 190, 195–6, 197, 199n10
Nigeria 70, 138
Nirvana, 5, 63, 74, 76
Nora, Pierre, 103–4, 112, 114
The Notorious B.I.G., 190, 191, 192,
    194–8
Novoselic, Krist, 76
No Way Sis, 68
N.W.A., 197

Oasis (band), 68, 169
obituaries, 6, 8, 10–11, 45, 119–28, 135–7,
    139–40, 143

INDEX

Obasanjo, General Olesugun, 138
Oranje, 21–2
Orbison, Roy, 171
Orlan, 50
Osmond, Donny, 51
'Other', 12, 26, 94, 137, 141
    fetishised, 12, 139
Outkast, 179

Master P, 192
Page, Jimmy, 169
Pagoda, 81
Pantera, 6
Parker, Charlie, 193
Colonel Parker, 152, 154
Parker, Sarah Jessica, 125
Pavement, 179
Pentangle, 67
Père Lachaise Cemetery, 105
Pergolesi, 193
Perkins, Carl, 150
Photoshop, 185
Pinkett-Smith, Jada, 143
Pitt, Michael, 77, 79, 81
Pixies, 179
Plastic People of The Universe, 141
polder blues, 19; *see also levenspop*
The Police (band), 192
pop, 46, 47, 51, 62, 65, 68, 92, 119, 122,
    140, 170
Pop, Iggy, 81–2
posthumous
    career, 65, 67, 150–52, 166
    cover version, 1, 6
    duet, 1, 11, 28, 165–8, 170–74, 182, 194
    fame, 1, 18, 173
    performance, 12, 54, 64, 165, 170, 185
    releases, 1, 52, 53–4, 64, 77, 179, 180,
        195, 197n9, 199n10
    representations, 9, 136, 139, 144, 149
    sales, 45–6, 54, 65, 151, 179
    tributes, 1, 10–11, 62, 67, 88–9, 97, 103
    voice sampling, 12, 190, 193–6, 199
Presley, Elvis, 2, 11, 61, 62, 64, 114, 122,
    149–58, 166–7, 169–74, 177, 179,
    184, 190, 194
Presley, Lisa Marie, 49n5, 50, 52, 152, 167
Presley, Priscilla, 152

Prince, 48
Prior, Richard, 137
Proof (rapper), 194
Public Enemy, 141
punk, 33–5, 40, 66, 75, 81
    hardcore punk, 34–6, 40, 42–3
    post-punk, 76
Purcell, Henry, 190

Queen (band), 62, 64, 68, 69
'Queen of Disco', 125; *see also*
    Summer, Donna

Ransome-Kuti, Israel, 137
rap, 2, 12, 139, 165, 177–86, 189–99
    bohemian rap, 192
    gangsta rap, 5, 12, 178, 182, 189,
        190–92, 197, 199
    reality rap, 191–2
Reed, Lou, 2
Reid, L.A., 53–4
resurrection, 2, 11, 18, 166, 179–82, 194;
    see also hologram
Busta Rhymes, 180
rhythm and blues, 150
Rihanna, 91
Riley, Amber 94
Riley, Billy Lee, 150
Riley, Sam, 78
Riley, Teddy, 46
Robeson, Paul, 182
Robinson, Smokey, 46
rock, 7, 62, 65, 66, 68, 108, 111, 112, 115,
    116, 119, 123, 135–7, 140–42, 144,
    151, 170, 178, 181, 184–5, 193
    folk-rock, 67
    hard rock, 111
    indie rock, 76
Rock, Pete, 191
rock 'n' roll, 19, 42, 66, 69, 105, 111, 112,
    122, 126, 141, 150, 154
rockabilly, 150
Rolling Stone (magazine), 140–41, 144,
    179
Rolling Stones, 65, 151
Ross, Rick, 192
Rowe, Debbie, 121
Russen, Rod, 154

Sandman, Mark, 5
Scarface (rapper), 192
Scorsese, Martin, 46
Scott, Bon, 66–7, 103, 107
Seth, Larry, 154–5
Sex Pistols, 81
Shakur, Afeni, 179, 182, 196
Shakur, Tupac, 2, 5, 11–12, 165–6, 177–86, 189–90, 191, 192, 194–7
Shankar, Ravi, 2, 140, 142
Shetty, Shilpa, 126
The Shrine, 135, 137, 138, 143
Simone, Nina, 138
Smith, Robert, 67
Smith, Sandra, 138
Smith, Will, 143
C.L. Smooth, 191
soul (genre), 122, 123, 170
Spence, Johnny 'Elvis', 155
Springfield, Dusty, 171
Stone, Joss, 167
Stone the Crows, 5
Streisand, Barbra, 46
The Sugababes, 169–70, 171
suicide, 5, 9, 39, 73, 74–82, 103, 108, 125, 198
    ideation, 75, 79, 81
    statistics, 75
    and stereotypes, 9
Summer, Donna, 2, 10, 119, 124–7
Sumner, Bernard, 76
Sun Ra, 137
Super Bowl, 47, 89
Sylvian, David, 67

Terrell Taylor, Jayceon, *see* The Game
Thompson, Hunter S., 141
Throbbing Gristle, 179
Till, Emmett, 178, 183
Tosh, Peter, 141
transpropertisation, 11, 158
transproperty, 152, 154, 158
tribute acts/artists, 9, 61, 67–9, 149, 151, 154–8; *see also* posthumous
Twitter, 2, 9, 45, 54, 87–97, 128–9, 177

Valens, Ritchie, 5
Van Sant, Gus, 74, 77–81
Vaughan, Sarah, 192n5
The Velvet Underground, 81
Vicious, Sid, 81
Vine, 185
vocaloid, 186
'The Voice', 89, 92; *see also* Houston, Whitney

Waits, Tom, 153
Wallace, Christopher, *see* The Notorious B.I.G.
Ward, C. Barry, 155
Warsaw (band), 77
Wattstax, 183
Lil Wayne, 91
webshrines, 62
Westlife, 171
White, Vanna, 153
The Who, 169
Wild Child, 68
Will.i.am, 177
Williams, Hank (Junior), 167
Williams, Hank (Senior), 167
Williams, Robbie, 167
Wilson, Jackie, 47
Winehouse, Amy, 2, 5, 10, 65, 119, 122–9, 199n10
Winfrey, Oprah, 49, 89, 90, 122–3
Wonder, Stevie, 169–70
Woodruff (Curtis), Deborah, 75, 76, 80, 81
Woodstock, 181
World Music, 136, 139, 140, 142, 144

Malcolm X, 137

Yasumasa, Mori, 157
Yates, Paula, 125
Yauch, Adam, 194
Yoruba, 135, 137–8, 143
YouTube, 68, 69, 139, 165, 166, 168, 169, 177

Zeitgeist, 123, 182